THE GREAT DEPRESSION

OPPOSING VIEWPOINTS®

Other Books in the American History Series:

THE GREAT DEPRESSION

OPPOSING VIEWPOINTS®

David L. Bender, *Publisher*
Bruno Leone, *Executive Editor*

Teresa O'Neill, *Series Editor*
John C. Chalberg, Ph.D., professor of history,
    Normandale Community College,
    Consulting Editor

William Dudley, *Book Editor*

AMERICAN HISTORY SERIES

Cover photos: (top left) Library of Congress, (top right) Franklin D. Roosevelt Library, (middle and bottom) Library of Congress.

Library of Congress Cataloging-in-Publication Data

Great depression : opposing viewpoints / William Dudley, book editor.
  p.   cm. — (American history series)
  Includes bibliographical references and index.
  ISBN 1-56510-084-0 (lib. bdg. : acid-free paper) —
  ISBN 1-56510-083-2 (pbk. : acid-free paper)
  1. New Deal, 1933-1939—Sources. 2. Depressions—1929—United States—Sources. 3. United States—History—1933-1945—Sources. 4. United States—History—1919-1933—Sources.
I. Dudley, William, 1964-   II. Series: American history series (San Diego, Calif.)
E806.G83 1994   93-13000
973.917—dc20   CIP

"America was born of revolt, flourished in dissent, became great through experimentation."

Henry Steele Commager, American Historian, 1902-1984

Contents

Foreword

Aboard the *Arbella* as it lurched across the cold, gray Atlantic, John Winthrop was as calm as the waters surrounding him were wild. With the confidence of a leader, Winthrop gathered his Puritan companions around him. It was time to offer a sermon. England lay behind them, and years of strife and persecution for their religious beliefs were over, he said. But the Puritan abandonment of England, he reminded his followers, did not mean that England was beyond redemption. Winthrop wanted his followers to remember England even as they were leaving it behind. Their goal should be to create a new England, one far removed from the authority of the Anglican church and King Charles I. In Winthrop's words, their settlement in the New World ought to be "a city upon a hill," a just society for corrupt England to emulate.

A Chance to Start Over

One June 8, 1630, John Winthrop and his company of refugees had their first glimpse of what they came to call New England. High on the surrounding hills stood a welcoming band of fir trees whose fragrance drifted to the *Arbella* on a morning breeze. To Winthrop, the "smell off the shore [was] like the smell of a garden." This new world would, in fact, often be compared to the Garden of Eden. Here, John Winthrop would have his opportunity to start life over again. So would his family and his shipmates. So would all those who came after them. These victims of conflict in old England hoped to find peace in New England.

Winthrop, for one, had experienced much conflict in his life. As a Puritan, he was opposed to Catholicism and Anglicanism, both of which, he believed, were burdened by distracting rituals and distant hierarchies. A parliamentarian by conviction, he despised Charles I, who had spurned Parliament and created a private army to do his bidding. Winthrop believed in individual responsibility and fought against the loss of religious and political freedom. A gentleman landowner, he feared the rising economic power of a merchant class that seemed to value only money. Once Winthrop stepped aboard the *Arbella*, he hoped, these conflicts would not be a part of his American future.

Yet his Puritan religion told Winthrop that human beings are fallen creatures and that perfection, whether communal or individual, is unachievable on this earth. Therefore, he faced a paradox: On the one hand, his religion demanded that he attempt to live a perfect life in an imperfect world. On the other hand, it told him that he was destined to fail.

Soon after Winthrop disembarked from the *Arbella*, he came face-to-face with this maddening dilemma. He found himself presiding not over a utopia but over a colony caught up in disputes as troubling as any he had confronted in his English past. John Winthrop, it seems, was not the only Puritan with a dream of a heaven on earth. But others in the community saw the dream differently. They wanted greater political and religious freedom than their leader was prepared to grant. Often, Winthrop was able to handle this conflict diplomatically. For example, he expanded, participation in elections and allowed the voters of Massachusetts Bay greater power.

But religious conflict was another matter because it was grounded in competing visions of the Puritan utopia. In Roger Williams and Anne Hutchinson, two of his fellow colonists, John Winthrop faced rivals unprepared to accept his definition of the perfect community. To Williams, perfection demanded that he separate himself from the Puritan institutions in his community and create an even "purer" church. Winthrop, however, disagreed and exiled Williams to Rhode Island. Hutchinson presumed that she could interpret God's will without a minister. Again, Winthrop did not agree. Hutchinson was tried on charges of heresy, convicted, and banished from Massachusetts.

John Winthrop's Massachusetts colony was the first but far from the last American attempt to build a unified, peaceful community that, in the end, only provoked a discord. This glimpse at its history reveals what Winthrop confronted: the unavoidable presence of conflict in American life.

American Assumptions

From America's origins in the early seventeenth century, Americans have often held several interrelated assumptions about their country. First, people believe that to be American is to be free. Second, because Americans did not have to free themselves from feudal lords or an entrenched aristocracy, America has been seen as a perpetual haven from the troubles and disputes that are found in the Old World.

John Winthrop lived his life as though these assumptions were true. But the opposing viewpoints presented in the American History Series should reveal that for many Americans, these assumptions were and are myths. Indeed, for numerous Americans, liberty has not always been guaranteed, and disputes have been an integral, sometimes welcome part of their life.

The American landscape has been torn apart again and again by a great variety of clashes—theological, ideological, political, economic, geographical, and social. But such a landscape is not necessarily a hopelessly divided country. If the editors hope to prove anything during the course of this series, it is not that the United States has been destroyed by conflict but rather that it has been enlivened, enriched, and even strengthened by Americans who have disagreed with one another.

Thomas Jefferson was one of the least confrontational of Americans, but he boldly and irrevocably enriched American life with his individualistic views. Like John Winthrop before him, he had a notion of an American Eden. Like Winthrop, he offered a vision of a harmonious society. And like Winthrop, he not only became enmeshed in conflict but eventually presided over a people beset by it. But unlike Winthrop, Jefferson believed this Eden was not located in a specific community but in each individual American. His Declaration of Independence from Great Britain could also be read as a declaration of independence for each individual in American society.

Jefferson's Ideal

Jefferson's ideal world was composed of "yeoman farmers," each of whom was roughly equal to the others in society's eyes, each of whom was free from the restrictions of both government and fellow citizens. Throughout his life, Jefferson offered a continuing challenge to Americans: Advance individualism and equality or see the death of the American experiment. Jefferson believed that the strength of this experiment depended upon a society of autonomous individuals and a society without great gaps between rich and poor. His challenge to his fellow Americans to create—and sustain—such a society has itself produced both economic and political conflict.

A society whose guiding document is the Declaration of Independence is a society assured of the freedom to dream—and to disagree. We know that Jefferson hated conflict, both personal and political. His tendency was to avoid confrontations of any sort, to squirrel himself away and write rather than to stand up and speak his mind. It is only through his written words that we can grasp Jefferson's utopian dream of a society of independent farmers, all pursuing their private dreams and all leading lives of middling prosperity.

Jefferson, this man of wealth and intellect, lived an essentially happy private life. But his public life was much more troublesome. From the first rumblings of the American Revolution in the 1760s to the North-South skirmishes of the 1820s that ultimately produced the Civil War, Jefferson was at or near the center of American political history. The issues were almost too many—and too crucial—for one lifetime: Jefferson had to choose

11

between supporting or rejecting the path of revolution. During and after the ensuing war, he was at the forefront of the battle for religious liberty. After endorsing the Constitution, he opposed the economic plans of Alexander Hamilton. At the end of the century, he fought the infamous Alien and Sedition Acts, which limited civil liberties. As president, he opposed the Federalist court, conspiracies to divide the union, and calls for a new war against England. Throughout his life, Thomas Jefferson, slaveholder, pondered the conflict between American freedom and American slavery. And from retirement at his Monticello retreat, he frowned at the rising spirit of commercialism he feared was dividing Americans and destroying his dream of American harmony.

No matter the issue, however, Thomas Jefferson invariably supported the rights of the individual. Worried as he was about the excesses of commercialism, he accepted them because his main concern was to live in a society where liberty and individualism could flourish. To Jefferson, Americans had to be free to worship as they desired. They also deserved to be free from an over-reaching government. To Jefferson, Americans should also be free to possess slaves.

Harmony, an Elusive Goal

Before reading the articles in this anthology, the editors ask readers to ponder the lives of John Winthrop and Thomas Jefferson. Each held a utopian vision, one based upon the demands of community and the other on the autonomy of the individual. Each dreamed of a country of perpetual new beginnings. Each found himself thrust into a position of leadership and found that conflict could not be avoided. Harmony, whether communal or individual, was a forever elusive goal.

The opposing visions of Winthrop and Jefferson have been at the heart of many differences among Americans from many backgrounds through the whole of American history. Moreover, their visions have provoked important responses that have helped shape American society, the American character, and many an American battle.

The editors of the American History Series have done extensive research to find representative opinions on the issues included in these volumes. They have found numerous outstanding opposing viewpoints from people of all times, classes, and genders in American history. From those, they have selected commentaries that best fit the nature and flavor of the period and topic under consideration. Every attempt was made to include the most important and relevant viewpoints in each chapter. Obviously, not every notable viewpoint could be included. Therefore, a selective, annotated bibliography has been provided at the end of each book to aid readers in seeking additional information.

The editors are confident that as this series reveals past conflicts, it will help revitalize the reader's views of the American present. In that spirit, the American History Series is dedicated to the proposition that American history is more complicated, more fascinating, and more troubling than John Winthrop or Thomas Jefferson ever dared to imagine.

John C. Chalberg
Consulting Editor

Introduction

"In more recent years the United States has suffered 'recessions,' the current term of preference, at frequent intervals. But no economic downturn has been as severe as that of the Great Depression, one of the few truly national crises in American history."

In the entire history of American capitalism, there has been only one Great Depression. True, in the nineteenth century relatively brief but often severe financial panics occurred at roughly twenty-year intervals, culminating with the prolonged economic slump of the mid-1890s. And in more recent years the United States has suffered "recessions," the current term of preference, at frequent intervals. But no economic downturn has been as severe as that of the Great Depression, one of the few truly national crises in American history.

Historians attribute this use of the term *depression* to President Herbert Hoover, who used the word to characterize the state of the American economy in the months following the stock market crash of October 1929. He thought that *panic*, a term used by some, was too frightening, especially since he saw no need for the American people to panic in response to the bad news from Wall Street. In fact, Hoover compared the American economy to a highway and the postcrash economic problems to a brief depression on the normally smooth and happy road to American prosperity.

Unfortunately, President Hoover turned out to be a poor prognosticator. The Great Depression was far from brief. Most people point to the Great Crash as its starting point, and, although there is no consensus on its concluding date, most historians agree that the American economy did not fully emerge from its depressed state until the demands of World War II had to be faced. For more than ten long years the American people suffered an economic crisis unlike any they had ever known or anticipated.

In 1929 the responsibility for solving the economic problems that were triggered by the stock market collapse fell on many shoulders, but prime among them were those of the Republican president, Herbert Hoover. This man, who had saved Europe from starvation during and after the Great War of 1914-1918, proved, however, to be other than a miracle worker during this new crisis. In fact, between the autumn of 1929 and the autumn of the presidential election year of 1932, the American economy went from bad to worse.

Signs of collapse were everywhere. National unemployment approached 20 percent. Joblessness among black Americans was close to 50 percent. Private construction investment had plummeted from $6.6 billion in 1929 to $1.3 billion in 1932. Private investment in old and new businesses fell 35 percent in 1931, and another 88 percent in 1932. By 1932 overall manufacturing stood at a paltry 54 percent of what it had been in 1929. More specifically—and depressingly—the automobile industry was operating at only 20 percent of capacity in 1932, and steel at 12 percent. Farm income, which had not been all that robust during the 1920s, slid from $12 billion in 1929 to just under $5 billion in 1932. At the same time, farm mortgage foreclosure rates continued to escalate.

Nor did banks escape the economic blows they had helped deliver to others. Although more than seven thousand financial institutions had gone under between 1920 and 1929 (providing evidence of underlying economic weakness well before the fateful October 1929 crash), more than nine thousand additional bank failures occurred in the three years between the stock market crash and the end of Hoover's term as president in 1933.

On a more personal level, marriages were being postponed at record rates. With economic security an uncertainty, 250,000 fewer marriages took place in 1932 than in 1929. And for the 1932 baseball season even Babe Ruth was forced to take a pay cut—and a hefty one at that—$10,000 in 1932 money!

Hoover's Response

Throughout his term as president, Hoover had attempted to address the growing crisis using traditional Republican capitalist solutions. Following the tradition of "trickle-down" economics established by the tax-cutting policies of presidents Harding and Coolidge, the Hoover administration opted to administer loans to businesses and banks through the Reconstruction Finance Corporation. If such institutions could get back on their financial feet, the thinking went, they would in turn be able to put people back to work. Another Republican solution was a national sales tax intended to cut the growing federal deficit. (Its critics dubbed it "soak the poor." Socialist party presidential candidate Norman Thomas exclaimed, "It's a wonder they don't put a tax on tickets to the bread line!")

Hoover did experiment with federally financed public works programs, but only on a small, pilot project basis. Fearful of sap-

15

ping the will and the initiative of the average American worker, he hesitated to make the federal government the employer of first—or last—resort. An enemy of bureaucracy, especially in its federal form, Hoover preferred to ride out the bad times rather than abandon the individualistic, capitalistic system he thought had worked so well for so long.

By 1932, given the dire state of the American economy, it would not have been surprising had the country decided to lurch dramatically to the left—beyond the Democrats—in the fall elections. To many, capitalism seemed beyond repair.

And yet the isms of the left—socialism and communism—claimed few adherents in 1932. After three years of the Great Depression, only 2.2 percent of the voters cast their presidential ballots for Socialist Norman Thomas. Franklin Delano Roosevelt, a politician to the core and the Democratic governor of New York, had understood correctly that he did not have to move decisively to the left in order to defeat Hoover. Nor had he felt compelled to lay out the specifics of any economic renewal program. To explain in great detail to voters his program for recovery would only invite criticism and remove the focus from Hoover's mounting failures.

Roosevelt also intuitively knew that most Americans still thought of themselves, for better or worse, as self-reliant individuals rather than pessimistic victims. Much anecdotal and other evidence indicates that unemployed workers were quick to blame themselves, not the system, for their plight.

Thus it was that the politically astute Roosevelt crushed Hoover, who had been swept into office a scant four years earlier on the optimistic slogan "A chicken in every pot and a car in every garage."

In tackling the economic problems he had inherited, President Franklin Roosevelt proposed to offer the American people a "New Deal." Times were tough, and Roosevelt believed that many Americans found themselves unemployed though no fault of their own. They deserved to be helped by their government.

The New Deal

Some called the New Deal "socialism on the installment plan." To FDR the charge was absurd. Socialists called for an end to competition; the New Deal sought to enlarge the playing field. Socialists called for government ownership of production and distribution; the New Deal called only for greater governmental regulation. Socialists believed in equality of result; New Dealers insisted on equality of opportunity.

True, the New Deal saw the primitive beginnings of a national welfare system to care for those unable to compete. But Roosevelt was not about to call for an end to competition for everyone. Instead, the New Deal set out to recruit more Americans to play the capitalist's game. If they faltered, a New Deal program would be there to pick them up and head them in the right direction once again. If they could not find work, the federal government offered itself as an interim employer. But in no sense did the president envision a society in which all members would finish with the same economic status, an important goal of socialist belief.

From the outset of the Roosevelt administration, there was disagreement over the root causes of the depression. Was the basic problem one of underconsumption or overproduction? If it was the former, then money had to be put into the hands of the unemployed and underemployed—and the deficit be damned! At the very least, public works projects should be drafted, promoted, and funded.

However, if the main problem was overproduction, then a very different and more conservative solution was needed. Government should encourage, perhaps even require, both industry and agriculture to cut back on production to get supply and demand back into proper alignment and to ensure fair prices.

Two major pieces of legislation passed during the furious first hundred days of the New Deal. This legislation offers evidence of Roosevelt's conservative approach to dealing with the overwhelming problems created by the Great Depression. Both the National Industrial Recovery Act and the Agricultural Adjustment Act (AAA) were grounded in the theory that the basic economic problem facing the country was one of overproduction. Hence, the National Recovery Administration (NRA) was created to draft and enforce codes for production, employment, and wages in industry after industry across the country. Once in compliance, American businesses could fly the "blue eagle," the stamp of approval that meant others could engage in commerce with them and feel patriotic.

But who wrote the codes? In most cases business leaders took the lead in the drafting process. Consequently, critics said, these codes may have helped slow the growth of unemployment, but they did little by way of putting the already jobless back to work. After all, businesses were having hard times, too, and they found it difficult to hire additional workers when they were already facing the tough challenge of selling their products in the depressed economy.

The Roosevelt administration followed a similar line in dealing with American agriculture. Why were farm prices so low? the administration asked. Its answer was that American farmers produced too much food too efficiently. Therefore, the solution was simple: Cut back on production. How was that to be achieved?

By paying farmers *not* to produce food. Some, both inside and outside the administration, contended that a system of guaranteed price supports to farmers was a better solution. But Roosevelt disagreed. The result was a decline in farm production and an accompanying rise in farm prices even as people in American cities were going hungry.

Not all of the early New Deal programs were based on the presumption that the root problem was one of too many goods in the marketplace. Public works programs on a scale previously unimagined were created. The Federal Emergency Relief Administration (FERA) provided cash grants directly to states whose relief agencies had gone bankrupt. When it became apparent that FERA money was not going to be sufficient, the New Deal created federal work relief programs. Between November 1933 and April 1934 some four million people were put to work on temporary projects by the Civil Works Administration. The Civilian Conservation Corps (CCC), one of Roosevelt's favorite New Deal programs, was also an experiment in work relief in national parks and forests. In 1935 the administration established the Works Progress Administration (WPA) with an initial budget of $5 billion. Under the direction of Harry Hopkins, the WPA built over 500,000 miles of roads, more than 100,000 bridges, and nearly 600 airports, all the while keeping an average of 2.1 million people employed.

Despite these efforts the Great Depression proved highly resistant to remedy. Unemployment rates remained in double digits. Wages stayed well below pre-1929 levels. The private sector continued to lack the confidence necessary to undertake large-scale new construction. Two years of the New Deal had produced a blizzard of what were planned as temporary relief agencies, but no long-term solutions seemed to be on the horizon.

The Rise of Discontent

However, by 1934 something else *was* on the rise: restiveness—restiveness on farms, in small towns, and in large cities. That restiveness led to several violent labor disputes. It also bred political leaders and would-be leaders with an inclination to demagoguery. Among them were Senator Huey Long, Father Charles Coughlin, and Dr. Francis Townsend—a politician, a priest, and a physician—three very different Americans, three men whose politics and ideologies defied easy classification. Yet they shared one trait: Each represented a challenge to the New Deal and to the leadership of Franklin Roosevelt.

The most serious political challenge came from Senator Long of Louisiana. His Share Our Wealth plan called for using the federal tax system to redistribute wealth so that every family could be guaranteed a homestead of $5,000 and an annual wage of $2,500.

Long also made no secret of his presidential ambitions. He planned to run as a third-party candidate in 1936. Although he did not expect to win, he knew he would drain enough votes from Roosevelt to bring about a Republican victory. The result, he predicted, would be four more years of depression and his own presidency by 1940. An assassin's bullet killed Long and foiled his convoluted plot in September 1935, but Long's presence—and his politics—had already served their purpose. By 1935 President Roosevelt had decided that a shift to the left was a political necessity.

The challenges presented by Coughlin and Townsend had a similar effect on the newly embattled president. In the spring of 1935 the "radio priest," Father Coughlin, created his own political organization, the National Union for Social Justice. Coughlin had been a Roosevelt supporter in 1932, but by 1935 he concluded that the president had not been harsh enough in his treatment of the "money powers." Through his organization and his weekly national radio sermons, Coughlin offered two panaceas: the nationalization of the banking system and the inflation of the currency.

In 1935 the unassuming Townsend was a retired California physician who suddenly found himself leading a movement five million strong when his proposal for federal pensions for the elderly captured the imagination of the populace. According to the Townsend Plan, every American over the age of sixty would receive a monthly government pension of $200, provided they would retire and spend the money in full each month. The concept made little headway in Congress, but it, along with Long's Share Our Wealth scheme, helped prepare the way for the Social Security Act of 1935.

The Social Security Act offers the best example of what has come to be called the Second New Deal, Roosevelt's programs that were mandated in the year and a half or so before his reelection. The Social Security Act established the structure for the future American welfare system, attempting to guarantee economic survival for the old, the young, the sick, and the indigent. During this time Roosevelt also signed the National Labor Relations Act, which gave greater power to the American laborer. Popularly known as the Wagner Act (for its chief sponsor, Senator Robert Wagner of New York), it compelled employers to recognize and bargain with legitimate unions through the auspices of the National Labor Relations Board. The president worried that the legislation might suddenly tip the scales too much in the direction of labor, but he signed the act because he realized that his political future might well depend upon a rejuvenated labor movement.

As it turned out, Roosevelt swamped his 1936 Republican challenger, Alf Landon, by a vote of 61 percent to 36 percent. His overwhelming margin of victory cannot be attributed entirely to his shift to the left. But Roosevelt the politician did know in which direction the political winds were blowing. With too many Americans still in the grips of the Great Depression, with memories of the makeshift shanties, called "Hoovervilles," erected by the newly poor still fresh in too many minds, the voters were not ready to return the Republicans to power.

Nor were they ready to lean much farther leftward. Membership in the Communist party rose by the mid-1930s, but total membership barely topped ninety thousand. And so impressed were many Socialists with Roosevelt's performance that the Socialist party's presidential candidate, Norman Thomas, garnered fewer votes than he had won in 1932.

Experimentation with new federal programs to aid economically plagued citizens continued into Roosevelt's second term. For example, the Resettlement Administration (RA) worked to relocate displaced sharecroppers and tenant farmers on federal land. In 1937 the RA was replaced by the Farm Security Administration, which set up some ninety-five camps to provide housing and cooperative self-government for migrant workers. Another break from old-fashioned American individualism was government-subsidized housing in newly planned suburban communities that would be owned and governed collectively. Ninety-nine such communities were planned, but only three (in Wisconsin, Ohio, and Maryland) were ultimately constructed. It seemed that the country was willing to accept pilot projects of a communitarian nature, but on a larger scale they seemed too threatening to American ideals of individualism and self-sufficiency to garner support. Even Roosevelt did not push hard to complete the program. His ultimate goal, after all, remained consensus. He hoped to achieve this by preserving the capitalist system while curbing some of its worst excesses and putting into place the beginning of a safety net under most Americans.

Many of Roosevelt's programs were genuinely reformist, but few seriously challenged existing power relationships. The largest farmers in each county controlled the workings of the AAA, and it was business leaders, not laborers, who drafted the NRA codes.

Saving Capitalism Through Reform

Roosevelt's desire to save the capitalistic system by reforming it generated plenty of debate within the administration. As the Great Depression persisted, those on the left wing favored more drastic measures, whether they be higher levels of spending, tighter regulatory controls, a greater number of communitarian experiments, or programs for especially disadvantaged groups, including blacks and women. At the same time, the New Deal produced renewed criticism from those on the right who worried that reform would lead inevitably to bureaucracy, which in turn would eventually strangle free enterprise as it had been practiced in pre-New Deal America.

Ultimately, just how revolutionary was the New Deal? Rexford Tugwell, one of the more left-leaning members of Roosevelt's "brain trust," the inner circle of his advisers, conceded after the fact that "practically the whole New Deal had been extrapolated from programs which Hoover had started." And yet there were differences. Where Hoover had tried persuasion, Roosevelt legislated. Where Hoover feared bureaucracy, Roosevelt embraced it.

Without question the impact of and the solutions to the Great Depression generated wildly conflicting points of view across the country. But at the highest levels of government the debate was largely confined to figuring out how to preserve some version of democratic capitalism. The administrations of both Herbert Hoover and Franklin Roosevelt had difficulty figuring out how to do this and still free the economy from the tight grip of the Great Depression. By 1937 the Gross National Product (GNP) had risen 44 percent over that of 1933 and the start of the Roosevelt years, but that figure only returned the economy to 1929 levels. By 1939 and the eve of World War II, the GNP had crept only 3 percent beyond what it had been in 1929. Furthermore, nine million Americans were still unemployed. The national crisis—the Great Depression—was not over even as the next national crisis—World War II—loomed. Ironically, perhaps even tragically, it took preparations for the war and finally participation in the conflict itself to ultimately remove the country from the throes of the depression. In the final analysis, the American defense industry proved to be the ultimate public works project. But not even the trauma of war and the return of peacetime prosperity following the defeat of Germany and Japan could purge the Great Depression from the memories of those who had lived through it.

John C. Chalberg
Consulting Editor

CHAPTER 1

Economic Collapse and Hoover's Response

Chapter Preface

Herbert Hoover's presidency is inseparably linked to the Great Depression. Ironically, when Hoover was overwhelmingly elected president of the United States in 1928, he seemed a perfect symbolic match for what Americans anticipated as a "new era" of prosperity and technological progress. Hoover, a mining engineer and self-made millionaire, seemed to epitomize the American dream of self-made success. His political reputation grew with his achievements as an innovative and energetic commerce secretary under presidents Warren G. Harding and Calvin Coolidge during the 1920s.

The U.S. economy Hoover was to lead as president had rebounded from World War I and a short 1920 recession to experience unprecedented economic growth during the 1920s. Between 1921 and 1929 industrial output almost doubled. Technological progress had created or transformed whole new industries including the automobile, chemical, and airplane industries. Workers' incomes increased 23 percent, while corporate profits rose 62 percent. Mass consumption, aided by installment or credit buying, grew as an increasing number of Americans were able to buy cars, radios, refrigerators, and other consumer goods. America's gross national product in 1929 was 25 percent higher than the GNP of 1919. Many economists and observers, including Hoover, expected that prosperity to continue. Hoover's 1929 inaugural address optimistically pledged to abolish poverty in America.

However, the 1929 stock market crash and ensuing economic events revealed the limitations both of Hoover's leadership and the American prosperity which had propelled him to the White House. The economic gains of the 1920s turned out to be deceptive as they had not been evenly distributed. American farmers had suffered a net income decline of nearly 50 percent. A 1929 study by the Brookings Institution found that 42 percent of American families were still at or below a "subsistence-and-poverty" level. This lack of broadly distributed wealth eventually became an economic weakness when the ability of American consumers to purchase goods could not keep up with American industry's ability to produce them.

Historians presently dispute how much effect the stock market crash ultimately had. However, beyond dispute is the decline in economic activity in the early 1930s, contrary to expectations that the economy would soon recover like it did following the 1920 recession. Consumer spending between 1929 and 1933 declined from $203.6 billion to $141.5 billion. Business investment fell from $40.4 billion to $5.3 billion. Unemployment rose from 3.2 percent to 24.9 percent. Many of these economic trends reinforced each other. Historian J. Bradford De Long writes in *The Reader's Companion to American History*:

> At its nadir, the depression paired individual rationality with collective insanity. Workers were idle because firms would not hire them to work their machines; firms would not hire workers to work machines because they saw no market for goods; and there was no market for goods because workers had no income to spend.

Hoover's response to the "collective insanity" of the depression was limited by his belief that the government should not force itself on or interfere with private enterprise. He saw his role as limited to being an "influential advisor and well-placed cheerleader." As an adviser he held numerous conferences with business leaders and urged them to work together to not lay off workers or lower wages. He urged labor leaders to desist from strikes, bankers to cooperate with each other to prevent weaker banks from failing, and local governments to provide relief and public works. His exhortations, not backed up by government mandates, failed to achieve their desired goals. His efforts as a cheerleader, which consisted mainly of periodic predictions that recovery was just around the corner and statements such as "What this country needs is a good big laugh," failed to boost American morale.

For the first two years of his presidential term, Hoover consistently refused on principle to grant federal money for the poor and for unemployment relief. As the depression continued to worsen, however, Hoover finally in 1931 proposed government help to the economy in the form of the Reconstruction Finance Corporation. The RFC would lend money to faltering banks, railroads, and other businesses in the hope of restoring confidence in the economy. The program loaned over a billion dollars to businesses, but it was widely attacked as an example of Hoover's willingness to provide federal aid for business instead of the poor and unemployed.

Hoover was not alone in advocating a limited government response. Many economists and businesspeople opposed even the limited measures of government action that Hoover presided over. This was in part reflective of longstanding American belief in self-reliance and limited government. Many Americans were ashamed of relief, blaming their poverty on themselves. The opinions expressed by industrialist Henry Ford, who wrote a series of editorials in 1932 advocating "self-help" for the poor and unemployed, were shared by many, including many of the unemployed themselves. Historian Sean Dennis Cashman writes in *America in the Twenties and Thirties:*

> The Protestant work ethic died hard. Millions who lost their jobs blamed themselves for their misfortune. . . . The social stigma attached to relief discouraged all but the most needy.

By 1932 America was in dire straits: 273,000 families were evicted from their homes that year alone. Thousands of banks had gone out of business, leaving many without their life savings. Historian Richard H. Pells writes that many Americans were demoralized: "The depression meant more than simply the failure of business; it was to many people an overwhelming natural catastrophe, much like an earthquake that uprooted and destroyed whatever lay in its path." Despite the nation's economic problems, the Republican party renominated Hoover for president. Hoover doggedly defended his policies and his belief in an imminent recovery and he harshly attacked his Democratic opponent, New York governor Franklin D. Roosevelt, for proposing policies dangerous to the American way of life. Despite his efforts, Hoover was defeated by a greater margin than his own landslide 1928 victory. The American people looked to a new president to lead the nation out of the Great Depression.

VIEWPOINT 1

"Our American system requires that municipal, county and state governments shall use their own resources and credit before seeking such assistance from the Federal Treasury."

Local Relief Efforts Help the Poor

Herbert Hoover (1874-1964)

Herbert Hoover served as secretary of commerce in the 1920s under presidents Warren G. Harding and Calvin Coolidge. The country elected him president in 1929, with the expectation that he would maintain the nation's prosperity. However, his presidency is best remembered for the 1929 stock market crash and the Great Depression that followed it.

In his effort to end the Depression, Hoover made far greater use of federal government programs than had any president before him. He created the Reconstruction Finance Corporation in 1932 to provide loans and credit to businesses, and he sponsored agriculture relief and public works programs. However, he had strong philosophical convictions on the proper limits of the federal government. He believed the political and economic freedoms of America depended on restricting the federal government's role. In the following viewpoint, taken from a February 3, 1931, press statement, he argues that welfare and unemployment relief should remain the responsibility of private charities and state and community governments.

Herbert Hoover, from a press statement dated February 3, 1931.

Certain senators have issued a public statement to the effect that unless the President and the House of Representatives agree to appropriations from the Federal Treasury for charitable purposes they will force an extra session of Congress.

I do not wish to add acrimony to a discussion, but would rather state this case as I see its fundamentals.

This is not an issue as to whether people shall go hungry or cold in the United States. It is solely a question of the best method by which hunger and cold shall be prevented. It is a question as to whether the American people on one hand will maintain the spirit of charity and mutual self help through voluntary giving and the responsibility of local government as distinguished on the other hand from appropriations out of the Federal Treasury for such purposes. My own conviction is strongly that if we break down this sense of responsibility of individual generosity to individual and mutual self help in the country in times of national difficulty and if we start appropriations of this character we have not only impaired something infinitely valuable in the life of the American people but have struck at the roots of self-government. Once this has happened it is not the cost of a few score millions but we are faced with the abyss of reliance in future upon Government charity in some form or other. The money involved is indeed the least of the costs to American ideals and American institutions.

President Cleveland, in 1887, confronted with a similar issue stated in part:

> A prevalent tendency to disregard the limited mission of this power and duty should, I think, be steadfastly resisted, to the end that the lesson should be constantly enforced that though the people support the Government, the Government should not support the people.

> The friendliness and charity of our countrymen can always be relied upon to relieve their fellow-citizens in misfortune. This has been repeatedly and quite lately demonstrated. Federal aid in such cases encourages the expectation of paternal care on the part of the Government and weakens the sturdiness of our national character, while it prevents the indulgence among our people of that kindly sentiment and conduct which strengthens the bonds of a common brotherhood.

And there is a practical problem in all this. The help being daily extended by neighbors, by local and national agencies, by municipalities, by industry and a great multitude of organizations throughout the country today is many times any appropriation yet proposed. The opening of the doors of the Federal Treasury is likely to stifle this giving and thus destroy far more resources than the proposed charity from the Federal Government.

The basis of successful relief in national distress is to mobilize and organize the infinite number of agencies of self help in the community. That has been the American way of relieving distress among our own people and the country is successfully meeting its problem in the American way today.

We have two entirely separate and distinct situations in the country; the first is the drought area; the second is the unemployment in our large industrial centers—for both of which these appropriations attempt to make charitable contributions.

Against Federal Unemployment Relief

The U.S. Chamber of Commerce established in May 1931 a special committee to study the American economy and draw up proposals for unemployment insurance and other economic reforms. In its report the committee, agreeing with President Herbert Hoover, argued against federal unemployment relief.

Unemployment is not, from an insurance point of view, a practical field for governmental intervention. Government compulsory insurance where it has so far been tried, in Europe, has proved inadequate through lack of sufficient reserves and has inevitably led to outright government payments, as in the English dole. It has thus engendered and encouraged unemployment.

Needed relief should be provided through private contributions and by state and local governments. There is every evidence that all requirements can in this manner be adequately met. Any proposals for federal appropriations for such purposes should therefore be opposed.

Immediately upon the appearance of the drought last August, I convoked a meeting of the governors, the Red Cross and the railways, the bankers and other agencies in the country and laid the foundations of organization and the resources to stimulate every degree of self help to meet the situation which it was then obvious would develop. The result of this action was to attack the drought problem in a number of directions. The Red Cross established committees in every drought county, comprising the leading citizens of those counties, with instructions to them that they were to prevent starvation among their neighbors and, if the problem went beyond local resources, the Red Cross would support them.

The organization has stretched throughout the area of suffering, the people are being cared for today through the hands and with sympathetic understanding and upon the responsibility of their neighbors who are being supported in turn by the fine spirit of mutual assistance of the American people. The Red Cross officials whose long devoted service and experience are unchallenged, inform me this morning that except for the minor incidents of any emergency organization, no one is going hungry and no one need go hungry or cold.

To reinforce this work at the opening of Congress I recommended large appropriations for loans to rehabilitate agriculture from the drought and provision of further large sums for public works and construction in the drought territory which would give employment in further relief to the whole situation. These Federal activities provide for an expenditure of upward of $100,000,000 in this area and it is in progress today.

The Red Cross has always met the situations which it has undertaken. After careful survey and after actual experience of several months with their part of the problem they have announced firmly that they can command the resources with which to meet any call for human relief in prevention of hunger and suffering in drought areas and that they accept this responsibility. They have refused to accept Federal appropriations as not being consonant either with the need or the character of their organization. The Government departments have given and are giving them every assistance. We possibly need to strengthen the public health service in matters of sanitation and to strengthen the credit facilities of that area through the method approved by the Government departments to divert some existing appropriations to strengthen agricultural credit corporations.

Unemployment Relief

In the matter of unemployment outside of the drought areas important economic measures of mutual self help have been developed such as those to maintain wages, to distribute employment equitably, to increase construction work by industry, to increase Federal construction work from a rate of about $275,000,000 a year prior to the depression to a rate now of over $750,000,000 a year; to expand state and municipal construction—all upon a scale never before provided or even attempted in any depression. But beyond this to assure that there shall be no suffering, in every town and county voluntary agencies in relief of distress have been strengthened and created and generous funds have been placed at their disposal. They are carrying on their work efficiently and sympathetically.

But after and coincidently with voluntary relief, our American system requires that municipal, county and state governments shall use their own resources and credit before seeking such assistance from the Federal Treasury.

I have indeed spent much of my life in fighting hardship and starvation both abroad and in the southern states. I do not feel that I should be charged with lack of human sympathy for those who suffer but I recall that in all the organizations with which I have been connected over these many years, the foundation has been to summon the maximum of self help. I am proud to have sought the help of Congress in the past for nations who were so disorganized by war and anarchy that self help was impossible. But even these appropriations were but a tithe of that which was coincidently mobilized from the public charity of the United States and foreign countries. There is no such paralysis in the United States and I am confident that our people have the resources, the initiative, the courage, the stamina and kindliness of spirit to meet this situation in the way they have met their problems over generations.

I will accredit to those who advocate Federal charity a natural anxiety for the people of their states. I am willing to pledge myself that if the time should ever come that the voluntary agencies of the country together with the local and state governments are unable to find resources with which to prevent hunger and suffering in my country, I will ask the aid of every resource of the Federal Government because I would no more see starvation amongst our countrymen than would any senator or congressman. I have the faith in the American people that such a day will not come.

The American people are doing their job today. They should be given a chance to show whether they wish to preserve the principles of individual and local responsibility and mutual self help before they embark on what I believe is a disastrous system. I feel sure they will succeed if given the opportunity.

VIEWPOINT 2

"We of the cities have done our best [to aid the unemployed]. . . . But . . . we must now admit that we have failed miserably."

Local Relief Efforts Are Inadequate

Joseph L. Heffernan (1887-1977)

During his presidency Herbert Hoover frequently voiced his opinion that the federal government should play a very limited role in providing direct relief to the American people and that local governments and charities were providing adequate welfare resources. However, at a time when the unemployment rate in many cities rose to more than 50 percent, local charities and governments were stretched to the breaking point. In the following viewpoint, Joseph L. Heffernan draws from his own experiences as mayor of Youngstown, Ohio, to challenge Hoover's views concerning local welfare. Heffernan, who was mayor from 1927 to 1931, wrote an article published in the May 1932 edition of the *Atlantic Monthly* magazine describing how Youngstown was affected by the Depression. Heffernan writes that his city government, hampered by inadequate help from the Ohio state government, was unable to adequately provide relief for the unemployed or otherwise respond to the Depression. The size of the Depression was overwhelming both to the city of Youngstown and the state of Ohio, and, Heffernan argues, similar situations existed in other parts of the United States. He calls for greater involvement by the federal government to help restore the nation's economy.

Following his term as mayor, Heffernan continued to be active in Democratic politics. He worked on the Federal Communications Commission and later served as assistant attorney general of Ohio.

From Joseph L. Heffernan, "The Hungry City: A Mayor's Experience with Unemployment," *The Atlantic Monthly*, May 1932.

In December 1929, when I was mayor of Youngstown, I attended a conference on unemployment at Cleveland, called at the request of President Hoover. It was held at the Chamber of Commerce, under the chairmanship of Mr. Elroy J. Kulas, president of the Otis Steel Company, and was attended by public officials of northern Ohio.

Speaker after speaker told what his community would do to end the depression, and how quickly it would be done. The unemployed were to be set marching gayly back to work without an instant's delay, and the two-car garage was to be made ready for further enlargement.

Telling the Truth

When it came my turn to speak, I said rather brutally: 'This is all plain bunk. We know that our cities and counties are in debt and have bond limitations imposed by the state. If all of us were to start this minute drawing up a programme of public improvements, it would require months to get the legislation through. Why not tell the people the truth?'

After the meeting many of the officials said to me: 'Mayor, you are right. There isn't much we can do. But we have to go along, don't we?'

Five months later I went to Germany and visited a number of cities. Everywhere I saw that the German people were in a bad way. On returning home, I made a public statement that Germany was on the verge of economic collapse, and predicted that the depression would take five years to run its course. Thereupon I asked for a bond issue of $1,000,000 for unemployment relief. Many leading business men went out of their way to show their disapproval. One of them voiced the opinion of the majority when he said to me: 'You make a bad mistake in talking about the unemployed. *Don't* emphasize hard times and everything will be all right.' An influential newspaper chastised me for 'borrowing trouble'; the depression would be over, the editor maintained, before relief would be needed.

Discussion dragged on for several months, and the gravity of the situation was so deliberately misrepresented by the entire business community that when the bond issue finally came to a ballot, in November 1930, it was voted down.

Thus we passed into the early days of 1931—fourteen months after the first collapse—with no relief in sight except that which was provided by the orthodox charities. Not a single move had been made looking toward action by a united community.

Strange as it may seem, there was no way in which the city government could embark upon a programme of its own. We had no funds available for emergency relief, and without specific authorization from the people we could not issue bonds. To get around that obstacle we urged the state legislature to amend the law so as to modify our bond limitation, but that body was reluctant to pass a relief bill. Finally, after a long delay, it agreed upon a halfway measure which permitted the cities to sell bonds for the limited purpose of providing for their indigents. It made no pretense of supplying new employment for the jobless, but it furthered this end to some degree by indirection. Up to this time all funds for poor relief had been appropriated from general receipts, such as taxes. The new bonds removed this strain upon taxes, so that the money which had formerly been set aside for this purpose was released for public works. A few of the unemployed were thus given part-time jobs improving the parks.

A Call for Federal Aid

Robert M. La Follette Jr. in 1925 succeeded his father as a senator from Wisconsin and served until 1947. He was a vigorous advocate of federal aid to deal with the Depression. In a July 15, 1931, article in the Nation *magazine, he criticized Hoover's detrimental economic actions.*

For a hundred years the federal government has granted financial aid to communities temporarily unable to cope with relief problems created by disaster. In spite of his inaugural declaration in favor of cooperation with "movements of self-help," the President devoted much of his energy during the past winter to the defeat of proposals to cooperate with local communities by supplementing out of federal revenues their relief funds, which were rapidly being exhausted. To defend his position, the President drew an arbitrary distinction between "natural" disasters and economic disasters, although the suffering created by the present economic disruption probably far exceeds the burdens imposed by all the "natural" disasters of the last century.

He insisted that relief for the unemployed must be locally and privately financed, although official figures finally disclosed that during 1930, 72 percent of the meager assistance given the unemployed was contributed by local governments and was therefore out of local taxes. The net result of this policy was to throw the burden upon direct, local taxpayers and to relieve the big income taxpayers of their fair share of the relief levy.

Inadequate as it was, this legislative relief was all that the great State of Ohio could bring itself to grant, and even this pittance was withheld until the crisis had already run through more than eighteen devastating months.

I have cited these instances from my experience as mayor of an industrial city because they illustrate perfectly the state of mind which has been America's greatest handicap in dealing with the depression. Everyone will remember the assurances that were freely given out in November and December, 1929, by the highest authorities in government and business. The country, we were told, was 'fundamentally sound.' Nevertheless, general unemployment continued to increase through the winter. Then in the spring of 1930 it was predicted that we might expect an upward turn any minute. Yet the summer slid past with hope unfulfilled. Winter came again, and conditions had grown steadily worse; still nothing was done, because we were reluctant to face the truth. Our leaders, having made a bad guess in the beginning, have been unwilling to admit their error. With the foolish consistency which is the hobgoblin of little minds, they have persistently rejected reality and allowed our people to suffer by pretending that all would be well on the morrow.

Pleas for Help

In spite of the insurmountable handicaps under which the cities have labored in trying to cope with the emergency, desperate men and women out of work have stormed city halls from coast to coast demanding jobs. It has been a waste of breath for mayors to explain that they have no authority to put men to work when municipal treasuries are empty. 'Don't hand us that,' is a response I have heard over and over again. 'Do you mean to tell us that the city couldn't raise the money if it wanted to?' This, of course, has been the real tragedy of the situation: the cities could *not* raise the money.

One man I had known for years stood at my desk and calmly said: 'My wife is frantic. After working at the steel mill for twenty-five years, I have lost my job, and I'm too old to get other work. If you can't do something for me, I'm going to kill myself.' I knew he was desperate. Through friends I managed to find him a little job where he could earn enough to keep body and soul together.

In another instance a newspaper man urged me to find work for one of his neighbors, a man who had a wife and four sons—all rugged citizens who preferred to starve rather than accept public charity. 'You could hardly believe what they live on,' the reporter told me. 'The mother mixes a little flour and water, and cooks it in a frying pan. That is their regular meal.' Eventually I found work for one of the sons, and he became the sole support of the others.

To my home came a sad-eyed woman, the mother of nine children. No one in the family had had work in more than a year. 'How do you manage to live?' I asked her. 'I can't tell you,' she replied simply; 'I really don't know.' Christmas 1930 was marked by the usual campaign for the most needy cases, and this family was included in the list. They got their Christmas basket all right, but when the holidays were over they were no better off than they had been before.

As time went on, business conditions showed no improvement. Every night hundreds of homeless men crowded into the municipal incinerator, where they found warmth even though they had to sleep on heaps of garbage. In January 1931, I obtained the cooperation of the City Council to convert an abandoned police station into a 'flop-house.' The first night it was filled, and it has remained filled ever since. I made a point of paying frequent visits to this establishment so that I could see for myself what kind of men these down-and-outers were, and I heartily wish that those folk who have made themselves comfortable by ignoring and denying the suffering of their less fortunate neighbors could see some of the sights I saw. There were old men gnarled by heavy labor, young mechanics tasting the first bitterness of defeat, clerks and white-collar workers learning the equality of misery, derelicts who fared no worse in bad times than in good, Negroes who only a short time before had come from Southern cotton fields, now glad to find any shelter from the cold, immigrants who had been lured to Van Dyke's 'land of youth and freedom'—each one a personal tragedy, and all together an overwhelming catastrophe for the nation. . . .

A Final Blow

In the autumn of 1931 a final blow laid the city of Youngstown prostrate. The atmosphere was poisoned with a new fever of apprehension, with rumors that began no one knew where and ended in panic. 'Have you heard?' everybody whispered excitedly. 'The banks . . . buzz, buzz, buzz . . . the banks!' People who were fortunate enough to have money deposited hurried to withdraw it. Day after day the drain continued, and the bankers had to stand by helplessly while their reserves melted away. Then three of the banks closed their doors, and fear ran riot.

At once concerted efforts were made to protect the other banks. Depositors were besought not to withdraw their savings and were urged to bring back what they had carried away to hide. Statements calling upon the people to have confidence were issued by everyone of supposed influence. The ministers joined the campaign with sermons on civic faith and hope. But confidence was shattered. Had not everybody in authority, from the President down, been making optimistic statements for two years, and had not subsequent events disproved all predictions? Could anybody be trusted to tell the truth? Did anybody really know? People

Hungry Families

In 1932 and 1933 the Senate Subcommittee on Manufacturers conducted hearings on federal and state cooperation in unemployment relief. On May 9, 1932, Karl de Schweinitz, executive secretary of the Community Council of Philadelphia, described for the committee what happened when relief funds were exhausted.

On April 11 [1932] we mailed to families the last food orders which they received from private funds. It was not until April 22 that the giving of aid to families from public funds began, so that there was a period of about 11 days when many families received nothing. We have received reports from workers as to how these families managed. The material I am about to give you is typical, although it is based on a small sample. We made an intensive study of 91 families to find out what happened when the food orders stopped. . . .

One woman said she borrowed 50 cents from a friend and bought stale bread for 3½ cents per loaf, and that is all they had for eleven days except for one or two meals.

With the last food order another woman received she bought dried vegetables and canned goods. With this she made a soup and whenever the members of the family felt hungry they just ate some of the soup. . . .

One woman went along the docks and picked up vegetables that fell from the wagons. Sometimes the fish vendors gave her fish at the end of the day. On two different occasions this family was without food for a day and a half. . . .

I should also like to say that when we talk to people who ask about unemployment they say, "Well, people manage to get along somehow or other don't they? You do not have very many people who really drop dead of starvation." That is perfectly true. Actually, death from starvation is not a frequent occurrence. You do not often hear about casualties of that sort. This is because people live in just the way that I have described. They live on inadequacies, and because they live on inadequacies the thing does not become dramatic and we do not hear about it. Yet the cost in human suffering is just as great as if they starved to death overnight.

stood on the street corners asking each other anxious questions. Never before had all the old landmarks of security been so shattered. Never had Youngstown suffered such a shock to the spirit which had made it one of the great industrial centres of the world. Nobody could now deny that America was in the throes of a panic.

Another winter was approaching. The numbers of the unemployed had increased, and suffering had grown acute. Many heads of families had not earned a penny in two years. Landlords clamored for their rents and sought evictions. Communists protested loudly and threatened to use force to put back anyone who was dispossessed. Thousands of the city's water bills were unpaid, and officials were torn between their desire to be charitable, their fear of disease if the water were cut off, and the city's urgent need of money. Property owners could not pay their taxes, and delinquencies became appalling.

Such a large proportion of the taxes were uncollectable that the city and county governments had to face the certainty that unless something was done they would soon lack funds to operate. A wild clamor went up to reduce public expenditures. (A year before, the cry had been to keep men at work.) The budget for 1932 would have to be cut 40 per cent. This meant that innumerable men who had been saved from starvation by doing part-time work would have to be turned away to join the ranks of the wholly unemployed. In consideration of this dilemma a special one-mill tax levy for relief was finally voted at the November election, but it was apparent that the returns from this source would have to be substantially discounted because of tax delinquencies. As in Cleveland, we adopted the slogan, 'Pay your taxes, so the hungry can be fed,' and the words meant just what they said, for by this time the private charities were swamped, desperate, and bankrupt.

Such was the state of affairs in Youngstown as we turned the corner of the new year, and it is common knowledge that many another once-thriving community now finds itself in the same predicament. What 1932 may do to alter these conditions no one can say, but perhaps we should take cold comfort in the thought that, no matter what turn events may take, they are bound to induce a change for the better, since it is hardly conceivable that the situation can grow much worse than it already is.

The Dole

Often, as I have watched the line of job seekers at the City Hall, I have had occasion to marvel at the mysterious power that certain words and phrases exercise upon the human mind. A wise man once observed that words rule mankind, and so it is in America today. Prominent politicians and business men have repeatedly stated that, come what may, America must not have the dole. To be sure, we should all be much happier if we could get along without a dole, but the simple truth is that we have it already. Every city in the land has had a dole from the moment it began unemployment relief. The men who apply for help know that it is a dole. The officials who issue work orders can be in no doubt about it, for the work done in no way justifies the money spent, except on the basis of a dole.

Why, then, so much concern about the word? Perhaps because, if we were honest enough to recognize unemployment relief for the dole it really is, we should also have to be honest enough to admit that the depression is a catastrophe of historic proportions, and courageous enough to deal with it accordingly. One alternative to the dole would be to let all the unfortunates starve to death, but so far no one has advanced this proposal, although some have come pretty close to it in saying that the way out of the depression is to let nature take its course.

Those who have not been willing to go so far as that have maintained, however, that each community must look after its own unemployed, and that under no circumstances must the Federal Government assume any responsibility for them. For two years local communities have carried the burden unassisted, and many of them, like Youngstown, have prostrated themselves in doing it. We of the cities have done our best, laboring against conditions which were beyond our control. But, even if we are given full credit for trying, we must now admit that we have failed miserably. Whether this was caused by a lack of simple charity in the hearts of our people or by our incapacity to manage our financial problems is beside the point. The fact of our failure is patent. We of the cities have not advanced a single new idea on unemployment or its relief. We have not dared to consider the fundamental questions raised by our social and economic collapse. We are still as stupidly devoted as ever to the philosophy of *laissez faire,* and we face the future bewildered and purposeless. Our one great achievement in response to this national catastrophe has been to open soup kitchens and flop-houses.

Moral Costs

And nobody has taken the trouble to weigh the consequences of our well-meant but ineffective charity upon the moral fibre of the American people. Seventy years ago we fought a civil war to free black slaves; to-day we remain indifferent while millions of our fellow citizens are reduced to the status of paupers. There is a world of difference between mere poverty and pauperism. The honest poor will struggle for years to keep themselves above the pauper class. With quiet desperation they will bear hunger and mental anguish until every resource is exhausted. Then comes the ultimate struggle when, with heartache and an overwhelming sense of disgrace, they have to make the shamefaced journey to the door of public charity. This is the last straw. Their self-respect is destroyed; they undergo an insidious metamorphosis, and sink down to spiritless despondency.

This descent from respectability, frequent enough in the best of times, has been hastened immeasurably by two years of business paralysis, and the people who have been affected in this manner must be numbered in millions. This is what we have accomplished with our bread lines and soup kitchens. I know, because I have seen thousands of these defeated, discouraged, hopeless men and women, cringing and fawning as they come to ask for public aid. It is a spectacle of national degeneration. That is the fundamental tragedy for America. If every mill and factory in the land should begin to hum with prosperity to-morrow morning, the destructive effect of our haphazard relief measures would not work itself out of the nation's blood until the sons of our sons have expiated the sins of our neglect.

VIEWPOINT 3

"Methods of self-help are numerous and great numbers of people have made the stimulating discovery that they need not depend on employers to find work for them—they can find work for themselves."

Self-Help Is the Best Response to Unemployment

Henry Ford (1863-1947)

Henry Ford, industrialist and founder of Ford Motor Company, was perhaps America's most famous businessman. In the following viewpoint, taken from two editorials the Ford Motor Company inserted in the *Literary Digest*, Ford argues that encouraging the unemployed to help themselves rather than to depend on charity or relief was the best approach. He also reveals his idealization of rural life, encouraging people to live off the land. In June 1932, when these articles first appeared, approximately 13 million people were unemployed in the United States. Ford's views toward unemployment were not uncommon within the business community during the Great Depression.

Henry Ford, "On Unemployment," editorial published in the *Literary Digest*, June 11 and June 18, 1932.

I have always had to work, whether any one hired me or not. For the first forty years of my life, I was an employe. When not employed by others, I employed myself. I found very early that being out of hire was not necessarily being out of work. The first means that your employer has not found something for you to do; the second means that you are waiting until he does.

We nowadays think of work as something that others find for us to do, call us to do, and pay us to do. No doubt our industrial growth is largely responsible for that. We have accustomed men to think of work that way.

In my own case, I was able to find work for others as well as myself. Outside my family life, nothing has given me more satisfaction than to see jobs increase in number and in profit to the men who handle them. And beyond question, the jobs of the world today are more numerous and profitable in wages than they were even eighteen years ago.

Problem of Unemployment

But something entirely outside the workshops of the nation has affected this hired employment very seriously. The word "unemployment" has become one of the most dreadful words in the language. The condition itself has become the concern of every person in the country.

When this condition arrived, there were just three things to be done. The first, of course, was to maintain employment at the maximum by every means known to management. Employment—hire—was what the people were accustomed to; they preferred it; it was the immediate solution of the difficulty. In our plants we used every expedient to spread as much employment over as many employes as was possible. I don't believe in "make work"—the public pays for all unnecessary work—but there are times when the plight of others compels us to do the human thing even though it be but a makeshift; and I am obliged to admit that, like most manufacturers, we avoided layoffs by continuing work that good business judgment would have halted. All of our non-profit work was continued in full force and much of the shop work. There were always tens of thousands employed—the lowest point at Dearborn was 40,000—but there were always thousands unemployed or so meagerly employed, that the situation was far from desirable.

When all possible devices for providing employment have been used and fall short, there remains no alternative but self-help or charity.

I do not believe in routine charity. I think it a shameful thing that any man should have to stoop to take it, or give it. I do not include human helpfulness under the name of charity. My quarrel with charity is that it is neither helpful nor human. The charity of our cities is the most barbarous thing in our system, with the possible exception of our prisons. What we call charity is a modern substitute for being personally kind, personally concerned and personally involved in the work of helping others in difficulty. True charity is a much more costly effort than money-giving. Our donations too often purchase exemption from giving the only form of help that will drive the need for charity out of the land.

Many of the unemployed tried to avoid going on relief by taking odd jobs such as selling apples.

Our own theory of helping people has been in operation for some years. We used to discuss it years ago—when no one could be persuaded to listen. Those who asked public attention to these matters were ridiculed by the very people who now call most loudly for some one to do something.

Our own work involves the usual emergency relief, hospitalization, adjustment of debt, with this addition—we help people to alter their affairs in common-sense accordance with changed conditions, and we have an understanding that all help received should be repaid in reasonable amounts in better times. Many families were not so badly off as they thought; they needed guidance in the management of their resources and opportunities. Human nature, of course, presented the usual problems. Relying on human sympathy many develop a spirit of professional indigence. But where co-operation is given, honest and self-respecting persons and families can usually be assisted to a condition which is much less distressing than they feared.

One of our responsibilities, voluntarily assumed—not because it was ours, but because there seemed to be no one else to assume it—was the care of a village of several hundred families whose condition was pretty low. Ordinarily a large welfare fund would have been needed to accomplish anything for these people. In this instance, we set the people at work cleaning up their homes and backyards, and then cleaning up the roads of their town, and then plowing up about 500 acres of vacant land around their houses. We abolished everything that savored of "handout" charity, opening instead a modern commissary where personal IOU's were accepted and a garment-making school, and setting the cobblers and tailors of the community to work for their neighbors. We found the people heavily burdened with debt, and we acted informally as their agents in apportioning their income to straighten their affairs. Many families are now out of debt for the first time in years. There has appeared in this village not only a new spirit of confidence in life, but also a new sense of economic values, and an appreciation of economic independence which we feel will not soon be lost. None of these things could have been accomplished by paying out welfare funds after the orthodox manner. The only true charity for these people was somehow to get under their burdens with them and lend them the value of our experience to show them what can be done by people in their circumstances.

Our visiting staff in city work has personally handled thousands of cases in the manner above described. And while no one institution can shoulder all the burden, we feel that merely to mitigate present distress is not enough—we feel that thousands of families have been prepared for a better way of life when the wheels of activity begin turning again.

Self-Help

But there is still another way, a third way, so much better than the very best charitable endeavor that it simply forbids us to be satisfied with anything less. That is the way of Self-Help. . . .

If it is right and proper to help people to become wise managers of their own affairs in good times, it cannot be wrong to pursue the same object in dull times. Independence through self-dependence is a method which must commend itself when understood.

Methods of self-help are numerous and great numbers of

people have made the stimulating discovery that they need not depend on employers to find work for them—they can find work for themselves. I have more definitely in mind those who have not yet made that discovery, and I should like to express certain convictions I have tested.

Ashamed of Relief

Many Americans firmly believed in the importance of self-reliance and were extremely reluctant to apply for welfare and relief. Ben Isaacs, a former salesman, described his experiences in an interview with Chicago writer Studs Terkel. Terkel published Isaac's views and those of many other Americans in his book Hard Times: An Oral History of the Great Depression.

We tried to struggle along living day by day. Then I couldn't pay the rent. I had a little car, but I couldn't pay no license for it. I left it parked against the court. I sold it for $15 in order to buy some food for the family. I had three little children. It was a time when I didn't even have money to buy a pack of cigarettes, and I was a smoker. I didn't have a nickel in my pocket.

Finally people started to talk me into going into the relief. They had open soup kitchens. Al Capone, he had open soup kitchens somewhere downtown, where people were standing in line. And you had to go two blocks, stand there, around the corner, to get a bowl of soup.

Lotta people committed suicide, pushed themselves out of buildings and killed themselves, 'cause they couldn't face the disgrace. Finally, the same thing with me.

I was so downcasted that I couldn't think of anything. Where can I go? What to face? Age that I can't get no job. I have no trade, except selling is my trade, that's all. I went around trying to find a job as a salesman. They wouldn't hire me on account of my age. I was just like dried up. Every door was closed on me, every avenue. Even when I was putting my hand on gold, it would turn into dust. It looked like bad luck had set its hand on my shoulder. Whatever I tried, I would fail. . . .

I didn't want to go on relief. Believe me, when I was forced to go to the office of the relief, the tears were running out of my eyes. I couldn't bear myself to take money from anybody for nothing. If it wasn't for those kids—I tell you the truth—many a time it came to my mind to go commit suicide. Than go ask for relief. But somebody has to take care of those kids.

The land! That is where our roots are. There is the basis of our physical life. The farther we get away from the land, the greater our insecurity. From the land comes everything that supports life, everything we use for the service of physical life. The land has not collapsed or shrunk in either extent or productivity. It is there waiting to honor all the labor we are willing to invest in it, and able to tide us across any dislocation of economic conditions.

No unemployment insurance can be compared to an alliance between a man and a plot of land. With one foot in industry and another foot in the land, human society is firmly balanced against most economic uncertainties. With a job to supply him with cash, and a plot of land to guarantee him support, the individual is doubly secure. Stocks may fail, but seedtime and harvest do not fail.

I am not speaking of stop-gaps or temporary expedients. Let every man and every family at this season of the year cultivate a plot of land and raise a sufficient supply for themselves or others. Every city and village has vacant space whose use would be permitted. Groups of men could rent farms for small sums and operate them on the co-operative plan. Employed men, in groups of ten, twenty or fifty, could rent farms and operate them with several unemployed families. Or, they could engage a farmer with his farm to be their farmer this year, either as employe or on shares. There are farmers who would be glad to give a decent indigent family a corner of a field on which to live and provide against next winter. Industrial concerns everywhere would gladly make it possible for their men, employed and unemployed, to find and work the land. Public-spirited citizens and institutions would most willingly assist in these efforts at self-help.

I do not urge this solely or primarily on the ground of need. It is a definite step to the restoration of normal business activity. Families who adopt self-help have that amount of free money to use in the channels of trade. That in turn means a flow of goods, an increase in employment, a general benefit.

No One Is Hurt

When I suggested this last year and enabled our own people to make the experiment, the critics said that it would mean competition with the farmer. If that were true it would constitute a serious defect in the plan. My interest in the success and prosperity of the farmer is attested by my whole business career. The farmer is carrying in the form of heavy taxes the burden of families who cannot afford to buy his produce. Enabling them to raise their own food would not be taking a customer away from the farmer, but would be actually lifting a family off the tax-payer's back. It is argued that farm products are so cheap that it is better to buy than to grow them. This would be impressive if every one had money to spend. Farm products are cheap because purchasing power is low. And the farmer paying taxes helps to pay the difference. The course I suggest is not competition with the farmer; it deprives him of no customer; it does not affect the big market crops. Gardens never hurt the farmer. Partnerships between groups of city men and individual farmers certainly help the farmer. When a family lifts itself off the welfare lists or increases its free cash by raising its food, it actually helps the farmer as it does every one else, including itself. In fact, it is fundamental that *no one is hurt by self-help*. In the relief of tax burdens and the revival of industry the farmer would share the benefit.

VIEWPOINT 4

"[The unemployed] were caught in the lay-off which everyone from their employers to the President of the United States assured them was a temporary dip in the cycle of prosperity."

Self-Help Is Not Enough

Charles R. Walker (1893-1974)

By the winter of 1932, a quarter of the Americans who sought work were without jobs. Unemployment was especially high in cities such as Detroit, where industries such as the auto industry cut down on their production. In the following viewpoint, Charles R. Walker examines the fate of one laborer who was laid off from the Ford Motor Company. Walker goes on to examine the effects of unemployment in Detroit and the nation. He suggests in his depiction the limits of self-help as advocated by Henry Ford.

Walker was a writer whose experiences included working as an editor for the *Atlantic Monthly*, working in a steel mill, and teaching at Yale University. He wrote fictional and nonfictional works examining the effects of industrial technology on the American worker. His books include *American City* and *The Man on the Assembly Line*.

Excerpted from Charles R. Walker, "Down and Out in Detroit." In *America Faces the Future*, edited by Charles A. Beard. Boston: Houghton Mifflin, 1932.

In 1914 an extraordinary thing occurred in America. An automobile manufacturer in Detroit announced that he was raising wages for common labor to five dollars a day. Newspaper headlines in Detroit went a little crazy; the streets of the city and of the little town of Dearborn were packed with workmen fighting for a chance to work at the new wage. And automobile manufacturers of Detroit and elsewhere raged and gave out desperate interviews prophesying doom. Detectives came to Detroit to investigate Henry Ford. But above all, workmen from all over the United States bought railroad tickets and boarded trains for Detroit. Among the latter was John (once Anton) Boris, American citizen of Slav descent, father of a family, who had ambitions to be a 'millerwright' and needed cash for an expanding family. He had been a logger in a Michigan lumber camp, then a worker in an Ohio steel mill where he earned from two to three dollars a day. With thousands of others, he now came to Detroit.

Working at Ford

'In dose days work was hard all right at Ford's, but dey treat us like mens.' One day the straw boss fired a workman in anger. The employment manager stood between the boss and the workman. 'You can't discharge a man out of spite,' he said. 'I am putting you back to work—both of you—in different shops.' Boris remembered the episode a long time. Another day a boy in his department suggested over their noon sandwiches that they should have a union at Ford's. The boy was a skilled worker with a good record. The next week he did not appear in the millwrights' gang. When Boris asked where he was, his companions raised their shoulders. Boris remembered this, too. He decided not to listen to men talking about unions even though they were 'good millerwrights.' He decided not to talk about unions himself.

John Boris's wages at Ford's rose steadily as the years passed, till he was making eight dollars a day. His young wife, whom he had found it a delight to cherish as he had promised the priest, had borne him eight children, five of whom were living and going to Michigan schools. One day a letter arrived from a friend in a Texas oil field, saying to come out there for a good job. 'I think I go all right,' he told me, 'can get twenty dollar a day.' But his wife expressed other ideas. 'You stay wid Ford; here steady job—better dan big money for you; las' all de years what you live.' Boris stayed at Ford's.

'The American way,' said the automobile manufacturers in 1927, 'is to pay wages sufficient to guarantee the workingman not only subsistence, but the comforts and some of the luxuries of life. Let him buy a car, a radio, and an American home!' The children wanted a radio, so John got one; but he resisted his foreman's appeal to buy a car, even though American salesmanship did what it could against his Slavic conservatism. Public advice to 'buy a home,' however, appealed to an instinct. The real estate agent made out his contract. There was a five hundred dollars down payment and fifty dollars a month. He started payments and moved in. The house seemed in a sense to be rounding out his millwright's career for him; and better, he thought, than a car—even though the neighbors boasted of both.

It was in this house, under the shaded light of the 'parlor lamp,' that Boris the other day gave me in his own words the final chapter of this history. The house was subject to foreclosure in default of payment, but the furniture was still intact. The radio stood at the left of the chair where Boris sat; a double door led into a pleasant dining-room.

'Fourteen year,' said Boris, leaning forward, 'I work for Henry Ford. All kin' jobs . . . millerwright, danger jobs; I put in all my young days Henry Ford. Las' July, what you know, he lay me off. When I go out of factory that day I don' believe; I don' believe he do such ting to me. I tink trouble wid man in de office who don' un'erstan'.' His voice ceased and he took a deep breath which was expended in the earnest emphasis of his next words: 'I tink,' he said, 'I go Henry Ford *pers'nally!* But what you know!' He looked like a boy whom a drunken father had whipped into physical submission. His voice was angry, but with a deep hurt at the core of it. 'I can' get close to him,' he cried, 'I can' get clos' even employment man. De guard say, "We got your name in dere all right, we let you know when we wan' you." Nine mont',' he concluded, 'I go no work.'

Coping with Unemployment

Figures show that 14.2 per cent of Detroit's normally employed are out of jobs. Other cities follow close, with Cleveland at 13.8 per cent and Chicago at 13.3. The distinction of Detroit, however, is not that she has been hardest hit in the depression, but that she has done something to buck it. Municipal and community leadership—not the manufacturers—are doing what they can.

During the first of his workless periods, Boris was able to support his family and to continue regular payments on his home. Against public pressure he had exercised thrift, and had in reserve a few hundred dollars. But misfortunes did not attack him singly. His wife fell ill and an operation for tumor was demanded. Boris met the emergency and hired the best doctor he could find. A kidney operation on the woman followed the first, running up medical charges for hospital and doctor to eight hundred dollars. Somewhere during this epoch the son of John Boris, who had gone to an American school and could put matters clearly in written English, composed a letter to the welfare department of the Ford Motor Company.

An 'investigator' arrived promptly, and took the chair, Boris informed me, in which I was sitting. 'Investigator say, "Boris, employment have no right do that to you. You get job back right away. Seven o'clock tomorrow morning you go employment; he put you back on job; tak' this slip."'

Going back the next morning through the high mill gate, with the slip tightly held in his fingers, Boris found delightedly that he was admitted to the office. 'We cannot give you your old job,' they told him, 'at eight dollars a day, but we will give you a new one at six dollars for three days a week.' 'Yes, all right,' said Boris. Lay-off and rehire with a dock of a dollar or two a day is common in the automobile industry. It enables the manufacturer to give the appearance of 'maintaining wages' while effecting the needed economies in his payroll. The same work is performed on 'the new job.' Boris was glad. 'Hard times for everybody,' he explained, 'sure, I take.' The employment manager continued courteously: 'After you work sixty days, you will receive seven dollars a day.'. . .

On the sixty-first day, Boris received the promised seven dollars. On the sixty-third his foreman fired him. 'You're finished, Boris,' he said. To Boris it seemed clear that he had been dropped because he was 'making too much money.' And because there were thousands waiting to take his job at minimum pay. But he repressed this resentment and went to the office. 'Anything wrong wid my work for comp'ny?' he asked earnestly. No, the employment man assured him; his work was satisfactory. 'Wid my records for comp'ny?' he persisted, knowing that in hard times a man's record is his friend. 'No,' said the employment man, 'you have a good record with the company. But there is no longer any work for you.' The office then stated that this was not a lay-off, but, as Boris had expressed it, 'finish.' Boris then exploded. In reminiscence of what he had said, his voice came somewhere from the middle of his chest; it was compacted of fourteen years of exploded loyalty.

'I haf' no money now,' he cried, 'lose my home quick, what I do chil'ren, what I do doctor? Fourteen years!' he returned to his original cry, 'I work Henry Ford!'

The employment man looked at him. 'That is a long time; you should have saved money, Boris, to take care of you in your old age.'

Boris trembled. 'You say dat to me!' he cried, struggling for possession of himself. 'I give up my strength to you; I put in all my young days work good for Henry Ford—you can' do dis to me now!'

'Why did you spend all your money?' asked the employment man.

'For why? I tell you. I spen' money for house,' replied John Boris, 'to raise fam'ly, to sen' my chil'ren school, to buy foods, *dat's how I spen' money*——'

'Your children are your own business,' said the other, 'not Henry Ford's.'

Betrayed Loyalty

Even in recollection of this episode which terminated his career and hastened the break-up of his family, I was struck by the special character of Boris's resentment. It seemed clear that he was torn as terribly by the blasting of his workman's loyalty as by the enormity of his personal loss.

'I go out from mill,' he continued. 'I try tink what I do help mysel'. Who I go to? I use tink,' he cried, 'if something come like dis, go to Henry Ford yoursel'. But I tell you no workman beeg enough see Henry Ford! Well, I go lawyer—I happen to know him once—who knows ting like dis more what I do. I say: "What can I do now?" He say: "Nutting, John, ain' nutting you can do!"'

John Boris refused to accept the dictum of the lawyer that there was nothing he could do. In accordance with the formula that 'there is plenty of work in the world if a man be willing to take it,' he buried the pride of a skilled maturity, and found a few hours' work in a cushion factory, accepting a wage twenty-seven and one half cents an hour less than Ford's minimum rate in 1914. But long before he managed this, his daughters had taken jobs in the same factory to which he came ultimately. They carried and are still carrying the bulk of the family load.

These latter items make the story of John Boris a relatively lucky one. The family enjoys a small income from wages; John Boris is not, and except only for a few weeks between the time of 'finish' at Ford's and the cushion factory job, has not been rated as one of the unemployed. And he is lucky enough to have escaped charity.

As I was sitting in the Boris parlor, the two girls came in from work. It was nine o'clock. He introduced his daughters to me; they excused themselves and went to the kitchen. John Boris explained: 'Only when they work late, comp'ny give time for supper.' Work begins at seven-thirty; lunch at twelve. 'How late do you work?' I asked the younger girl, when she reappeared. 'Sometimes till nine o'clock,' she answered, 'sometimes till ten. One night last week we worked till eleven-thirty.' I checked up on this and found that in the smaller concerns which have sprung up in the wake of depression, no regularity prevails: the workmen are expected to finish the work available, which sometimes takes five hours, sometimes ten.

'Alice, Louie's girl,' said one of the girls, 'said she felt faint tonight'—it seemed to me that Miss Boris thought Alice a little silly for it—'so I sent her upstairs to my coat where I keep cookies.'

John Boris had been silent a long time. He moved his shoulders restlessly and looked down at the thick fingers of his hands. 'Las' July,' he said, 'I was good man.' He raised his eyes slowly. 'I ain't man now,' he said.

With some effort I looked into the work of the Ford employment office and of the welfare department of the Ford Motor Company. A comprehensive stagger system I found had been organized to spread work among the largest possible number. Further than this, a sincere effort was being made everywhere to give jobs to the neediest. Boris was dismissed, I am ready to believe, not through carelessness—but because relatively worse cases needed his job more. In fact the wealth of data put before me by the mayor's unemployment committee of the city of Detroit confirms me in the belief that his particular case, in which job, savings, and home were wiped out, was one of the lucky ones.

Life of a Tramp

For hundreds of thousands of young people, "self-help" meant leaving home and wandering through America, working at odd jobs and sleeping at missions and hobo camps. Robert Carter wrote of such experiences in a diary, portions of which were printed in the New Republic, *March 8, 1933.*

Greenville, N.C.

Arrived here on a freight train late at night, tired and dirty from train smoke and cinders. I slept in the tobacco warehouse with two other young tramps, one having a suitcase crammed with dirty clothes and a blanket smelling of antiseptic. Next morning was cold, the wind hinted of winter. Leaving town I turned due south, walking the roads. All day I went steadily, getting an occasional ride from trucks or Fords. When dinnertime came I asked for work at a farmhouse for food and picked peas with the farmer's family for two hours.

That night I pried open a church window and slept there. Services had been held there that night, and I had crouched near by in a clump of pines till the last hymn had ended and the people had walked and driven away in cars and buggies. I placed two seats together, wrapped my blanket about me and fell asleep. It grew steadily colder during the night. About four o'clock I was awakened by the wind rattling the windows. I got up chilled to the bone and walked the roads till morning. When the sun rose I spread my blanket on the ground and fell asleep.

In addition to Mr. Boris's case, there are 227,000 men totally unemployed. Let us consider some of these. Out of the number, fifteen thousand are reported homeless. Boris as yet is not of this class and will probably escape it by living with relatives. These men are now housed in the 'emergency lodges,' better known as 'flop houses,' which are maintained at the city's expense. What are they like? Take the 'Fisher East Side Lodge.' It is a huge unused factory building lent to the city by Fisher Brothers and housing, when I visited it, sixteen hundred men. Here I found bank tellers with twenty to thirty years' experience, traveling salesmen, expert toolmakers, a vice-president or two, and workmen of every variety.

The mayor's committee estimates that of the 'homeless men' on their records, about ten per cent are chronic vagrants who would be looking for hand-outs in fat times as well as lean. The rest are *bona-fide* unemployment cases with a large white-collar sprinkling. Fifteen thousand homeless is considered large for the size of the city and is generally attributed by manufacturers I talked with to the army of unmarried men attracted to Detroit by the high wages and short hours of the automobile factories. But I discovered that over ten per cent of the homeless group are married men. These are perhaps the least fortunate cases, as contrasted with the relatively fortunate who, like Boris, still command resources of a sort. What is their history? What, for example, becomes of the wife, and what happens to the kids? The story of the married homeless averages as follows. (I am omitting the cases of suicide and actual starvation.)

A majority of the men are automobile workers; the average age is thirty-eight. Fifteen years ago they came to Detroit attracted by the good wages. A considerable number are college men; as skilled workers, tool designers, and engineers, they made from ten to fifteen dollars a day. They laughed at their white-collar classmates making forty per—and obliged to 'keep up appearances.' The ordinary workers among them were making five dollars a day, or six dollars, or seven dollars, with steady jobs. They married, bought a car, and ultimately started payments on a 'home of their own.'

About six years ago the 'inventory period' of the manufacturers began to stretch. From two weeks' 'vacation' in summer—without pay—it edged up to a month. 'Changing tools' for the new model, repair periods, 'reorganization,' sliced another week or two from the winter months. As a rule the single man didn't care; for him it *was* a vacation. But his married brother got fidgety. He hadn't rigged his budget for a ten-month year. Then among Ford men came the five months' shutdown in 1927. This wiped out a good many surpluses. The surpluses were not large. Why? Most of the men had bought a car, had taken out insurance, and begun payments on the 'home.' By 1929, the family men were worried. Not in a panic, but thinking hard. They still had their homes, they still had the car, but their savings were gone. The expanding vacations gave them an increasing sense of insecurity.

The Depression Hits

Then descended the first months of the depression a year and a half ago. They were caught in the lay-off which everyone from their employers to the President of the United States assured them was a temporary dip in the cycle of prosperity. The first act of the conservative householder was to sell his car—the purchase of which a year before had been all but compelled by company salesmanship. 'It is your duty,' the married man had been told; 'it will guarantee your job.' Two months passed. Just as the newspapers agreed that the 'worst was over,' the married man borrowed four hundred dollars on his furniture. This to keep his end up, to continue payment on his home, pay his insurance premiums, buy food, and keep the boy at school. At this point he had adopted his employers' optimism. 'Things *must* pick up. In another month I'll be back at work.' But the month passes, and the furniture goes to meet the loan. However, there is the hundred dollars which Alice hasn't told him about. With it he manages one more payment on the house, hoping that the rumor about a 'pick-up' at Fisher's will come true. It doesn't.

In a Michigan 'land contract' the owner holds the deed; in case of the tenant's default, payments go to the deed-holder. At this point his contract is foreclosed, and with the house passes forever the three thousand dollars paid to date toward ownership. The children, who have been denied milk for a couple of months, are now sent to grandmother's, or parked around among relatives. The married man and his wife move into two rooms in the suburbs she had always scorned. With the change there passes into discard the emotions which cling to a united family, and to the home as a physical possession, somehow defensible.

The married man, however, at this point is really just beginning to fight. He tells his wife this in as many words. With the burden of the kids off his mind, and with no payments to make on the lost home, he is ready for any kind of work at any pay. It is the mood endorsed by so many well-wishers who themselves are in more fortunate positions. And he gets the work. Any number of young men found a month's neighborhood work, repairing the front steps, trimming hedges, mowing the lawn, or cleaning out the furnace—at a dollar a day, or two.

But this permits a physical subsistence only; it doesn't constitute what the married man hopes for and desires passionately— the beginnings of rehabilitation. After a couple of months the odd-job market is exhausted, and he has learned either to pity or to despise himself. The mental attitude of his new employers is, I find, almost without exception a compound of self-interest and charity. They demand two things of the ex-tool-maker who has asked the privilege of tending furnace for them: first, that he take a rate lower than they would pay an ordinary workman at the job; second, that he show himself abundantly grateful.

At some point during this odd-job epoch, the wife goes back upstate to live with her mother. She suggests he come too. But in the group I am considering, when the man's nerve is still strong, the husband answers: 'No. You go ahead, but I'll stick it in Detroit. This has been our home since 1918, and I certainly can find something. Before you know it I'll be sending for you.' He tries another six months, paying five dollars (a month) for his room. Finally pawns his overcoat, his watch; applies at last to the Welfare for an old pair of shoes.

You and I can call on him today at the Fisher Lodge, where at the moment the city will be able, if tax receipts hold up, to expend twenty-two and a half cents a day on him. Out of this comes a clean cot, clean laundry, and two meals a day. And he—with most of his fellows with whom I talked—is still looking for that job, working a week or two without pay for the city to pay for the winter's board.

VIEWPOINT 5

"If the state desires to check deflation it can check it; to create employment on useful and worthy projects, it can create it."

The Federal Government Should Act to End the Depression

Stuart Chase (1888-1985)

Stuart Chase was a writer and an economist. During the 1920s he worked for the Federal Trade Commission and the Labor Bureau, a federal office which gave economic advice to labor unions. He later worked for consumer groups, including Consumer's Union. Many of his books dealt with economic issues facing American society.

In the following viewpoint, taken from his 1932 book *A New Deal*, he criticizes the steps the Hoover Administration took during the Great Depression as inadequate and inconsistent. Chase argues for an active role for the federal government in fighting the Depression. Many of Chase's arguments were inspired by the new theories of the British economist John Maynard Keynes, who challenged the orthodox economic thinking of his day by calling for government spending, even deficit spending, to help stimulate the economy.

Excerpted from Stuart Chase, *A New Deal*. New York: Macmillan, 1932. Reprinted by permission of the author and the Watkins/Loomis Agency.

Our sometime leaders—bankers, big business men, politicians—have concentrated in the last three years on just one thing: how to get by; how to hold out until the cyclical upswing starts. Their influence, so far as they have any left, has been directed to:

1. Holding the right thought, in publicity confidence drives, and anti-hoarding campaigns.

2. Deflating wages.

3. Attacking the Wall Street bears.

4. Arguing passionately for government economy and a balanced budget.

5. Intoning the virtues of deflation to the bitter end as the "natural" way out. Antagonism to inflation, devaluation or tampering with the gold standard.

6. Supporting the banks with government credit.

7. Supporting bond and mortgage holders with government credit, particularly railroad securities.

8. Loosening credit through "open market" operations by the Federal Reserve System.

The last three contradict the fifth, to be sure—for one cannot both have government props and allow nature to take her course—but such paradoxes disturb the Elder Statesmen not at all. Paradoxes are obvious only to thoughtful minds. Every item on the program is *negative*, or at best static, with the possible exception of the first—which seems to fall more under the head of constructive magic. There is no analytic intelligence, no wish to experiment, no boldness, no sense of the imperatives of economic trend, no understanding of the modern world, to be found in any part of it. In brief, our leaders up to June, 1932 have offered no leadership; only incantations, chiefly survivals from the Nineteenth Century and the pioneer tradition.

Herbert Hoover's Leadership

Mr. Hoover provided us with a marvellous demonstration of misapplied psychology. Recognizing—quite correctly—that fear is a leading factor in deflation, he sought to check the fear, without concurrently checking the physical deflation. Fear does not start a depression, it appears afterwards, with an appreciable lag. Exorcising fear with optimistic statements is a useless gesture, for it does nothing about the falling price level which caused the fear. It is not only useless but demoralizing in the end. Time and again, from the first Pollyanna pipings in the fall of 1929, the American public has been lulled to a false and spurious hope which has bewildered it, shaken its morale, caused many business men tangible extra loss by encouraging ill-advised expansion, destroyed confidence in Mr. Hoover and American leadership generally. There was an embryo of thought in the campaign, we must admit, but it perished stillborn. . . .

The great drive led by the bankers—and opposed officially by Mr. Hoover—to liquidate wages in 1931, we have already commented upon. When deflation gets really under way, wages have to come down like everything else. Unemployment, full and part time, begins almost immediately to undermine the total wage bill. Rates become a secondary consideration, but, sooner or later, they too must fall in those industries which simply cannot support the level after making all other possible economies. The point to grasp in the premises is that the action, while it may prevent bankruptcies here and there, *does not check deflation*. By further reducing purchasing power, it leaves us no better off. Touted, as it was, as a major movement toward industrial recovery, it comes, like holding the right thought, under the head of witch doctoring.

The spirited attack of early 1932 on the Wall Street bears was a very human attempt to find, in personal terms, the devil which plagued us. As a matter of fact, the bulls (of 1929) had a good deal more to do with the deflation than the bears. Bears, in simple minds, particularly those of farmers, are the sinister creatures which pull down prices of wheat and cotton. (Sometimes, to be sure, they do.) But bears on Wall Street were no more responsible for preventing industrial recovery than bears in Alaska. To regulate them intelligently is undoubtedly a sorely needed reform— but that is quite another story. To imagine that a world-wide price collapse can be reversed or even halted by driving to cover a thoroughly frightened and enormously attenuated short interest, is the most naïve of animisms.

Budget Deficits

We come now to more serious matters—the alleged necessity of government economy and balanced budgets. Here we have animism on a grand scale. You and I, when the cycle begins lopping off our incomes, have to cut expenses. Business houses, even great corporations, have to do the same. In such times, no individual's credit is very good, and no choice remains but to retrench. What is more logical than to conclude that governments must do likewise? But the animistic logicians forget that the government is in a *totally different category*. The government is *not* held to the limitations of the money medium; it is above them, for it *makes* the money medium. The code for gods is not the code for mortals. The state can double the money supply if it so elects, or halve it. It is perfectly true that reckless inflation or deflation is a dangerous business and should be strenuously avoided, but in an emergency the government can borrow, as no individual dares to borrow; can expand public works; can defy its budget; can, as a last resort, devalue the dollar or increase the currency and inflate—if public welfare demands it. Indeed, I do not hesitate to say that in a nation as largely self-contained as is the United States—and I think Mr. [John Maynard] Keynes would agree with me—the government could, in a few months' time, have broken the back of the deflation. To do so, it would perforce run some risk, but there is graver risk in doing nothing.

FDR Library

The Depression left many thousands of Americans dependent on relief organizations for survival. Here, hundreds wait in line for a meal from a soup kitchen in New York City.

If the government borrowed or inflated for a bold program of public works which absorbed two or three million of the unemployed directly—thus feeding a huge new stream into the river bed of purchasing power—thus stimulating industry—thus causing more of the unemployed to be absorbed as food and clothing workers—thus adding to purchasing power again—thus checking the domestic price fall—thus strengthening the banks. . . . We should come close to a recurring decimal upward. The budget, left to go hang today, would be balanced out of the taxes of a revived nation tomorrow. "The idea," says Keynes, "that a public works program represents a desperate risk to cure a moderate evil is the reverse of truth. It is a negligible risk to cure a monstrous anomaly." And again: "To bring up the bogy of inflation as an objection to capital expenditure [by the state] is like warning a patient who is wasting away from emaciation of the dangers of excessive corpulence." And again: "It is not the miser who gets rich; but he who lays out his money in fruitful investment."

Mr. Keynes was directing his remarks to the gentlemen of the City in their tightly burdened frock coats, but all the solemn nonsense they have uttered in England since 1921 finds its counterpart in Wall Street and Washington today. "Sound" bankers are much the same the world over. The important thing for us to realize is that Mr. Keynes has almost invariably been right in his prediction as to the course of events in England, and the City has almost invariably been wrong. He warned it solemnly against the War reparations schedules, against returning to the gold standard, against the folly of too much government "economy." His warnings were disregarded, and, with mathematical precision, Britain sank deeper into the pit, until finally tension became unendurable, and in September, 1931, the gold standard collapsed. In 1924, Sir Harry Goschen of the National Provincial Bank—one of the Big Five—delivered himself as follows. It is an excellent sample of the Elder Statesman philosophy, both here and abroad.

> I cannot help thinking that there has lately been far too much irresponsible discussion as to the comparative advantages of Inflation and Deflation. Discussions of this kind can only breed suspicion in the minds of our neighbors as to whether we shall adopt either of these courses, and, if so, which. I think we had better let matters take their natural course.

In other words, let us drift to ruin mutely and respectably.

To repeat and emphasize again: The state can do what no individual or private group can do. As Czar of the nation's money, it can expand or shrink the supply, rising above the limitations of the individual who must live within the rules. Governments make the rules. If the state desires to check deflation it can check it; to create employment on useful and worthy projects, it can create it; to augment purchasing power, it can augment it. Nobody else can do it. Fire engines are for conflagrations too great for the householder to extinguish. The bankers and their friends want to keep the fire horses safe in their stalls while the world burns down. A difficulty with this proposal is that the engine house may burn down too. "If we carry 'economy' of every kind to its logical conclusion, we shall find that we have balanced the budget at nought on both sides, with all of us flat on our backs starving to death from a refusal, for reasons of economy, to buy one another's services. Economy is only useful from the national point of view in so far as it diminishes our consumption of imported goods. For the rest its fruits are entirely wasted in unemployment, business losses and reduced savings."

One parting shot, before we leave this monstrous animism. The witch doctors say that the state should embark on no extensive public works because it takes capital away from private business, and the state—according to the doctrine of laissez-faire—is notoriously inefficient. This assumption is packed with nonsense. To begin with, it presupposes a fixed loan fund; the more the state gets, the less for private enterprise. There is no such fixity; the credit pyramid, as we have seen, can shrink and expand within wide limits, even on a gold apex. Secondly, it assumes that private capital *wants* to expand. If there is one thing which private capital will not do in a depression it is extend its facilities. It would rather take a red-hot poker than a new bank loan. The incentive is all in the direction of getting out of debt, rather than borrowing more. If there is expansion to be done, the state must do it, for nobody else in his senses can afford to. Thirdly, whether the state is more or less efficient than private enterprise is an excellent subject for college debating teams, but has nothing to do with this particular emergency. "Even if half the public works program were wasted, we would still be better off." Why? Because, in the end, it is either public works or the dole, and with the former, you at least secure something for your money. Think of the useful and necessary things which the state can do—and which private enterprise, even under "normal" conditions, will not do—highways, grade crossings, water ways, parks, playgrounds, afforestation, slum clearance, education, research, regional planning. Every day the government postpones such measures makes the problem of halting deflation more difficult. By the time this book is in print it may be too late for salvation by public works alone.

Outdated Theories

Mr. J. Lawrence Laughlin, one of the most classical of our economists, combines with Sir Harry Goschen in advocating deflation to the bitter end as the "natural" way out. What is so natural about uncounted families on the brink of starvation and mountains of wheat in storage escapes me altogether. It seems a most perverse and unnatural course. The Nineteenth Century had its cycles and recovered, and the Nineteenth-Century-minded lean up against this historical analogy as though it were the Rock of Ages. They may be warranted—for one more cycle at the most—but because a patient has recovered from five attacks of pneumonia is no earnest, a doctor assures me, that he will recover from the sixth. I think the medical analogy is just as safe to lean upon.

The great advantage of allowing nature to take her course is that it obviates thought. Men fear thought, says Bertrand Russell, as they fear nothing else on earth. There is no need to think; no need to take concrete action. Just sit and wait with folded hands, chanting: They also serve. The second advantage is that if recovery arrives before matters have gone too far, the creditor class scores a neat victory on the debtor class, and transfers a very considerable additional slice of the national income—secured at rock bottom market prices—to its own not inconsiderable share. When the banking structure began to wobble in 1931 it was fairly obvious that matters *had* gone too far. At the present time, the creditor class, with its *principal* imperilled, probably stands to gain more by inflation than by further deflation. The third advantage is that marginal and inefficient business units are weeded out in a depression, leaving production in the hands of the more able business men. In view of the fact that one of the causes of the slump was the advanced state of technical progress, the clearing of decks for still greater production, advisable as this might be in a functional society, helps the present situation not at all. How far up the margin do you propose to go, Mr. Laughlin; how many businesses do you advise ruining; and how much more unemployment do you think it desirable to provoke? There is always the chance that the "course of nature" in this particular attack of pneumonia is the ultimate death of the system. If it can be destroyed by too much inflation on the Lenin formula, it can as effectively be destroyed on the Laughlin-Goschen formula of deflation—pushed far enough.

The last three items on the agenda of the Elder Statesman—with which Messrs. Goschen and Laughlin could hardly agree if they are to keep their logic pure—are government support of banks and creditors, specifically, in the United States, the Reconstruction Finance Corporation. This does at least connote action, but action of a negative kind. Government credit, instead of being devoted to purchasing power, is devoted to shoring up a swaying structure. It can halt bank failures, and the more hysterical forms of fear and panic for a time, but it will not halt the remorseless processes of deflation. The motor needs gasoline, far more than it needs bolts in the frame. . . .

Stages of the Depression

Broadly speaking, we have passed through two stages and are now entering the third. The first was marked by the belief that everything was fundamentally satisfactory and only public confidence was needed. The confidence game extended until the fall of

1931. The second phase was marked by a realization that the situation was really serious, and that steps must be taken to underwrite unfortunate creditors. Government credit was extended in the form of square dollars beneath the Doric pillars of banks. This halted bank failures, but produced none of the round dollars so desperately needed to roll from consumer to retailer to manufacturer to farmer. Now (June, 1932) we enter the third phase and are being forced to consider round dollars—in the form of deliberate inflation, public works programs, even loans to the unemployed. A year ago, five billions for public works might have saved the situation. Today the remedy must probably be more heroic.

Planning Our Economy

George Soule was a writer and editor who from 1924 to 1947 was an editor of the New Republic. *He was one of the leaders of a group of thinkers who argued that the Great Depression demonstrated the need for greater centralized government planning of the economy. He wrote in a February 11, 1931, issue of the* New Republic *that depressions could be managed and even abolished by intelligent economic planning.*

The major task of our civilization is to create a brain and a coördinating nervous system for our economy. It is to organize our great economic organs. The need of doing so has, indeed, been seen for so long by a few, and is now being declared by so many, that to say this is almost trite. The difficulty is not so much to appreciate the need as to know just how it can be met.

If we are ever able to relate our economic activities to a policy carried out through careful planning and expertly devised control, a policy whose purpose is to produce the greatest possible amount of wealth, satisfaction and leisure for everyone, at the least possible sacrifice, we shall no longer have the business order as we know it. We shall have achieved a higher type of economic organism, one with a brain and nervous system, one which does have a natural equilibrium. The business cycle will have disappeared with the old business order, or will have become only barely traceable. We may utilize a large number of the devices hitherto recommended by the various theorists; we shall undoubtedly discard some of them. We shall have abolished unemployment by a process of envelopment. I do not believe there is any other way to abolish it.

We have canvassed the program of the Elder Statesmen, from holding the right thought to open market operations. It is without light, hope, intelligence or imagination. It is plain holding on. The only thought in it is to keep a colossal debt structure intact until the corner is rounded. It has not worked and I am convinced it will not work. Deflation has roared past every section of it. The witch doctors have chanted their incantations for three years—in England for a decade, and the economic stomach-ache is worse than ever. It is time for authentic surgeons to go to work.

The terms of the surgical operations now in order are reasonably clear in broad outline, complicated as they may be in detail.

To begin with, no one can possibly qualify for the work in hand until he has a lucid picture in his mind of what the operation aims to achieve; until he has asked and answered the question: What is an economic system for? Again, he needs a firm grasp on the basic formula that population plus natural resources plus the state of the technical arts, equals the standard of living, with imaginative regard for the past and probable future movement of all three factors. Finally, he must understand the behavior of money and credit and the causes and effects of inflation and deflation. Above all, he must realize that in the last analysis money is not a force in itself, assured of a private rampage whenever the mood arises, but an artificial, man-made system of symbols (largely paper); a sheer labor saving device to mitigate the clumsy processes of barter; the slave and creature of man, and strictly subject to his control.

The two great inventions for saving human labor are money and the machine. Both have got out of hand, and are prancing and trampling around through the social order as though they had equestrian rights from God. The job before us is to stop this nonsense, and lead them back into the stalls where they belong. It cannot be done by casting spells.

A Need for New Leadership

Where shall we find our surgeons? Our business men and politicians have obviously failed us. As for our scientists and professional men, nobody has ever expected anything from them. Their only function in the American saga has been to grease the wheels. (But if my eyes do not deceive me, some are even now crawling out from under the tonneau.) Well, what does one expect, a psychological miracle? Nature does not act that way; she is not in the habit of producing stars from a vacuum. We have no leadership, because, forsooth, after the opening of the West, we never needed any. We were a self-generating perpetual-motive machine. . . .

The present . . . emergency will, I am convinced, create leaders. Where they are, I do not know—though I could, if pressed, suggest a name or two. In the ranks of the engineers and technicians; in the ranks of industrial management—as contrasted with ownership; in the colleges where young men are beginning to ask plain questions as they never asked them before—are likely places to look. You, my friend, may be hiding a marshal's baton under your coat at this moment. The path along which they shall lead us can bear only to the left. No more excursions into the petrified forests of rugged individualism. No more attempts to keep government and business single and celibate. No more jogging in the middle of the road amid the placid certainties of the Nineteenth Century. No more mass movements to the good old days when the easiest thing to do with an over-mortgaged house was to leave it to the mortgage holder and take the sunset trail.

Right trails, center trails, are posted No Thoroughfare. The left road is the only road, and willy-nilly we must take it.

VIEWPOINT 6

"Any attempt at [government-initiated] violent fundamental business or banking changes is more likely to retard than accelerate improvement."

Government Actions Cannot End the Depression

Ray Vance (1886-1954)

Ray Vance was an investment counselor and economist. Over his career he served as chairman of several investment firms including Mutual American Securities Trust and Templeton, Dobbrow & Vance, Inc. The author of several books, he also lectured on economics at Yale, Dartmouth, and other universities.

In the following article from the June 29, 1932, issue of the *Nation* magazine, Vance presents views that are fairly representative of the conventional economic thinking of that time. He states that the Depression is an inevitable result of the business cycle and that the economy, if left to itself, will work its way toward recovery. He cites evidence which he believes indicates that the Depression is already coming to an end. Vance argues against government action and spending, stating that it would only prolong the Depression and make it worse. The most important thing the federal government can do, Vance states, is to balance its budget.

From Ray Vance, "The Problem of the Business Cycle," *The Nation*, June 29, 1932.

It is particularly fitting to discuss the business cycle in connection with this depression because failure to provide against the dangers inherent in business cycles has been, in my personal opinion, the prime cause for the extraordinary length and violence of the depression. In the first place, all warnings issued during 1928 and 1929 were met with ridicule as the opinions of men clinging to an "exploded superstition." In the second place, the same men who refused to take precautions which might have prevented much of the damage are equally stubborn in refusing to recognize the signs that the crisis has about run its course and that what the patient needs is a period of natural convalescence rather than surgical operations on all parts which were ever diseased. These two statements are not based on any discounting of the importance of international debts, inflated bank loans, unwise speculation, or any other cause commonly assigned for the occurrence or for the long continuation of this depression. A combination of physical and financial conditions brought on the panic, and the wreckage of that combination must be cleared away before prosperity can return. The point I wish to make is that the creation of that combination was the result of human activities, and that the creation of the *causes* was, in itself, the *effect* of a state of mind which considered the danger of another depression negligible *under the current business organization*. Furthermore, the failure to clear away the wreckage in a reasonable time is the direct effect of a widespread doubt that prosperity can ever return until the business organization has been fundamentally altered.

All of this is of practical importance because it goes exactly to the crucial point in judgment of any effort to cure this depression or to prevent another. Of course, it is hard to believe today that business will revive unless some one does "something drastic," but is it any harder than it was to see danger in 1928 or 1929? As a matter of fact, there is just as much nonsense being talked today about the impossibility of revival as was ever talked about the impossibility of a panic. The natural forces which will produce that revival are already at work, with the mass of our population coöperating as unconsciously through their daily acts as they coöperated unconsciously in the bringing on of the panic. Legislative or other conscious efforts must be approved when they help along the natural forces, condemned when they seek some miraculous or unsound way out.

How the Depression Will End

Any attempt to give in the limited space of this article a detailed description of the developments which bring about the end of a depression would be ridiculous. However, we may divide them into two general groups which have a definite time sequence. During the first of these periods almost every business or financial indicator declines. All kinds of property, except cash, are pressed for sale at falling prices. Less of all types of goods, except raw food products and basic minerals, are produced than are consumed. Old debts are paid, or canceled through default, more rapidly than new ones are contracted. Working forces are decreased, salary and wage rates are reduced, and incomes from interest, dividends, rent, or professional services all decline. During this period living costs are lowered but purchasing power falls at least as fast, and fear induces a restriction rather than an increase in standards of living even for those whose incomes would permit an expansion or at least a maintenance of standards.

To a certain extent the change into the next phase is caused by sheer exhaustion of goods available for consumption, but a much more powerful factor is found in the fact that holders of cash begin to fear that never again will they be able to acquire so much property in exchange for their cash. As a result, purchases are made in excess of current supply and the business tide rises as inevitably as it declined. Four characteristics of these purchases tend to bring a turning-point in the business tide:

1. They do not arise from the fact that economies in production have reduced prices relatively below current incomes—every economy in production reduces some one's income by exactly the same amount.

2. They are made from accumulated cash which its owners may use at their own judgment.

3. They are not made merely because prices are lower than before but because the owners of cash fear future prices will be higher.

4. The motive for these purchases is the selfish one of getting the most for one's money rather than any altruistic one of "helping the situation."

In brief, the upswing after any period of depression starts with the reëmployment of idle capital, and that reëmployment occurs when the owners of capital believe that profits rather than losses will follow its use in place of its hoarding.

Capital and Labor Interests

The interests of capital and labor are never identical, but in a situation like the present they happen to be practically concurrent. For most of us the depression will be over when we have steady jobs at living pay, or when the business activities in which we have invested our money begin to show profits. Profits for capital tend to return more slowly than employment for labor, but during the lagging period capitalists are gaining something, and are looking forward to still greater profits. For example, eighteen months after the bottom of the last great depression—1921—factory employment in the United States was more than 5 per cent *above* the peak of employment during the previous prosperity. By contrast, the year 1923, which opened with this new high level of factory employment, ended with eight out of ten outstanding manufacturing corporations showing profits which ranged from a fraction of 1 per cent to a full 55 per cent *below* the previous peak. However, no one of these corporations failed to show reasonable profits in 1923, and no one of them failed to reach a new peak of earnings before the next depression.

Governments Cannot End Depressions

In his State of the Union address to Congress on December 2, 1930, approximately one year after the stock market crash, Herbert Hoover reiterated his beliefs on the limits of government in ending the Depression.

Economic depression can not be cured by legislative action or executive pronouncement. Economic wounds must be healed by the action of the cells of the economic body—the producers and consumers themselves. Recovery can be expedited and its effects mitigated by cooperative action. That cooperation requires that every individual should sustain faith and courage; that each should maintain his self-reliance; that each and every one should search for methods of improving his business or service; that the vast majority whose income is unimpaired should not hoard out of fear but should pursue their normal living and recreations; that each should seek to assist his neighbors who may be less fortunate; that each industry should assist its own employees; that each community and each state should assume its full responsibilities for organization of employment and relief of distress with that sturdiness and independence which built a great Nation.

Our people are responding to these impulses in remarkable degree.

So long as a decline is still in progress, it remains hard to see that foundations for improvement are being laid, but some of the things which precede the end of a depression have already been accomplished. Among them are:

1. A liquidation of speculative positions in securities. With brokers' loans below $400,000,000 (a decrease of more than 95 per cent from the peak) we need worry no more about this factor.

2. Current debts have been sharply decreased. Total bank loans were off over 25 per cent by the end of 1931 and reporting member banks indicate a further decline of 33 per cent by May 1, 1932.

Debts on open book accounts and installment purchases are reduced even more sharply.

3. The supply of goods available for consumption has been sharply reduced. With wholesale prices for merchandise off 20 per cent, department-store stocks are off 35 per cent, indicating a physical-volume decrease of 19 per cent; and the supply of other unsold finished products has declined by almost exactly the same percentage. These are record-breaking figures, but the amount and condition of goods in the hands of consumers after two and one-half years of low buying are even more significant.

4. Wage rates and the general overhead of business concerns have been curtailed to a point where profits could be made on relatively small volumes of business.

What Needs to Be Done

At least three things, however, are not yet accomplished:

1. An adjustment between long-term or "capital" debts and general price levels. In the rush to do this with intergovernmental debts, we overlook its impossibility for privately owned bonds and mortgages without wholesale bankruptcies. This will be an overhanging cloud until some inflation, or "reflation" has intervened.

2. With the exception of Great Britain no large nation has readjusted its budget to current conditions. To do this does not require an exact balancing of the budget but does require the drastic cutting of expenses built up through long years of free spending, the placing of heavy taxes, and the distribution of taxes over practically all classes and sections of the country. In spite of the tax bill just passed, I do not believe the real readjustment has been accomplished, or that it will be accomplished on the eve of an election, and I do not believe it will be accomplished except by bipartisan action.

3. Owners of hoarded capital must be convinced that they face an opportunity for profit in its use. This cannot be accomplished until the other readjustments just outlined are clearly promised, and even then it will take more courageous leadership than is now in sight. However, there is little room for doubt that the leadership will be available as it always has been when conditions were right.

Business men and investors have been told that prosperity is just "around the corner" until the phrase has become a national joke. For that reason it seems worth while to consider first some of the factors of delay. Conditions for revival will probably not be right until after the election in November. Theoretically, this might be extended until the new terms of office begin in March or even later than that, when new legislation can be enacted. The effect of an election, however, reaches business confidence long before it affects actual governmental action. We cannot now forecast the election results, but we can assume that the country will vote for what it wants and will have confidence in the resulting government.

Other factors are not so definite. Intergovernmental debts will probably have to wait for a time when a United States Administration with a fresh mandate from the voters can deal with the governments of Europe, which, fortunately, are of relatively recent selection. Some factors of inflation for commodity prices are already at work in Great Britain and some are being tried in the United States. So far those working in this country have had no effect except to slow up the decline in prices. Actual history of past panics shows that commodity prices usually do no better than that until months after the volume of business has increased, so this factor may be considered as already satisfactory. Summing up these indications and allowing for the fact that it usually takes longer for business to rise than to fall, "prosperity" in the sense of normal business is more than a year away. Even the beginning of the climb promises to be four to six months away unless something is done to hasten the natural progress.

How Government Can Help

A study of past depressions offers only four ways in which prosperity might be hastened:

1. International governmental debts might be canceled or definitely suspended. This would impose a long-term burden on creditors. Personally, I believe these debts are largely uncollectable, but it is doubtful whether that opinion will become sufficiently general in time to permit action which will affect this depression.

2. International trade barriers might be lowered. This would be of little value unless by coöperation of practically all countries. Probably no action can be obtained for more than a year.

3. Any individual nation may hasten the process by a realistic readjustment of its budget. This is the opportunity which Congress has not adequately seized. As already explained, no elective body has ever had the courage to do a real job on the eve of an election. The individual voters may well do their part by disregarding party lines to bring in a stronger group of men at the next election, but there is small possibility that the present makeshift tax law or a few grudgingly enacted economies will have the desired effect.

4. A genuine inflation of currency, possibly even the suspension of the gold standard, would bring a quick response. Great Britain has already demonstrated this point. Its longer effect has always been seriously bad, and most economists will agree with the writer that impatience with the slow operation of the inflationary forces already at work is likely to produce transient benefit at the

expense of trouble over a long period.

On the whole, the only cycle-control measure being seriously neglected in the United States at the present time is the balancing of federal, State, and local budgets. Other artificial aids to recovery at this point would be more likely to hinder than to help the operation of natural forces which are at work to end this depression.

Advice to Do Nothing

Andrew Mellon was a wealthy financier and industrialist who served as secretary of the treasury under presidents Harding, Coolidge, and Hoover. Under his guidance the U.S. government pursued a policy of cutting taxes in order to promote business. In 1951 Herbert Hoover recalled in his book Memoirs: The Great Depression *Mellon's advice for dealing with the Depression.*

Let the slump liquidate itself. Liquidate labor, liquidate stocks, liquidate the farmers, liquidate real estate. . . . It will purge the rottenness out of the system. High costs of living and high living will come down. People will work harder, live a more moral life. Values will be adjusted, and enterprising people will pick up from less competent people.

The emphasis I have laid upon natural rather than artificial means of ending a depression must not be construed as a condemnation of efforts to control the swings of the business cycle. The fact that periods of boom and depression are "natural" to business activity is no more reason for accepting them as right or inevitable than the fact that disease is natural to the human body is a reason for giving up preventive hygiene for the healthy or medical treatment for the sick. The fatal error in our treatment of business cycles has been that we have worked at it only after the damage has been done. The time to have prevented the current depression was between January 1, 1927, and January 1, 1929. During those two years business, banking, and political leadership had their final opportunity to provide against the natural reaction from a long period of business and speculative boom. A whole book has been printed ridiculing these leaders for their public statements during those years, but let us rather study their actual operations in fields where control might have been exercised.

The Federal Reserve

The most natural place to expect leadership in cycle control is from the Federal Reserve System. The most noticeable failure of the leaders of that system occurred in 1927. During that year stock prices showed signs of inflation by soaring to new record heights, while business had difficulty in keeping pace, and private banks showed some conservatism by reducing their rediscounts with the Federal Reserve by $45,000,000, or nearly 7 per cent. In this situation the Federal Reserve contributed to further inflation by voluntarily adding $311,000,000—about 45 per cent—to its open-market purchases and by lowering its rediscount rates ½ of 1 per cent as an invitation to an increase of rediscounts. In the following year member banks took the cue so plainly given by the Federal Reserve. They increased their rediscounts by $474,000,000—81 per cent, and increased their loans to brokers by 42 per cent; and by so doing supported an inflation of stock prices which left common stocks yielding an average of 3.60 per cent from their dividends, while the money borrowed to carry them cost 7.4 per cent for time loans and 8.6 per cent for call loans. The Federal Reserve made a feeble attempt to check the tide by withdrawing $233,000,000 from the open market and by raising the rediscount rate of the New York Bank to 5 per cent, but this had no real effect on the movement which the Federal Reserve authorities had done so much to start. The movements continued till the very breaking-point of the 1929 panic, but it is really the operations of 1927 and 1928 which represent the type of mistake which must be avoided if the business cycle is to be controlled.

The most important factor upon which "new era" disciples relied for cycle control was construction work, but the record here is little better than in banking. It seems reasonably clear that if construction work controlled by governments and large corporations is to be done in times of depression, it must be postponed in a period of boom activity in other lines. However, no such postponement was even considered. By 1925 construction work of the "controllable" type had reached a new high record, and 1926 showed a 26 per cent increase over that. Surely then, if ever, the time for "saving up" of desirable activity along this line had arrived. Instead, 1927 saw another 4 per cent added to the dizzy record of 1926, and 1928 piled still another 5 per cent increase on top of that. Public utilities and railroads responded gallantly in 1930 when President Hoover called on them to continue unnecessary construction work, but the really needed work of that year had been anticipated during the boom, and the unnecessary work brought disaster to the coöperating corporations and to government finance, with a balance of damage rather than of benefit to the country as a whole.

Reducing Government Debt

After covering these mistakes of banking and construction policy, it is pleasant to note one instance in which genuine provision for cycle control was made. When business reached normal in late 1922, the debt of the United States government stood at approximately $23,000,000,000. Tax rates were high and the demand for reduction pressing. Two definite tax reductions were actually made, but the brightest spot in our provision for cycle control has to do with the handling of our federal debt. Every six months saw a net reduction in this debt, and so well was the situation handled that reduction continued until long after the panic had fallen upon business and finance. By December 31, 1930, the total was down to $16,000,000,000—a decline of $7,000,000,000, or over 30 per cent in eight years. Up to June 1, 1932, the figure was still $4,000,000,000 under the 1922 total and $7,000,000,000 under the extreme peak debt of 1919. If the same wise policy prevails during our next prosperity, the recent increase in federal debt need not be of great moment.

Unfortunately, the record on State debts is not of that character, and the handling of municipal debts was one of the worst features of our failure to prepare for depression. Throughout the entire period of prosperity municipal debts showed a consistent yearly increase, with the result that at the first sharp fall in tax yields a disconcerting percentage of our cities either defaulted or had difficulty in meeting their current bills. A curtailment of expenses in this field is even more pressingly necessary than in the federal budget, and a reduction of debt in the next period of prosperity is even more essential if we are to avoid another such depression as this one.

The conclusions which appear to arise from a study of the current business cycle are:

1. This period of depression is drawing to a close from natural causes and will probably show improvement before the end of this year (1932) without any legislative aids.

2. Balancing of federal, State, and municipal budgets by real economy and by common-sense tax methods would not only hasten the turn but would accelerate the rise after it has started.

3. Any attempt at violent fundamental business or banking changes is more likely to retard than accelerate improvement.

4. Avoidance of another depression of such severity and length is possible if we are willing to begin our efforts at cycle control while prosperity is still with us, but it will involve sacrificing part of the possible temporary profits of that period. If we again insist on dancing the last possible step, we shall again be compelled to pay the fiddler's bill in full.

VIEWPOINT 7

"Republican leaders not only have failed in material things, they have failed in national vision. . . . I pledge myself to a new deal for the American people."

America Needs a New Deal

Franklin D. Roosevelt (1882-1945)

Franklin Delano Roosevelt was born in 1882, the only child of a wealthy family. His political career began in 1910 with his election to the state senate of New York. In 1913 he was appointed assistant secretary of the navy under Woodrow Wilson and in 1920 he was chosen as the Democratic vice presidential nominee. Stricken with polio in 1921, he was left with only partial use of his legs. Following a brief hiatus from politics, Roosevelt returned in 1928 and was elected governor of New York. As governor, Roosevelt pressed for greater state programs to deal with unemployment and other problems of the Great Depression. Nominated for president by the Democratic party in 1932, Roosevelt broke with tradition by personally addressing the Democratic National Convention. It was in this speech that he introduced the term "New Deal" to the American public.

In his address, Roosevelt describes what he holds as fundamental differences between the Republican and Democratic parties concerning government and the people's welfare; he argues that the causes of the Depression were the neglect of the consumer and the worker by the American business establishment; and he proposes new actions by the federal government to help farmers, the unemployed, and others hurt by the Great Depression.

Franklin D. Roosevelt, from his address to the Democratic National Convention, July 2, 1932.

The great social phenomenon of this depression, unlike others before it, is that it has produced but a few of the disorderly manifestations that too often attend upon such times.

Wild radicalism has made few converts, and the greatest tribute that I can pay to my countrymen is that in these days of crushing want there persists an orderly and hopeful spirit on the part of the millions of our people who have suffered so much. To fail to offer them a new chance is not only to betray their hopes but to misunderstand their patience.

To meet by reaction that danger of radicalism is to invite disaster. Reaction is no barrier to the radical. It is a challenge, a provocation. The way to meet that danger is to offer a workable program of reconstruction, and the party to offer it is the party with clean hands.

This, and this only, is a proper protection against blind reaction on the one hand and an improvised, hit-or-miss, irresponsible opportunism on the other.

Two Views of Government

There are two ways of viewing the Government's duty in matters affecting economic and social life. The first sees to it that a favored few are helped and hopes that some of their prosperity will leak through, sift through, to labor, to the farmer, to the small business man. That theory belongs to the party of Toryism, and I had hoped that most of the Tories left this country in 1776.

But it is not and never will be the theory of the Democratic Party. This is no time for fear, for reaction or for timidity. Here and now I invite those nominal Republicans who find that their conscience cannot be squared with the groping and the failure of their party leaders to join hands with us; here and now, in equal measure, I warn those nominal Democrats who squint at the future with their faces turned toward the past, and who feel no responsibility to the demands of the new time, that they are out of step with their Party.

Yes, the people of this country want a genuine choice this year, not a choice between two names for the same reactionary doctrine. Ours must be a party of liberal thought, of planned action, of enlightened international outlook, and of the greatest good to the greatest number of our citizens.

Now it is inevitable—and the choice is that of the times—it is inevitable that the main issue of this campaign should revolve about the clear fact of our economic condition, a depression so deep that it is without precedent in modern history. It will not do merely to state, as do Republican leaders to explain their broken promises of continued inaction, that the depression is worldwide. That was not their explanation of the apparent prosperity of 1928. The people will not forget the claim made by them then that prosperity was only a domestic product manufactured by a Republican President and a Republican Congress. If they claim paternity for the one they cannot deny paternity for the other.

Franklin D. Roosevelt campaigned for president in 1932 with sweeping promises to enlist the federal government in aiding Americans suffering from the Depression.

Library of Congress

I cannot take up all the problems today. I want to touch on a few that are vital. Let us look a little at the recent history and the simple economics, the kind of economics that you and I and the average man and woman talk.

In the years before 1929 we know that this country had completed a vast cycle of building and inflation; for ten years we expanded on the theory of repairing the wastes of the War, but actually expanding far beyond that, and also beyond our natural and normal growth. Now it is worth remembering, and the cold figures of finance prove it, that during that time there was little or no drop in the prices that the consumer had to pay, although those same figures proved that the cost of production fell very greatly; corporate profit resulting from this period was enormous; at the same time little of that profit was devoted to the reduction of prices. The consumer was forgotten. Very little of it went into increased wages; the worker was forgotten, and by no means an adequate proportion was even paid out in dividends—the stockholder was forgotten.

And, incidentally, very little of it was taken by taxation to the beneficent Government of those years.

What was the result? Enormous corporate surpluses piled up—the most stupendous in history. Where, under the spell of delirious speculation, did those surpluses go? Let us talk economics that the figures prove and that we can understand. Why, they went chiefly in two directions: first, into new and unnecessary plants which now stand stark and idle; and second, into the call-money market of Wall Street, either directly by the corporations, or indirectly through the banks. Those are the facts. Why blink at them?

The Crash

Then came the crash. You know the story. Surpluses invested in unnecessary plants became idle. Men lost their jobs; purchasing power dried up; banks became frightened and started calling loans. Those who had money were afraid to part with it. Credit contracted. Industry stopped. Commerce declined, and unemployment mounted.

And there we are today.

Translate that into human terms. See how the events of the past three years have come home to specific groups of people: first, the group dependent on industry; second, the group dependent on agriculture; third, and made up in large part of members of the first two groups, the people who are called "small investors and depositors." In fact, the strongest possible tie between the first two groups, agriculture and industry, is the fact that the savings and to a degree the security of both are tied together in that third group—the credit structure of the Nation.

Never in history have the interests of all the people been so united in a single economic problem. Picture to yourself, for instance, the great groups of property owned by millions of our citizens, represented by credits issued in the form of bonds and mortgages—Government bonds of all kinds, Federal, State, county, municipal; bonds of industrial companies, of utility companies; mortgages on real estate in farms and cities, and finally the vast investments of the Nation in the railroads. What is the measure of the security of each of those groups? We know well that in our complicated, interrelated credit structure if any one of these credit groups collapses they may all collapse. Danger to one is danger to all.

How, I ask, has the present Administration in Washington treated the interrelationship of these credit groups? The answer is clear: It has not recognized that interrelationship existed at all. Why, the Nation asks, has Washington failed to understand that all of these groups, each and every one, the top of the pyramid and the bottom of the pyramid, must be considered together, that each and every one of them is dependent on every other; each and every one of them affecting the whole financial fabric?

Statesmanship and vision, my friends, require relief to all at the same time.

Taxes and Spending

Just one word or two on taxes, the taxes that all of us pay toward the cost of Government of all kinds.

I know something of taxes. For three long years I have been going up and down this country preaching that Government—Federal and State and local—costs too much. I shall not stop that preaching. As an immediate program of action we must abolish useless offices. We must eliminate unnecessary functions of Government—functions, in fact, that are not definitely essential to the continuance of Government. We must merge, we must consolidate subdivisions of Government, and, like the private citizen, give up luxuries which we can no longer afford.

Hoover's Do-Nothing Approach

In his 1931 book Washington Merry-Go-Round, *co-authored with columnist Drew Pearson, Washington reporter Robert A. Allen wrote his assessment of President Herbert Hoover's response to the Depression.*

In the long and tragic travail of the economic depression, the most tragic thing was the President's fear of admitting that a great disaster had befallen the country. For months, while gloom, unemployment, and deflation settled on the land, he refused to admit their reality or do anything fundamental about the situation. His approach to the problem was wholly that of the boomer, the bull-marker operator, concerned only with his own political interests and willing to resort to any device or misrepresentation to further them.

Facts, statistics, plan, organization—there have been none, and when proposed by others have been rejected and stifled, secretly when possible, openly when that was impossible.

One policy alone has dominated his course: not to do or say anything that would reveal the truth about the great catastrophe. Suppression and inaction have been his unshaken rule.

By our example at Washington itself, we shall have the opportunity of pointing the way of economy to local government, for let us remember well that out of every tax dollar in the average State in this Nation, forty cents enter the treasury in Washington, D.C., ten or twelve cents only go to the State capitals, and forty-eight cents are consumed by the costs of local government in counties and cities and towns.

I propose to you, my friends, and through you, that Government of all kinds, big and little, be made solvent and that the example be set by the President of the United States and his Cabinet. . . .

Unemployment

And now one word about unemployment, and incidentally about agriculture. I have favored the use of certain types of public works as a further emergency means of stimulating employment and the issuance of bonds to pay for such public works, but I have pointed out that no economic end is served if we merely build without building for a necessary purpose. Such works, of course, should insofar as possible be self-sustaining if they are to be financed by the issuing of bonds. So as to spread the points of all kinds as widely as possible, we must take definite steps to shorten the working day and the working week.

Let us use common sense and business sense. Just as one example, we know that a very hopeful and immediate means of relief, both for the unemployed and for agriculture, will come from a wide plan of the converting of many millions of acres of marginal and unused land into timberland through reforestation. There are tens of millions of acres east of the Mississippi River alone in abandoned farms, in cut-over land, now growing up in worthless brush. Why, every European Nation has a definite land policy, and has had one for generations. We have none. Having none, we face a future of soil erosion and timber famine. It is clear that economic foresight and immediate employment march hand in hand in the call for the reforestation of these vast areas. In so doing, employment can be given to a million men. That is the kind of public work that is self-sustaining, and therefore capable of being financed by the issuance of bonds which are made secure by the fact that the growth of tremendous crops will provide adequate security for the investment.

Yes, I have a very definite program for providing employment by that means. I have done it, and I am doing it today in the State of New York. I know that the Democratic Party can do it successfully in the Nation. That will put men to work, and that is an example of the action that we are going to have.

Now as a further aid to agriculture, we know perfectly well—but have we come out and said so clearly and distinctly?—we should repeal immediately those provisions of law that compel the Federal Government to go into the market to purchase, to sell, to speculate in farm products in a futile attempt to reduce farm surpluses. And they are the people who are talking of keeping Government out of business. The practical way to help the farmer

81

is by an arrangement that will, in addition to lightening some of the impoverishing burdens from his back, do something toward the reduction of the surpluses of staple commodities that hang on the market. It should be our aim to add to the world prices of staple products the amount of a reasonable tariff protection, to give agriculture the same protection that industry has today.

And in exchange for this immediately increased return I am sure that the farmers of this Nation would agree ultimately to such planning of their production as would reduce the surpluses and make it unnecessary in later years to depend on dumping those surpluses abroad in order to support domestic prices. That result has been accomplished in other Nations; why not in America, too? . . .

Bold, Persistent Experimentation

In a May 22, 1932, address to the graduating class of Oglethorpe University in Atlanta, Georgia, Franklin D. Roosevelt called for "drastic means" to fix "the faults in our economic system."

The country needs and, unless I mistake its temper, the country demands bold, persistent experimentation. It is common sense to take a method and try it: If it fails, admit it frankly and try another. But above all, try something. The millions who are in want will not stand by silently forever while the things to satisfy their needs are within easy reach.

We need enthusiasm, imagination and the ability to face facts, even unpleasant ones, bravely. We need to correct, by drastic means if necessary, the faults in our economic system from which we now suffer. We need the courage of the young.

Rediscounting of farm mortgages under salutary restrictions must be expanded and should, in the future, be conditioned on the reduction of interest rates. Amortization payments, maturities should likewise in this crisis be extended before rediscount is permitted where the mortgagor is sorely pressed. That, my friends, is another example of practical, immediate relief: Action.

I aim to do the same thing, and it can be done, for the small home-owner in our cities and villages. We can lighten his burden and develop his purchasing power. Take away, my friends, that spectre of too high an interest rate. Take away that spectre of the due date just a short time away. Save homes; save homes for thousands of self-respecting families, and drive out that spectre of insecurity from our midst.

Out of all the tons of printed paper, out of all the hours of oratory, the recriminations, the defenses, the happy-thought plans in

Washington and in every State, there emerges one great, simple, crystal-pure fact that during the past ten years a Nation of one hundred twenty million people has been led by the Republican leaders to erect an impregnable barbed wire entanglement around its borders through the instrumentality of tariffs which have isolated us from all the other human beings in all the rest of the round world. I accept that admirable tariff statement in the platform of this convention. It would protect American business and American labor. By our acts of the past we have invited and received the retaliation of other nations. I propose an invitation to them to forget the past, to sit at the table with us, as friends, and to plan with us for the restoration of the trade of the world.

Go into the home of the business man. He knows what the tariff has done for him. Go into the home of the factory worker. He knows why goods do not move. Go into the home of the farmer. He knows how the tariff has helped to ruin him.

At last our eyes are open. At last the American people are ready to acknowledge that Republican leadership was wrong and that the Democracy is right.

The Welfare of All

My program, of which I can only touch on these points, is based upon this simple moral principle: the welfare and the soundness of a nation depend first upon what the great mass of the people wish and need; and second, whether or not they are getting it.

What do the people of America want more than anything else? To my mind, they want two things: work, with all the moral and spiritual values that go with it; and with work, a reasonable measure of security—security for themselves and for their wives and children. Work and security—these are more than words. They are more than facts. They are the spiritual values, the true goal toward which our efforts of reconstruction should lead. These are the values that this program is intended to gain; these are the values we have failed to achieve by the leadership we now have.

Our Republican leaders tell us economic laws—sacred, inviolable, unchangeable—cause panics which no one could prevent. But while they prate of economic laws, men and women are starving. We must lay hold of the fact that economic laws are not made by nature. They are made by human beings.

Yes, when—not if—when we get the chance, the Federal Government will assume bold leadership in distress relief. For years Washington has alternated between putting its head in the sand and saying there is no large number of destitute people in our midst who need food and clothing, and then saying the State should take care of them, if there are. Instead of planning two and a half years ago to do what they are now trying to do, they kept putting it off from day to day, week to week, and month to month, until the conscience of America demanded action.

I say that while primary responsibility for relief rests with localities now, as ever, yet the Federal Government has always had and still has a continuing responsibility for the broader public welfare. It will soon fulfill that responsibility. . . .

One word more: Out of every crisis, every tribulation, every disaster, mankind rises with some share of greater knowledge, of higher decency, of purer purpose. Today we shall have come through a period of loose thinking, descending morals, an era of selfishness, among individual men and women and among nations. Blame not Governments alone for this. Blame ourselves in equal share. Let us be frank in acknowledgment of the truth that many amongst us have made obeisance to Mammon, that the profits of speculation, the easy road without toil, have lured us from the old barricades. To return to higher standards we must abandon the false prophets and seek new leaders of our own choosing.

A New Deal

Never before in modern history have the essential differences between the two major American parties stood out in such striking contrast as they do today. Republican leaders not only have failed in material things, they have failed in national vision, because in disaster they have held out no hope, they have pointed out no path for the people below to climb back to places of security and of safety in our American life.

Throughout the Nation men and women, forgotten in the political philosophy of the Government of the last years look to us here for guidance and for more equitable opportunity to share in the distribution of national wealth.

On the farms, in the large metropolitan areas, in the smaller cities and in the villages, millions of our citizens cherish the hope that their old standards of living and of thought have not gone forever. Those millions cannot and shall not hope in vain.

I pledge you, I pledge myself, to a new deal for the American people. Let us all here assembled constitute ourselves prophets of a new order of competence and of courage. This is more than a political campaign; it is a call to arms. Give me your help, not to win votes alone, but to win in this crusade to restore America to its own people.

VIEWPOINT 8

"Our opponents . . . are proposing changes and so-called new deals which would destroy the very foundations of our American system."

Roosevelt's New Deal Would Harm America

Herbert Hoover (1874-1964)

Herbert Hoover was president of the United States during the first years of the Great Depression. His popularity suffered sharply as economic conditions worsened in the early 1930s. Nonetheless, he was renominated for the presidency by the Republican party in 1932. During the campaign he both defended his presidency and attacked his Democratic opponent Franklin D. Roosevelt.

In the following viewpoint, taken from a speech given in Madison Square Garden in New York on October 31, 1932, Hoover defends his record and sums up his philosophy of government and what he called the "American system." He argues that the American system depends on individual freedom and decentralized government. Giving too much authority to the federal government, he asserts, would destroy this system.

Hoover was defeated by Roosevelt in the 1932 election. He remained a lifelong critic of Roosevelt and the New Deal.

Herbert Hoover, from a campaign speech delivered at Madison Square Garden in New York City, October 31, 1932.

This campaign is more than a contest between two men. It is more than a contest between two parties. It is a contest between two philosophies of government.

We are told by the opposition that we must have a change, that we must have a new deal. It is not the change that comes from normal development of national life to which I object, but the proposal to alter the whole foundations of our national life which have been builded through generations of testing and struggle, and of the principles upon which we have builded the Nation. The expressions our opponents use must refer to important changes in our economic and social system and our system of Government, otherwise they are nothing but vacuous words. And I realize that in this time of distress many of our people are asking whether our social and economic system is incapable of that great primary function of providing security and comfort of life to all of the firesides of our 25,000,000 homes in America, whether our social system provides for the fundamental development and progress of our people, whether our form of government is capable of originating and sustaining that security and progress.

This question is the basis upon which our opponents are appealing to the people in their fears and distress. They are proposing changes and so-called new deals which would destroy the very foundations of our American system. . . .

The American System

Let us pause for a moment and examine the American system of government, of social and economic life, which it is now proposed that we should alter. Our system is the product of our race and of our experience in building a nation to heights unparalleled in the whole history of the world. It is a system peculiar to the American people. It differs essentially from all others in the world. It is an American system.

It is founded on the conception that only through ordered liberty, through freedom to the individual, and equal opportunity to the individual will his initiative and enterprise be summoned to spur the march of progress.

It is by the maintenance of equality of opportunity and therefore of a society absolutely fluid in freedom of the movement of its human particles that our individualism departs from the individualism of Europe. We resent class distinction because there can be no rise for the individual through the frozen strata of classes, and no stratification of classes can take place in a mass livened by the free rise of its particles. Thus in our ideals the able and ambitious are able to rise constantly from the bottom to leadership in the community.

This freedom of the individual creates of itself the necessity and the cheerful willingness of men to act cooperatively in a thousand ways and for every purpose as occasion arises; and it permits such voluntary cooperations to be dissolved as soon as they have served their purpose, to be replaced by new voluntary associations for new purposes.

President Herbert Hoover's popularity plummeted in the last years of his term in office when his periodic proclamations of economic recovery failed to materialize.

There has thus grown within us, to gigantic importance, a new conception. That is, this voluntary cooperation within the community. Cooperation to perfect the social organization; cooperation for the care of those in distress; cooperation for the advancement of knowledge, of scientific research, of education; for cooperative action in the advancement of many phases of economic life. This is self-government by the people outside of Government; it is the most powerful development of individual freedom and equal opportunity that has taken place in the century and a half since our fundamental institutions were founded.

It is in the further development of this cooperation and a sense of its responsibility that we should find solution for many of our complex problems, and not by the extension of government into our economic and social life. The greatest function of government is to build up that cooperation, and its most resolute action should be to deny the extension of bureaucracy. We have developed great agencies of cooperation by the assistance of the Government which promote and protect the interests of individuals and the smaller units of business. The Federal Reserve System, in its strengthening and support of the smaller banks; the Farm Board, in its strengthening and support of the farm cooperatives; the Home Loan Banks, in the mobilizing of building and loan associations and savings banks; the Federal Land Banks, in giving independence and strength to land mortgage associations; the great mobilization of relief to distress, the mobilization of business and industry in measures of recovery, and a score of other activities are not socialism—they are the essence of protection to the development of free men.

The primary conception of this whole American system is not the regimentation of men but the cooperation of free men. It is founded upon the conception of responsibility of the individual to the community, of the responsibility of local government to the state, of the state to the National Government.

It is founded on a peculiar conception of self-government designed to maintain this equal opportunity to the individual, and through decentralization it brings about and maintains these responsibilities. The centralization of government will undermine responsibilities and will destroy the system. . . .

Democratic Proposals

A proposal of our opponents which would break down the American system is the expansion of Government expenditure by yielding to sectional and group raids on the Public Treasury. The extension of Government expenditures beyond the minimum limit necessary to conduct the proper functions of the Government enslaves men to work for the Government. If we combine the whole governmental expenditures—National, state, and municipal—we will find that before the World War each citizen worked, theoretically, 25 days out of each year for the Government. In 1924 he worked 46 days a year for the Government. Today he works for the support of all forms of government 61 days out of the year.

No nation can conscript its citizens for this proportion of men's time without national impoverishment and destruction of their liberties. Our Nation cannot do it without destruction to our whole conception of the American system. The Federal Government has been forced in this emergency to unusual expenditures but in partial alleviation of these extraordinary and unusual expenditures, the Republican Administration has made a successful effort to reduce the ordinary running expenses of the Government. Our opponents have persistently interfered with such policies. I only need recall to you that the Democratic House of Representatives passed bills in the last session that would have increased our expenditures by $3,500,000,000, or 87 per cent. Expressed in day's labor, this would have meant the conscription of 16 days' additional work from every citizen for the Government. This I stopped. . . . But the major point I wish to make—the disheartening part of these proposals of our opponents—is that they represent successful pressures of minorities. They would appeal to sectional and group political support, and thereby impose terrific burdens upon every home in the country. These things can and must be resisted. But they can only be resisted if there shall be live and virile public support to the Administration, in opposition to political log-rolling and the sectional and group raids on the Treasury for distribution of public money, which is cardinal in the congeries of elements which make up the Democratic party.

These expenditures proposed by the Democratic House of Representatives for the benefit of special groups and special sections of our country directly undermine the American system. Those who pay are, in the last analysis, the man who works at the bench, the desk, and on the farm. They take away his comfort, stifle his leisure, and destroy his equal opportunity. . . .

The Growth of Government

No man who has not occupied my position in Washington can fully realize the constant battle which must be carried on against incompetence, corruption, tyranny of government expanded into business activities. If we first examine the effect on our form of government of such a program, we come at once to the effect of the most gigantic increase in expenditure ever known in history. That alone would break down the savings, the wages, the equality of opportunity among our people. These measures would transfer vast responsibilities to the Federal Government from the states, the local governments, and the individuals. But that is not all; they would break down our form of government. Our legislative bodies can not delegate their authority to any dictator, but without such delegation every member of these bodies is impelled in representation of the interest of his constituents constantly to seek privilege and demand service in the use of such agencies. Every time the Federal Government extends its arm, 531 Senators and Congressmen become actual boards of directors of that business.

Capable men can not be chosen by politics for all the various talents required. Even if they were supermen, if there were no politics in the selection of the Congress, if there were no constant pressure for this and for that, so large a number would be incapable as a board of directors of any institution. At once when these extensions take place by the Federal Government, the authority and responsibility of state governments and institutions are undermined. Every enterprise of private business is at once halted to know what Federal action is going to be. It destroys initiative and courage. . . .

The Democratic Political Strategy

In a campaign speech given in St. Louis, Missouri, on November 4, 1932, Herbert Hoover accused the Democrats of misleading the American people concerning the causes of the Great Depression.

From the congressional elections in 1930 down to the present moment the strategy of the Democratic Party has been an effort to implant in the unthinking mind through deliberate misrepresentation the colossal falsehood that the Republican Party is responsible for this world-wide catastrophe. They then appeal to distress, hardship, and radicalism by nebular and inconsistent promises. These are the reasons they give why the Republicans of the country should desert their party and why the Nation should abandon a constructive program with its accomplishment already demonstrated in overcoming the crisis. Theirs is not a campaign of issues; it is a campaign of avoidances.

Even if the Government conduct of business could give us the maximum of efficiency instead of least efficiency, it would be purchased at the cost of freedom. It would increase rather than decrease abuse and corruption, stifle initiative and invention, undermine development of leadership, cripple mental and spiritual energies of our people, extinguish equality of opportunity, and dry up the spirit of liberty and progress. Men who are going about this country announcing that they are liberals because of their promises to extend the Government in business are not liberals, they are reactionaries of the United States. . . .

Ending Poverty

I am not setting up the contention that our American system is perfect. No human ideal has ever been perfectly attained, since humanity itself is not perfect. But the wisdom of our forefathers and the wisdom of the 30 men who have preceded me in this office hold to the conception that progress can only be attained as the sum of accomplishments of free individuals, and they have held unalterably to these principles.

In the ebb and flow of economic life our people in times of prosperity and ease naturally tend to neglect the vigilance over their rights. Moreover, wrongdoing is obscured by apparent success in enterprise. Then insidious diseases and wrongdoings grow apace. But we have in the past seen in times of distress and difficulty that wrongdoing and weakness come to the surface and our people, in their endeavors to correct these wrongs, are tempted to extremes which may destroy rather than build.

It is men who do wrong, not our institutions. It is men who violate the laws and public rights. It is men, not institutions, which must be punished.

In my acceptance speech four years ago at Palo Alto I stated that—

> One of the oldest aspirations of the human race was the abolition of poverty. By poverty I mean the grinding by under-nourishment, cold, ignorance, fear of old age to those who have the will to work.

I stated that—

> In America today we are nearer a final triumph over poverty than in any land. The poorhouse has vanished from amongst us; we have not reached that goal, but given a chance to go forward, we shall, with the help of God, be in sight of the day when poverty will be banished from this Nation.

Our Democratic friends have quoted this passage many times in this campaign. I do not withdraw a word of it. When I look about the world even in these times of trouble and distress I find it more true in this land than anywhere else under the traveling sun. I am not ashamed of it, because I am not ashamed of holding ideals and purposes for the progress of the American people. Are my Democratic opponents prepared to state that they do not stand for this ideal or this hope? For my part, I propose to continue to strive for it, and I hope to live to see it accomplished. . . .

America's Choice

My countrymen, the proposals of our opponents represent a profound change in American life—less in concrete proposal, bad as that may be, than by implication and by evasion. Dominantly in their spirit they represent a radical departure from the foundations of 150 years which have made this the greatest nation in the world. This election is not a mere shift from the ins to the outs. It means deciding the direction our Nation will take over a century to come.

CHAPTER 2

Roosevelt Offers a New Deal

Chapter Preface

In the four months between the November 1932 election and Franklin D. Roosevelt's presidential inauguration in March 1933, the Great Depression reached its lowest point. Economic conditions, which had shown signs of improvement in the summer and fall of 1932, collapsed again in the winter amidst the uncertainty of what Roosevelt would do as president. Unemployment rose to a record level of fifteen million, and the nation's farmers faced acute problems of low crop prices and impending foreclosures. The most urgent problem, however, was a national banking crisis. As the number of bank failures mounted (there had been 1,345 in 1930, 2,298 in 1931, and 1,456 in 1932) national confidence fell, and depositors rushed to withdraw their savings, imperiling even the largest and relatively solvent institutions. On February 14 the governor of Michigan declared a state bank holiday to prevent further failures; governors from thirty-seven other states soon followed suit. America's banking system, one of the cornerstones of its economy, was in distress.

It was against this backdrop that Franklin D. Roosevelt took the oath of office on March 4, 1933. His inaugural address opened with his now-famous words:

> So, first of all, let me assert my firm belief that the only thing we have to fear is fear itself—nameless, unreasoning, unjustified terror which paralyzes needed efforts to convert retreat into advance.

As the gathered crowd of about 100,000 people and a national radio audience listened, Roosevelt pledged to call a special session of Congress to begin vigorous federal action to provide relief and combat the depression. Roosevelt made an analogy to national mobilization for war in the following passage which drew one of the largest cheers from the crowd:

> In the event that the Congress should fail [to pass needed legislation] . . . and in the event that the national emergency is still critical, I shall not evade the clear course of duty that will then confront me. I shall ask the Congress for the remaining instrument to meet the crisis—broad Executive power to wage a war against the emergency, as great as the power that would be given to me if we were in fact invaded by a foreign foe.

Roosevelt's first actions as president dealt with the banking crisis. On March 5, 1933, he declared a national bank holiday effective the next day and summoned Congress to a special session to deal with the bank crisis. The special session of Congress convened March 9 and passed the Emergency Banking Act the same day. The act provided for the reopening of banks under tightened federal supervision. Perhaps just as important as the legislation itself was Roosevelt's first "fireside chat"—an informal radio address to Americans, in which Roosevelt explained the banking situation and what had been done to solve it. Banks began reopening on March 13, the day after Roosevelt's radio address, and by April newly confident citizens deposited more than $1 billion. The bank crisis was over—without the drastic measure of nationalizing the banks, as some progressive Roosevelt supporters had hoped would happen.

The success of the bank legislation encouraged Roosevelt to keep Congress in session for further economic recovery legislation. Historian Robert Kelley writes in *The Shaping of the American Past:*

> Roosevelt now pushed forward on a broad front during the famous Hundred Days, a three-month period in the spring of 1933 when Congress enacted the most sweeping program of reform legislation in American history. Fifteen major laws went on the books; they dealt with banking, the gold standard, relief, mortgages, hydroelectric power and regional planning, the stock market, and reorganizing industry and agriculture. It all swept forward in the presence of a wartime psychology, when people tended to pull together and look on the country as a great team under centralized direction in which each member cooperates with every other for the good of the whole.

Roosevelt encouraged cooperation and optimism with his speeches, "fireside chats," and press conferences, and the speed and breadth of the New Deal's changes made an impression on many Americans. Influential columnist Walter Lippmann, who had criticized Roosevelt as a political lightweight, wrote:

> At the end of February we were a congeries of disorderly panic-stricken mobs and factions. In the hundred days from March to June we became an organized nation confident of our power to provide for our own security and to control our own destiny.

The New Deal was not without its critics, however. Ex-president Hoover and other conservatives decried the government intervention as threatening tyranny. Socialist presidential candidate Norman Thomas and others from the left-side of the political spectrum argued that Roosevelt was trying to shore up a tottering capitalist system that needed to be replaced. Despite these critics and the continuing economic slump and hard times of many Americans, Roosevelt remained highly popular, and the 1934 congressional elections were marked by sharp gains for the Democratic party.

VIEWPOINT 1

*"What . . . happened in this nation in 1933
was . . . a magnificent vindication of democracy."*

The New Deal Is a Momentous Achievement

Allan Nevins (1890-1971)

Allan Nevins was a renowned historian whose biographies and historical studies won Pulitzer prizes in 1932 and 1936. A journalist and editor for several publications including the *Nation* and the New York *World*, Nevins joined the history faculty at Columbia University in New York in 1931. His books include biographies of Grover Cleveland and Henry Ford and a six-volume series on the Civil War.

The following viewpoint is taken from a December 31, 1933, article in the *New York Times Magazine*. In it, Nevins attempts to summarize the historical events of that year, including the actions of President Franklin D. Roosevelt. Nevins compares the actions of the United States with those of other countries facing depression and argues that the New Deal measures represent a vindication of the ability of the United States to adapt to new conditions. He argues that the resourcefulness of the New Deal marks a fundamental shift in which the government assumed a greater responsibility for ensuring economic prosperity for all Americans, including farmers and workers who had been neglected by previous administrations.

From Allan Nevins, "1933-1934: Two Momentous Years," *The New York Times Magazine*, December 31, 1933. Copyright © 1933, 1961 by The New York Times Company. Reprinted by permission.

The year that now draws to a close has been marked by extraordinary fluctuations and changes. It has been on the whole a year of storm, with nations struggling in the waves left by the World War. Many countries had been half-submerged ever since that conflict. The United States, which for a time had ridden on the top of the surge, fell at the beginning of the year deeper into the trough than any other. In its extremity it turned, like Europe, to new experiments. Certainly in no other year since 1919 has the world seen so many radically new ideas and principles broached.

There has been what seemed to many a great change in ideas of government. Fascism has been striding onward; the United States has entrusted unprecedented peacetime authority to Mr. Roosevelt. There has been a radical revision of men's ideas upon international relationships. World organization has suffered heavily, and theories of "autarchy" or self-containment have made many converts.

In the field of economics also there has been a momentous shifting of ideas—in the United States in particular, which has turned to reduction of production, to restriction of competition and to government intervention for the raising of commodity prices. Bold new financial theories are accepted in high places; most of the world is off the gold standard; the validity of that standard in its old form is being questioned, and in the two most powerful nations attempts are being made to manage the currency.

Ideas Born of Crisis

These new ideas, however varied, have one common quality. They are fundamentally the products of a time of unexampled crisis. A number of them bear plain evidence of exaggeration or distortion and one or two even of hysteria. During great tempests there are moments when the earth itself seems to heave and tremble. After they have passed men realize that this was a delusion, that through all the rush and shock of wind and wave the earth stood solid as ever—its quivers were imagined.

Of late, Americans have had a tendency to pass from one exaggeration to another. Six years ago they talked of a new economic era of unprecedented possibilities, of prosperity that nothing could check and stocks that "will go to a thousand." Bank presidents said that we had but started on our way, and economists of repute wrote that the soaring stock prices registered a permanent revolution in national well-being. It is possible that at the nadir of the depression many ideas are as warped as were those expressed at the crest of the wave. When we get back to a fairly calm sea we may perceive that both were askew, and that "If hopes [1928] were dupes, fears [in 1933] may be liars."

At any rate, the year 1934 is certain to offer a severe test for many of the ideas and principles propounded in 1933. There is evidence that it will be a year of slowly returning prosperity. The best reason for thinking this is that the recent upward tendency seems to be world-wide. It is the same in England, America, Scandinavia and Australia, which are off the gold basis, and in France, Belgium and Switzerland, which are still on it; the same in nations with managed currencies and in nations without them; the same in high-tariff countries and in moderate-tariff countries. A general trend, whose origins economists trace back to midsummer of 1932, seems to be at work.

Theories formed to fit a depression will soon, we may hope, be working in a period of growing normality. Laws and governmental agencies devised for populations badly frightened, and hence ductile and obedient, will have to be applied to populations which are resuming their individualistic habits. And there are other factors as well. Men's whole attitude toward great public questions may change rapidly, as our recent dramatic verdict upon Prohibition has just indicated. Altogether, the next twelve-month will undoubtedly sift much which the last year has produced.

Without violating Lowell's wise maxim, "Don't prophesy onless ye know," it is possible to make one flat statement: The recent assertions that ideas of government have undergone a radical change will not be sustained by future events. These assertions rest upon a misreading of the facts. The assumption in certain quarters that in the United States something has befallen democracy, that the concentration of power in the President's hands has meant a "revolution," already begins to appear absurd. No country, for evident reasons, is less inclined to revolution than the United States. What actually happened in this nation in 1933 was just the opposite, a magnificent vindication of democracy. We proved anew the flexibility of our government, its capacity for meeting unexpected tensions.

The sudden expansion of Presidential authority to overcome a great emergency conformed entirely with the intent of the founders of the Republic. They meant that in war, in periods of internal strife and in great economic crises the President should be endowed with sufficient power to conquer all difficulties. Again and again Presidents have assumed such power. Jefferson did so when he stretched the Constitution till it cracked, Jackson when he met nullification, Lincoln during the Civil War, Wilson during the World War. When the present crisis subsides, Mr. Roosevelt's powers will subside also.

In fact, it is in times like the present and under such bold and resourceful leaders as Mr. Roosevelt that our democratic institutions are at their best. There is some reason to feel discouraged about them when weak Presidents fail to exercise their authority in due degree—and we do not need to go back to Pierce and Buchanan to name such Presidents. There is no reason to feel anything but optimism when we see Congress and President cooperating as they did last spring, the Chief Executive showing sustained leadership and the people responding loyally to the demands of the government. This is representative government as Locke and Montesquieu outlined it two centuries ago and as James Bryce and Woodrow Wilson expounded it more recently.

We have plenty of balance in reserve. The legislative branch will be playing its usual rôle in a few days, and the judiciary is still to be heard from. But the best defenders of democracy have always contended that balance has to give way at times to stern executive leadership. . . .

A New Economic Philosophy

In the economic sphere there is much that is still confused and bewildering. In many respects the American people are still at a half-way point. Yet, again a few statements may be ventured without treading on the dangerous ground of prophecy. For one, the year 1933 seemed to show that the United States is at last accepting a long-contested principle: the principle that no prosperity is a true prosperity unless it embraces substantially the entire population.

This may sound axiomatic. Yet we can now see that during the decade of the Twenties it was disregarded by most Easterners and by a number of those in the highest governmental places. The prosperity which we boasted from 1921 to 1929, and which many recklessly misused, left large sections of the country untouched. The great mass of the American farmers, the great majority of bituminous miners, a large part of our textile workers, to name only three groups, were shut out in the cold.

The first of these groups was all-important. Mr. [George] Peek said a few pungent words in Chicago the other day about the folly of trying to make a profit system work while depriving 6,000,000 farmers, who are at the foundation of our whole national life, of any hope of profits. It has been generally acknowledged during 1933 that if the administrations which scolded the farmer so vigorously for demanding just such aid as had been granted to industry in the post-war tariffs had spent a little more energy in devising rational assistance to agriculture, we might have been far better off today. A dollar spent six or eight years ago . . . would have saved many dollars this last year. Instead, the farmer was rebuffed with a lecture on political economy—the lecturers themselves forgetting some of the most elementary tenets of national economy in the larger sense.

Of all the new ideas put into effect by the Roosevelt administration, the idea that the prosperity of the farmers is worth just as much governmental thought and effort as that of the industrialists ought to be surest of continued approval. The administration has turned to a series of frankly experimental devices to help agriculture.

The policy that men should be paid not to grow wheat, cotton, corn and hogs would have astounded an earlier generation. It may not win indefinite acceptance; the coming year may bring it under heavy fire. The farmer himself, still a stanch individualist, who would far rather grow all he could for a large foreign market than grow half of what he could for a restricted domestic market, may insist on changes. Some of them have already been hinted at by Secretary Henry Wallace in his utterances on foreign trade as it affects the farmer. But the general principle that the country can never again afford to let the prairies and the plantations drop lower and lower in poverty and discouragement just because its factories and brokerage houses are still flourishing may be taken as fairly established for 1934 and all future years.

Industrial Reform

The fate during the coming year of the various ideas bound up in the NRA [National Recovery Administration] will likewise be interesting to watch. That system of government advisership and assistance to industry, as Mr. Roosevelt calls it—repudiating the word "control"—has hitherto been under the guidance and surveillance of the Executive alone. It will now pass under that of Congress as well, while the legislation creating it remains to be tested in the highest court.

Unquestionably, if and as the economic crisis passes, the tendency to regard this as purely emergency legislation will gain strength. With much of it certain to lapse, the really interesting question is what permanent residuum will remain. That it will at least leave some permanent benefits of a social nature in higher minimum-wage standards, in shorter hours and in the reduction of child labor may be devoutly hoped.

Some of these benefits will have to be embodied in entirely new legislation. To make sure of the one last named, the abolition of child labor, another constitutional amendment will be required, and already there is evidence that Mr. Roosevelt's bold measures have given impetus to the movement in the States for ratifying it. We may hope that 1934 will prove that much in the NRA standards which has been hailed by social meliorists most jubilantly will remain as a permanent legacy.

Doubtless the fundamental question in the economic sphere, however, is whether the country will long support the new principle that prosperity may be attained and kept by cutting down production, restricting competition and thus raising price levels. This principle, if carried to its logical conclusion, really comes near being "revolutionary" in a minor sense of the word. It is certainly in direct conflict with some of the convictions most deeply ingrained in the American breast.

Most plain citizens of this country still regard the anti-trust laws and all other legislation against collusion, combination, interlocking directorates and the like with the deepest jealousy. Many people have a keen remembrance of some of the evils of monopoly in the days when trusts were most lawless; many have an unshakable faith in the value of competition. The West in particular looks upon this legislation as one of the bulwarks of economic and political liberty.

In general, again, most Americans, however illogically, hold that there is a direct connection between unfettered production and a rising standard of comfort. Various writers, like Walter Lippmann, have lately pointed out that the outcry against overproduction is always raised when depressions occur, that we have often heard it in the past when production was but a fraction of what it now is, and that it has always been forgotten when good times recur.

As for prices, the American public is capable of coming very quickly and sharply to the conclusion that prices and living costs are too high. In this whole field it is clear that the Roosevelt administration has raised many questions which are far from settled. The coming year must go a long way toward providing the answers.

The Gold Standard

Questions of finance may well be left to the experts who are now quarreling so acrimoniously upon the subject. Obviously this debate has as yet come nowhere near its conclusion. Its vehemence has so far perhaps succeeded in impressing upon the general public just one truth. There is no fiat from Heaven which has ordained that the gold dollar of 23.22 grains shall be immutably indispensable to American well-being.

A New Direction

Harold L. Ickes, a former Republican and a progressive supporter of Theodore Roosevelt, was Franklin D. Roosevelt's secretary of the interior. In a May 27, 1934, article for the New York Times Maga-zine, *Ickes contrasts the New Deal with what he considers the misguided policies of the three previous Republican administrations.*

In our attempt to say where we, as a nation, are now headed, it may be well to consider briefly where we were headed before we changed our direction on March 4, 1933. For almost four years before that day we had been drifting, going nowhere at all. Caught in the worst economic jam the country had ever known, we were milling around in a confusion that grew steadily worse. And throughout the eight years before that, ending in the fatal autumn of 1929, we had been wandering in a fool's paradise of false prosperity and hastening directly for the jam. . . .

We have learned much about economics since we went on that twelve-year detour of ours. Theodore Roosevelt and Woodrow Wilson had tried to teach us, and we promptly forgot. We had to go down into the depression to learn our lesson. And now, as we struggle back to the highroad where we should have been traveling all the while, we humbly and thoughtfully take up again our traditional task of making our country a good place to live in for every man, woman and child.

That dollar was fixed, not by supernatural decree, but by act of Congress in 1834. This legislation superseded an earlier law of Congress, which in 1792 fixed a decidedly different gold content (to wit, 24.75 grains) for the dollar. It is possible to conceive of the government fixing a third gold content in 1934 without bringing the nation to utter ruin. The most important characteristic that money can have is stability, and gold has been far from stable.

101

When, once before, in the years preceding 1896, declining prices called the gold standard into sharp question, the problem was solved by a greatly enlarged production of gold. William Jennings Bryan was able to remark, with complete justice, that the Republicans wanted the gold standard and got it, and that the Democrats wanted more money and got it. Today the solution may have to be very different. It is clearly evident that it will have to be a compromise solution and that it will have to take into account the arguments for higher commodity prices and for a scaling down of debts.

Moreover, most people are now convinced that we need not expect an ideal solution, for in the very nature of the question that is impossible. We did not have an ideal currency before the crash and we should not expect or demand to have it afterward.

The World Situation

As we look back over the year 1933, viewing the world as a whole, it is impossible to avoid the conclusion that the most disturbing development has been the weakening of international ties. So far as the hope of world cooperation and unity goes, the past twelve-month has recorded several heavy defeats. The World Economic Conference in London, while not completely fruitless, did in general prove empty and abortive. The Disarmament Conference came to nothing. Moreover, Germany's rupture with it led to a still more deplorable event. The League of Nations has now been weakened by the withdrawal of the Reich, following hard on that of Japan. Of the world's seven greatest powers, four—United States, Germany, Russia and Japan—are left on New Year's Day of 1934 outside its portals. . . .

Moreover, all over the globe the sentiment of nationalism has been heightened by the comparatively new doctrine of "autarchy" or self-containment. The doctrine, like so much else, belongs to the ideology of the emergency. In one nation after another "autarchy" has grown out of or been correlated with plans for far-reaching internal readjustments to restore prosperity. These readjustments, according to the prevailing doctrine, can be made more easily if the national life is largely isolated from the world economy. Collective control, so the theory runs, is possible only in an insulated or semi-insulated State.

The United States was unfortunately one of the first nations to take a long step along this path. The Smoot-Hawley tariff, so universally condemned by economists, provoked in 1930 a long series of retaliatory enactments or decrees by other nations. As the crisis grew worse, the tendency progressed further; the British Imperial Conference at Ottawa gave it fresh impetus. Today "autarchy," despite the verdict of such economists as Sir Arthur

Salter that it is as foolish economically as it is dangerous politically, is being discussed and all too forcibly urged in most of the great capitals.

It is to be hoped that the year 1934, if it does little else, will subject this and all other tendencies or theories making for greater national isolation to a severe and destructive test. Unless the conclusions of virtually all careful students of the subject are wrong, "autarchy" is indeed economic folly.

The largest single source of the world's present ills, economic as well as political, is to be found in nationalistic conflicts and barriers. The world depression has descended directly from the World War, its effects accentuated by nationalistic jealousies and disputes over reparations, debts and tariffs. If the coming year is to bring us a permanent hope of better times it must do something to reverse these unfortunate tendencies of 1933—to strengthen the League, to reduce the burden of armaments, to lessen the constant danger of an explosion in Europe, to lower trade barriers and to bring the nations of the world into closer relations and greater friendliness.

VIEWPOINT 2

"It seems questionable whether the Forgotten Man is likely to share very handsomely in the New Deal."

The New Deal Is a Limited Achievement

Suzanne La Follette (1894-1983)

Suzanne La Follette was a feminist and journalist who was a contributing author and editor for several magazines, including the *Nation* and *American Mercury*. Her books include *Concerning Women* and *Art in America*. She was a cousin of Robert M. La Follette, a Wisconsin senator and leader of the Progressive Movement. In the following viewpoint, taken from an October 1933 article in *Current History*, La Follette argues that people expecting a radical revolution from Franklin D. Roosevelt's New Deal have been or will be disappointed. The New Deal merely attempts to patch up America's capitalist system, she asserts, while leaving broader problems of exploitation unsolved.

There is a strange air of unreality about the New Deal somewhat suggestive of adventure on a rocking-horse. President Roosevelt and his subordinates are attacking real problems—no doubt of that—energetically, enthusiastically, and with wonderful devotion to their tasks. But they appear to be no more aware of the economic implications of those problems than the public

Excerpted from Suzanne La Follette, "The Roosevelt 'Revolution.'" Reprinted with permission from *Current History* magazine (October 1933), © 1933, Current History, Inc.

whose fears and desperate hopes they unquestionably represent. Their program thus lacks the coherence that understanding would give it, and the contradictions involved make the United States of America in 1933 seem like the world of Lewis Carroll, where anything is possible and nothing is real.

As one considers this appearance of unreality, one realizes that it is not strange at all. It is the distinguishing and perennial characteristic of liberal thought and action. Self-deception is the primary requisite of the liberal mind. The liberal does not dare see the reality of the economic injustice whose effects make him so indignant. If he did, he would be obliged to admit that economic injustice should be abolished, not tinkered with; and for a complex of reasons ranging from self-interest to the chance that God may have made him a tinker by temperament, he does not want it abolished. He wants it "regulated in the public interest." His labor is accordingly out of all proportion to his results, and these are likely to be not at all what he expected. He is like a gallant St. George, trying not to kill the dragon but to pull a few of his teeth without hurting him. It is much more difficult, and the results are unpredictable.

Roosevelt's Radicalism

President Roosevelt has been described as "the most radical man in Washington." From the radical point of view this is such faint praise that it does not do him justice. He is a radical in the American tradition of radicalism—that is, a radical by temperament and instinct. He is for the underdog and against the powerful interests that exploit the underdog. He is genuinely concerned for the fifteen million unemployed; he is genuinely concerned for the debt-burdened farmer victimized by low prices for his own product and high prices for the things he must buy. He is quite in the Jeffersonian tradition of radicalism in that he is instinctively on the side of the producing interest in society and against the speculating interest. But like Jefferson's, his championship of the producing interest is only instinctive. It is a far cry from instinctive radicalism to the radicalism which is inspired by an understanding of what economics and politics are really about. To put it concretely, there is a vast difference between having Wall Street investigated and setting out to abolish the economic system which makes Wall Street possible.

Mr. Roosevelt is far from wishing to abolish the economic system which involves the injustice against which he is tilting. Otherwise he would not be in the White House. The will to change in the American people, which he represents and which is the source of his extraordinary influence, is by no means a will to radical change. There is no widespread discontent with the existing economic system; there is only discontent with its inevitable working-out in hardship for the vast majority and enormous wealth for the few. Psychologically we are still under the spell of the freedom of opportunity offered by a vanished frontier. The nineteenth century took this freedom to inhere in our political and economic institutions, and the twentieth has not yet discovered its error. Thanks to the influence of this self-deception, nine out of ten Americans still believe that the system is divinely ordained and has only somehow fallen into bad hands from which some of its spoils must be rescued for the masses.

Let us not minimize the revolutionary feeling which unquestionably existed during the last years of the Hoover regime. One has only to remember the general satisfaction with the political and economic reaction of the post-war period to realize what an extraordinary change the depression brought about in the national temper, which may possibly have momentous consequences, unless renewed prosperity shall change it once more into complacence. But when the American public becomes revolutionary in feeling it cannot, so long as its peculiar attitude toward existing political and economic institutions remains unchanged, translate that feeling into any kind of fundamentally revolutionary action. This perhaps explains the paradox of Mr. Roosevelt. He is a liberal meliorist acting in a revolutionary situation which allows of nothing more fundamental than liberal meliorism. . . .

One cannot foresee, of course, to what lengths or in what direction events may drive the public and the government, but at present it is quite just to say that the New Deal is another attempt to secure everybody's right to life, liberty and the pursuit of happiness by obviating the more onerous effects of the monopolistic system of ownership which denies that right. Mr. Roosevelt clearly expresses its purpose in his book, *Looking Forward*:

> I believe that the government, without becoming a prying bureaucracy, can act as a check or counterbalance of this oligarchy [the "few hundred corporations" and "fewer than three dozen banks" which control our economic life] so as to secure initiative, life, a chance to work, and the safety of savings to men and women, rather than the safety of exploitation to the exploiter, safety of manipulation to the manipulator, safety of unlicensed power to those who would speculate to the bitter end with the welfare and property of other people.

The method by which the President hopes to attain this highly desirable purpose, the method which has already been embodied in the Securities Act, the Banking Act, the National Industrial Recovery Act, is not revolutionary at all. . . . Mr. Roosevelt's method is the old familiar one of government supervision and regulation, valiantly fought for from the day of this country's birth by a long line of liberals whose Pyrrhic victories strew the pages of its his-

No Central Direction

In 1935, journalists and political activists Benjamin Stolberg and Warren Jay Vinton published a pamphlet sharply attacking the New Deal. They assert that in his attempt to please and placate everyone, including big business, Roosevelt has accomplished little with his New Deal.

In its attempt to evade the fundamental contradictions of our economy the New Deal was bound to rely on panaceas. Its whole program is in essence nothing but a well-intentioned synthesis of errors. What it accomplishes in one direction it undoes in another. It is like the Russian peasant who cut some cloth from the front of his pants to patch the hole in the seat; and then cut from the leg of his pants to patch the front. After repeating this operation a dozen times he wound up, very much like the New Deal, with his pants all in patches and the migratory hole still there. . . .

The New Deal is trying to right the unbalance of our economic life by strengthening all its contradictions. For Big Ownership it tries to safeguard profits and to keep intact the instruments of its financial domination. For the middle classes it tries to safeguard their small investments, which only serves to reintrench Big Ownership. For labor it tries to raise wages, increase employment, and assure some minimum of economic safety, while at the same time it opposes labor's real interests through its scarcity program. In trying to move in every direction at once the New Deal betrays the fact that it has no policy.

tory. In the very nature of the situation it could never be anything else.

Why, then, is everyone so hopeful? Because Americans are very slow to learn that it is economic relationships that govern political actions, and not political actions that govern economic relationships. This is another way of saying that those who own rule, and they rule because they own. In a political democracy they may appear to be beaten for a while, but in the end the victory is theirs because the economic power is theirs. They furnish the big campaign contributions; they can use their control of wealth to corrupt public officers; they can even use the people's money to corrupt the people's mind to their purposes, and they are welded into a united front against mercurial popular movements by "the cohesive power of public plunder." At present the owning oligarchy appears to be on the run. The collapse of the philanthropic pretensions with which it masked its unbridled theft, the amazing discovery that not a few of its revered leaders were little better than morons—these developments have served to discredit it in the public mind. But discredited as it is, it still owns—a fact worth bearing in mind as one watches the government's attempts to "regulate it in the public interest."

It is a tremendous economic power which Mr. Roosevelt is trying to "check and counterbalance," for it is concentrated in very few hands. There is, moreover, the curious spectacle of his trying to preserve it in order to check and counterbalance it, for he is continuing Mr. Hoover's policy of propping up with government credit the capital structure through which the American people are exploited. Let us not impugn his motive. As he sees it, the life of the country depends on the capital structure—the jobs of the workers, the savings of all the citizens, the profits of the industrialists and bankers and shopkeepers, the livelihood of the farmers, the incomes of landowners and bondholders. And it is quite true that the capitalist way of life depends upon the preservation of the capitalist system. The vast majority of Mr. Roosevelt's fellow-citizens see the thing as he does. They cannot envisage any other way of life. As Trotsky says, "society actually takes the institutions that depend upon it as given once for all."

The Forgotten Man

But with the structure preserved unaltered, with its liens on production unrevised, it seems questionable whether the Forgotten Man is likely to share very handsomely in the New Deal. He will still be obliged to carry the heavy load of unearned income—on capitalized franchises, capitalized earning power, bonds issued to enrich underwriters, mortgages held at usurious rates of interest, overcapitalized land values. In addition, he must bear a tax burden which has mounted fantastically since the beginning of the century and has increased rather than lessened during the depression. Contrary to popular belief, all income, unearned as well as earned, and all taxes come out of the labor of the producing classes; there is no other source for them to come from.

Thus, at a cursory glance the New Deal looks like a plan to employ more workers at higher wages so that they can pay higher prices so that interest can be paid on inflated bond-issues, dividends on watered stock, and rents on inflated land values. This is certainly not what Mr. Roosevelt has been promising. Yet might not a stranger, watching the New Deal as it gets under way and not knowing its author's expressed intention to abolish exploitation, be likely to assume that its primary purpose was to rationalize unearned income, which is to say, to stabilize the right of exploitation?

This may be challenged on the ground of the "peaceful revolution" supposedly proceeding under the National Industrial Recovery Act. One should be reluctant to attack this attempt to restore workers to employment if for no other reason than that it is meeting with resistance at the moment from some of the most ruthless of the exploiting interests, such as the steel trust and the coal operators. Moreover, it seems to be eliminating child labor, and we are emotionally stirred by that prospect even though intellectually we should realize that employers can well afford this apparently humanitarian gesture when adult labor can be had at wages as low as those provided in some of the codes submitted or already adopted under the act—codes which indicate that neither the employers nor the government officials have forgotten the sacred right of exploitation that inheres in ownership.

Here the obvious retort may be anticipated by remarking that the administration cannot demand higher minimum conditions than the employers will accept. If you are compromising with an exploiting system you have to respect the right to exploit.

Exploitation of Workers

We say to ourselves, "What must the exploitation of men and women have been during this depression if these minimums mean an improvement in their condition!" We know something of it, for official agencies have enlightened us from time to time. Women in Pennsylvania sweatshops have been reported as receiving less than $2 for two weeks' work. In the South the textile workers have lived in a state of virtual peonage for so long that a $12 minimum wage and a 40-hour week must seem like wealth and leisure to them. But while the government is raising minimum wages it is also trying to raise prices, and even holding inflation in reserve as a means to that end. Suppose the purchasing power of the dollar should drop once more to 50 cents—which seems not at all improbable—what then will be the condition of the worker who is now sure of a minimum wage ranging from $10 to $15 a week? One is reminded of the minimum-wage laws for women that liberal reformers have pounded through State Legislatures only to see them rendered valueless by a rise in the cost of living.

To be sure, the National Industrial Recovery Act gives the President dictatorial powers. It authorizes him not only to approve but to prescribe "maximum hours of labor, minimum rates of pay, and other conditions of employment." Theoretically he could use these powers to abolish the exploitation of labor; practically he could and would do no such thing. In order to do so he would have to prescribe wages and conditions of labor which would eliminate unearned income from production, and that would be to destroy the credit structure which the government is maintaining at the taxpayers' expense. Therefore he would not eliminate exploitation. . . .

Viewed objectively, then, the administration's program looks like an attempt to rationalize and stabilize exploitation on a nationalist basis. Through subsidizing a reduction of acreage the government proposes to relieve the farmer from dependence on the export market; at the same time it is trying to raise the domestic price of agricultural staples through the processing tax. Thus the agricultural community is to be enabled to bear its annual rent burden of $700,000,000, meet the interest on its $8,500,000,000 of mortgages and pay monopoly prices for farm machinery. And the domestic market for agricultural products at higher prices, and for industrial products, too, is to be enlarged through the National Industrial Recovery Act, which by shortening hours of labor will bring about extensive re-employment—if production continues to improve—and by setting minimum wages for the workers re-employed will increase their buying power—if higher prices do not cancel the value of higher wages. . . .

No New Frontier

The attempt to increase employment by shortening the hours of labor is extremely interesting and significant. It is the only new thing, indeed, about the New Deal, with the significant exception of the spirit which animates it. Depressions can be lifted only through the opening up of new economic opportunities for the workers who have been squeezed out of their livelihood by licensed greed. In the past these opportunities have been furnished by free land or the rise of new industries. But for the past forty years this country has had no frontier; the industrial worker can no longer avail himself of the free opportunity to "labor the earth" for himself; nor has any industry arisen during this depression, as the automobile and radio industries have in the past, on a scale so large as to absorb enough jobless workers to start the whole productive mechanism anew.

The National Industrial Recovery Act is an attempt to provide a substitute for this means of renewing economic activity. It seems to be regarded by its advocates as a means of restoring equality of opportunity. If the New Deal is successful, it may work in that direction, though only, for reasons already adduced, toward equality of opportunity to be exploited. The fact that even this should at the moment seem like a tremendous social improvement is a terrible indictment of our economic system.

Significant as it is that we have in Washington an administration trying to fight the battle of the suffering masses against their exploiters, it is nevertheless unfortunate that more should be expected of its plan of campaign than is warranted by the plan itself and by the essential liberal meliorism of the American public and the administration. If the New Deal, in spite of the spirit animating it, has here been rather mercilessly analyzed, it is because it seems important that we cease to expect miracles of it. If we do not delude ourselves with extravagant hopes, what is going on in Washington will be of great educational value in showing up the nature and workings of economic forces in this country. If we regard the New Deal as at best a first halting step in the general direction of revolutionary improvement, instead of *the* revolution sprung full-panoplied from the brow of Mr. Roosevelt, we may save ourselves some disagreeable surprises.

VIEWPOINT 3

"The New Deal is a very definite attempt to evolve a new governmental-economic relationship in response to the needs and opportunities created by the past methods of operating our economy."

The New Deal Marks a New Era of Economic Planning

Rexford G. Tugwell (1891-1979)

Rexford G. Tugwell was part of Franklin D. Roosevelt's "Brain Trust," a group of academics who assisted in Roosevelt's 1932 election campaign and were later employed by the president to help plan and implement the New Deal. Tugwell, who was a professor of economics at Columbia University in New York, served as an adviser and speechwriter for Roosevelt in addition to holding numerous government posts between 1933 and 1937. Among his official appointments were assistant secretary and undersecretary of agriculture and head of the Resettlement Administration, an agency which provided assistance to poor and displaced farmers. In his books, articles, and speeches, both before and during the Roosevelt administration, Tugwell was a strong advocate of government planning of the economy. Viewed by many as the most radical of Roosevelt's advisers, Tugwell was a frequent target of criticism. He left the Roosevelt administration in 1937 and later served as governor of Puerto Rico and professor at the University of Chicago.

From Rexford G. Tugwell, "America Takes Hold of Its Destiny." In *The Battle for Democracy*, © 1935 Columbia University Press, New York. Reprinted with permission of the publisher.

The following viewpoint is taken from an article first published in *Today* magazine on April 28, 1934, and reprinted in the 1935 book *The Battle for Democracy*. Tugwell argues that the actions taken by the Roosevelt administration in the year since his inauguration amount to a fundamental shift in the relationship between the U.S. government and the economy. Government must go beyond simply breaking up monopolies and promoting economic competition, he writes. Such an approach to the economy was discredited by the Great Depression. It is to be replaced, he states, by a new era in which government and business cooperate in planning the economy, reducing unemployment, redistributing income, and ensuring a higher living standard for everyone.

The twentieth century found the American people psychologically and financially unprepared to utilize the wealth which the technological revolution of the last thirty years has made possible. For the first time in human history, it was possible to foresee a period during which a nation need not live from hand to mouth, but could, instead, count upon a steady increase in the supply of physical wealth accompanied by a steady decrease in the amount of human effort required to produce that wealth. A surplus of economic goods and services had been brought into existence and remained to be dealt with by the methods and ideas which were appropriate to the eons of scarcity.

As it became apparent that a more abundant life was within the reach of all our people, if we could only display the social inventiveness necessary to deal with this new abundance in such form as to convert anxious unemployment into secure leisure, we were shaken by a profound moral crisis. On the one side stood the sincere group of wishful beneficiaries of the Old Order, who—in the words of a gifted Englishman—sat "waiting for the twentieth century to blow over." On the other side stood the mass of our people, who were increasingly bewildered by the failure of the old principles of our society to assure the distribution of those goods which were there for all to see and which were rotting away for want of buyers. The result of this crisis and conflict was the New Deal.

A New Deal Mandate

A new deal was absolutely inevitable. People will submit to grave privations and will even starve peaceably, if they realize that actual dearth exists, but no man and no race will starve in the presence of abundance. The possibility of revolution, either peaceful or violent, against any system which denies the visible means of life to those who have produced those means, will always be with us. Therefore, the only choice before the American people, after four years of patient privation, was whether their revolution should follow the course of violence and destruction or should express itself in orderly, legal channels. The answer was given in November, 1932, when the American people gave to President Roosevelt a peaceful mandate to attempt to devise a better means of distributing the national income than had previously existed.

Faith in the American People

President Roosevelt concluded his July 24, 1933, radio fireside chat with an assertion of faith in the abilities of Americans to cooperate in ending the Depression.

I have no faith in "cure-alls" but I believe that we can greatly influence economic forces. I have no sympathy with the professional economists who insist that things must run their course and that human agencies can have no influence on economic ills. One reason is that I happen to know that professional economists have changed their definition of economic laws every five or ten years for a very long time, but I do have faith, and retain faith, in the strength of the common purpose and in the strength of unified action taken by the American people.

The objective of this administration is accordingly a simple one: it is to give our citizens the opportunity for a richer life. But simple and easily stated as this objective is, the methods it imposes are difficult and complex. This because riches do not appear in answer to wishes; they result only from careful thought, arduous work and rigorous choosing. These processes are going forward now through the various agencies which have seemed appropriate to the task. The activities involved are carried on in so many different fields, they seem so different and sometimes so contradictory, that it is valuable from time to time to remind ourselves what the central intention is, how everything which is being done fits into the service of that intention, and to look forward, even if only a little way, toward what is coming.

In order to understand, it seems to me necessary to keep far up in the foreground always the idea that the possibilities of the future are always greater than were those of any time in the past. As we multiply inventions and add to our store of processes, as the different sciences are enriched by the accretions of scholarship, we move forward with a changing and growing equipment. The possibilities of every new year are therefore greater rather than less. That is why, in my opinion, it is a fundamental error to assume that we have now reached the end of the "swing to the left" and that we ought to forego any further important policy changes. The real economic revolution is just beginning and social policy will have to move rapidly to keep pace with it.

I have very little patience, therefore, with those who say that we have come to the end of a period of progress, that we must now retrench and economize, hoarding our gains against a poverty-stricken future. One of our troubles has been that we have hoarded and economized too much, rather than devoting ourselves to organizing and expanding our resources and capabilities. We do not seem to realize that it is our own abundance which compels us to make radical changes, first in our ideas and then in the institutions based on our ideas. This is as true of government as of individuals. As individuals we are apt to ride in airplanes with horse-and-buggy ideas in our heads. And our Government has done the same thing. It has attempted to function in a world which has long since outgrown it. All the prejudices and shibboleths which survive in people's heads seem to crystallize in government—perhaps because, very rightly, we think of it as somehow sacred. But it will not stay sacred long if it is set apart from change in a changing world. It will simply become atrophied and obsolete and will either be ignored or contemptuously brushed aside by those in the community who have important affairs afoot which they desire shall not be interfered with.

Ineffective Policies

Something like this has been happening to our Government. I think it fair to say that until last March it was fast becoming ineffectual in its relationships with industry. It insisted on an interpretation of industrial life which belonged to an era which had disappeared. It broke up trusts as a sufficient answer to the pressing problem of control; and when it discovered that the more they were broken up, the more they remained as they had been, it fell into a kind of trance. It was unwilling to give up competitive theory; it could therefore think of nothing to do except to restore competition; and when competition refused to be restored, industry continued to exist in a kind of purgatory—half the heaven of freedom and half the hell of ineffectual public disapproval.

The various recovery acts proceeded from a theory which was in the sharpest possible contrast to all this. This theory recognized the changes which had occurred in industrial society and it sought to secure the benefits of industry as it actually existed for the public good. It said, "Industry has developed out of the face-to-face stage; huge factories exist; central-office organizations control many even of these organizations, great as they are in themselves; financial controls are superimposed on this; scientific management has come to stay—therefore, the Government must legalize all these heretofore horrid developments so that it may shape them into social instruments."

In effect, this was the theoretical basis of the recovery program. The Sherman Act and the Clayton Act were not repealed; but in so far as the codes could become effective, their operation was suspended. The codes have now become operative over most of industry; and it can be said that we have turned our backs on competition and have chosen control. This transformation, very nearly complete as it is, provides, as I believe, an instrument suitable to the purpose of enriching American life as it is our ambition to do. With it we can, for the first time, proceed to the management of purchasing power. And when purchasing power is provided, the potentialities of our vast producing equipment can be released. It is toward this that we have been working. It would be folly to assume that, having created the means toward our chosen end, we should forego the end for which these means were created. To suggest, therefore, that it is time to call a halt on the application of social control to the physical distribution of American abundance, is on a par with that old legislative spirit which decreed that no man should drive an automobile on a public highway unless he were preceded by another man afoot, carrying a red flag to warn pedestrians to keep out of the way. The New Deal is conceived in no such spirit of obscurantism. It is a beginning, not an end.

A New Framework

This new legislation is best described in some such terms as this—as a charter for experiment and research, for invention and learning. The new institutions have not sprung full grown from these legislative acts—the Agricultural Adjustment Act, the National Recovery Act and the rest—any more than the original Government of the United States sprang full grown from the Constitutional Convention. They mark a turning point just as that Convention did. We had to learn about democratic government in practice, we had to grow into it by trying various devices and by learning to live together within a new framework. And the same thing is true of this better planned society we are entering upon now. In both cases we expressed a determination to go forward in a general direction and within an agreed framework of rules, but without specific commitment to policies concerning problems which could not yet be foreseen. In entering on such an untrod path it is unwise to lay down too specifically the structure of new things; it is always better merely to register a change of heart and mind and then begin to work out, patiently and carefully, the requirements of the conversion.

The National Industrial Recovery Act

The National Industrial Recovery Act was one of the centerpieces of the early New Deal and a main instrument in the Roosevelt administration's attempt to impose economic planning on American industry. In a July 24, 1933, radio fireside chat, President Roosevelt attempted to clarify what he aimed to accomplish by the act.

Last autumn, on several occasions, I expressed my faith that we can make possible by democratic self-discipline in industry general increases in wages and shortening of hours sufficient to enable industry to pay its own workers enough to let those workers buy and use the things that their labor produces. This can be done only if we permit and encourage cooperative action in industry, because it is obvious that without united action a few selfish men in each competitive group will pay starvation wages and insist on long hours of work. Others in that group must either follow suit or close up shop. We have seen the result of action of that kind in the continuing descent into the economic hell of the past four years.

There is a clear way to reverse that process: If all employers in each competitive group agree to pay their workers the same wages—reasonable wages—and require the same hours—reasonable hours—then higher wages and shorter hours will hurt no employer. Moreover, such action is better for the employer than unemployment and low wages, because it makes more buyers for his product. That is the simple idea which is the very heart of the Industrial Recovery Act.

On the basis of this simple principle of everybody doing things together, we are starting out on this nationwide attack on unemployment. It will succeed if our people understand it—in the big industries, in the little shops, in the great cities, and in the small villages. There is nothing complicated about it and there is nothing particularly new in the principle. It goes back to the basic idea of society and of the nation itself that people acting in a group can accomplish things which no individual acting alone could even hope to bring about.

No one could have foreseen at first in what the processes of code and agreement-making would result. Even now no one can foresee the final structure of industry which may result. Whatever it may be, it will be worked out by the essentially voluntary and democratic processes now going on. But we can begin, at least, to look forward to the time when the preliminary structure will be complete. Every industry will then have set up a kind of government of its own, within which those aims which it holds in common can be pressed for and those discords and controversies which exist can be compromised and mediated. It was necessary to pass through this rather protracted period of conflict and discussion before these industrial groups could be made ready for planning. Up to now much of the energy of businessmen has been dissipated in the overpraised conflicts of competition. Each was trying to beat the other fellow—to reach success by standing on the exhausted bodies of fallen competitors. And the success for which all this striving took place was usually defined as the right to exploit consumers by selling them goods of doubtful quality at prices which lowered the general standard of living.

This competition is being outlawed. Code-making, if it had done nothing else, would have been worthwhile for the revelation it has given our industrialists of the essential futility of much of their activity. We are fast approaching the time, therefore, when each industry will be able to devote its best energy to the fundamental purpose of industry—which is to produce goods rather than competition. . . .

There are two broad ways in which industrial policy may be shaped from this point on to secure this objective. Industry may be required to define the quality of the goods it offers and to sell them at prices which are suitably low, so that when the transactions of a year, for instance, are totaled up it will be found that our energies and our producing plant have been used to the utmost and that the goods and services they yield have gone to consumers without increase of debt; or industry may be allowed to proceed with the policy of establishing high prices and maintaining them by limitation, and of selling goods whose qualities are mysterious to most consumers; and much of the resulting profits may be taken in taxes and returned to consumers as free goods by the Government—in the form of facilities for health and recreation, insurance against old age, sickness and unemployment, or in other ways. We shall have to accept one or the other of these policies because unless we do we shall sacrifice most of those objectives which we associate with what has been called the New Deal. The choice which lies before us is, therefore, a choice between a socially wise economic policy and the application of socialistic taxation. I prefer the former method. . . .

I think it is perfectly obvious that we can have nothing new in the Government which does not correspond to a new need on the part of our people and of their economic institutions. The New Deal is a very definite attempt to evolve a new governmental-economic relationship in response to the needs and opportunities created by the past methods of operating our economy. To inhibit further growth of these new methods is, therefore, impossible and to attempt to deny their application is the ultimate folly of fossilized ways of thought. Using the traditional methods of a free people, we are going forward toward a realm of coöperative plenty the like of which the world has never seen. It will be no antiseptic utopia and no socialistic paradise, but a changing system in which free American human beings can live their changing lives.

I have tried to make it clear that the objectives and the instruments being used in the reconstruction which is now going on are novel only in the sense that they are devices which have not hitherto been used.

Experiments

I have also stressed their experimental nature. That seems to me their most important characteristic, and that is something which is American if anything is—at least there was a time when Yankee ingenuity was a byword of praise. I have been too closely associated with all that has taken place to be anything like an impartial witness; nevertheless, I cannot help feeling that the nation has taken hold of its destiny again in ways which show that we have not lost our courage and resourcefulness. It was simply stifled for a while. There is no reason to think that year by year we shall not learn to better ourselves with the full use of energies and instruments which we have at our disposal. If this be Socialism, make the most of it!

VIEWPOINT 4

"The New Deal . . . has cured none of the ills that the country was suffering from a year and a half ago, and it has multiplied the pains . . . that went with them."

The New Deal Is a Fraud

H. L. Mencken (1880-1956)

H. L. Mencken was a noted journalist, writer, and satirist. He was a columnist for the *Baltimore Sun* from 1906 to 1948, founder and editor of the magazine *American Mercury*, and author of many books. Targets of his satire included American literature, democracy, Prohibition, and middle-class life. In 1926 fellow columnist and journalist Walter Lippmann called Mencken "the most powerful personal influence on this whole generation of educated men." Mencken's influence declined in the 1930s, in part because of his strong criticism of Franklin D. Roosevelt, which can be seen in the following viewpoint, excerpted from an August 1934 article in *Current History*.

Mencken directs much of his criticism toward members of Roosevelt's Brain Trust such as Columbia University professor Rexford G. Tugwell, who claimed to be initiating a new era of intelligent government planning of the economy. Mencken argues that the New Deal is beset by inconsistencies within itself, that its legislative achievements have done nothing to help the economy and most Americans, and that its only beneficiaries have been members of the Roosevelt administration.

Excerpted from H.L. Mencken, "Notes on the New Deal." Reprinted with permission from *Current History* magazine (August 1934), © 1934, Current History, Inc.

Despite the apparent belief of the busy young men at Washington that they are making a revolution, the Planned Economy they talk of is really almost as old as history. Indeed, the impulse to fashion something of the sort, whether of bricks or of straw, seems to be rooted deeply in human nature, and if there were no indecorum in mentioning Darwin I'd be inclined to identify it with his primary social instinct. Every savage tribe has a Planned Economy of great rigidity, to which even the tribal gods must yield, and everywhere on higher levels there is a constant movement in the same direction, though the gods are commonly left to individualism. Sometimes this movement stops with the enactment of sumptuary laws, as under Julius Caesar in Rome and the early Edwards in England, but at other times it proceeds to the concoction of economies as wide in their sweep and as tight in their effect as those of the Incas in Peru and the fathers of the caste system in India. If the brethren of the Brain Trust only had time for Bible searching they would find an elaborate Planned Economy in the Pentateuch, and some of its articles might very well suggest improvements in their own. . . .

When the Coolidge Prosperity collapsed under the unfortunate Hoover it was actually . . . a Planned Economy that collapsed. It had a staff of necromancers that was almost as bold in fancy and as long on promises as the outfit now operating in Washington, and at the head of it stood a virtuoso whose gift for running the business of other people was one of the seven wonders of the world. Certainly no Planned Economy was ever better named. And equally certainly none other ever blew up with a louder report.

Its disaster was so vast that, in a rational world, it might have discredited Planned Economies for a long while, and perhaps even forever. But fortunately for the gentlemen who stood waiting behind the arras not many people are rational when they apply their minds to public affairs, and very few of them live in the United States. Thus these gentlemen were able to rush forward with a new and even more dubious Planned Economy before the wreckage of the old one came down. The country was so scared that it hadn't the breath to challenge them, and they added to its alarm and hence to their opportunity by shrill and bloodcurdling outcries, the burden of which was that not only the late Planned Economy had blown up, but also the whole capitalistic system. On many other points they appeared to differ seriously among themselves, but on this point they all agreed: that on March 4, 1933, at high noon, the economic system which began with Crô-Magnon Man came to an end, and that some substitute for it had to be improvised at once, lest civilization itself go too.

121

This, of course, was nonsense, and the most that may be said for it today is that it made very effective political medicine at the time it was concocted. As every one knows, all politics under democracy is essentially the practice of quackery, and the first business of quackery is to scare the patient. Thus every politician, when he prepares to seize the easements and hereditaments of some other politician, looks about him first of all for an effective bugaboo. . . .

In a parody of an Alice in Wonderland *illustration, Gregory Duncan portrays Franklin D. Roosevelt as a cook stirring a pot of money that he hopes will quiet the crying "Administration Mistakes." The Cheshire Cat is former Republican Harold Ickes, Roosevelt's interior secretary, while the Duchess is Jim Farley, Roosevelt's campaign and presidential adviser.*

The Brain Trust boys, by a convenient stroke of luck, were enabled to effect a tremendous synthesis of banshees, some new but the most old, and with this creature they managed to throw the country into a panic of terror. It had multiple heads, borrowed from Hoover, Andy Mellon, Wiggin, Mitchell, Bishop Cannon, Al Capone and many another scarecrow, but its main corpus was the cadaver of capitalism, sieved with ghastly wounds and in graveyard clothes.

But it was after all only a banshee, and keeping it kicking has been heavy work. The moment the first scare was over some of the customers began asking themselves why, if capitalism was so dreadfully dead in America, it had not also died in England and

France. What the official answer is I do not know, for I can't find it in any of the communiqués that have reached me. But the actual answer is plain enough: the death of capitalism, as the phrase goes, was greatly exaggerated. Indeed, even its illness was exaggerated. . . . Of late that fact seems to have penetrated to the cavernous cerebrums of the Brain Trust, despite the formal persistence of its faith in the catastrophe of March 4, 1933. Its glorious young men still refuse to admit categorically that capitalism did not die then, but they have begun to protest urgently that they don't want to be counted among its murderers, or even among its evil-wishers, and whenever there is any fresh sign of its recovery they join in the rejoicing, and try to get some of the credit therefor.

As a matter of fact, they are all clients of capitalism, and must know it deep down in their massive brains. Their show has been kept running from the start by the capital of Americans who, while the going was good, worked hard and saved their money— in other words, by the accumulations of capitalism—and they would have to shut down tomorrow if this supply ran out. They have not shown any visible capacity for financing their grandiose operations otherwise, and it was only because capitalism was very far from dead in 1933 that they have been able to carry on so long. All their schemes for raising the wind are essentially and incurably capitalistic schemes. They never lose sight of the fact that the taxpayer, in order to be taxed, must have something to tax, and they are careful to let him acquire it in the only way that has ever worked on this earth, to wit, in the capitalistic way. In brief, they are full of the transparent false pretenses of the politicians they profess to abhor. Mention the only honest and plausible alternative to capitalism, which is communism, and they hasten to protest that they are against it. . . . And yet they keep on mouthing the nonsense that capitalism is done for, and can serve the uses of mankind no more.

Quack Remedies

Thus there is a fundamental fraudulence in the New Deal, and out of it flow a multitude of corollary fraudulences. It is a grotesque compound of false diagnoses and quack remedies. Those remedies come impartially from the platforms of forgotten revolutionaries of the cow country, and from the portfolios of young pedagogues eager for short cuts and quick promotions. Some of them were put to trial long ago in this or that backwater—for example the guarantee of bank deposits and the government control of money crops—and there failed ingloriously; others are so fantastic that even the Legislatures of Wisconsin and the Dakotas have refused to fool with them. . . .

Planned? Then so is a dog fight planned. The one thing that its shining ornaments have in common is not a common purpose nor even a common method, but simply a common privilege, to wit, the privilege of wreaking their genius for folly upon the taxpayer, each for himself, rugged individualists all. There is a complete lack of coherence in their operations, save only that kind of coherence which Grover Cleveland called "the cohesive power of public plunder." While one faction bellows that overproduction is ruining the farmer, and frames a multitude of discordant projects to restrain him, first by bribes and then by penalties, another faction proceeds to lay out hundreds of millions on schemes that can only have the effect of making the land produce more and more. And while one faction exclaims that the mortgage load is intolerable, and must be lightened if we are to escape catastrophe, another prepares to accommodate delinquent debtors with larger and grander mortgages, financed out of taxes. Indeed, it would be hard to think of any proposal of the starboard watch that has not been refuted and made a mock of by some proposal of the port watch. First there was a spectacular attack upon governmental extravagance, with multitudes of poor letter-carriers and other such laborious fellows reduced to starvation wages, and then there was a vast multiplication of jobholders at high salaries, performing imaginary tasks. First there was a violent effort to lift the wage level above the price level, and then there was a violent effort to raise prices. First there was a holy war on speculation, and then there was a formal licensing of speculation. And so on, and so on.

Experiments

Of late, I observe, the spokesmen for the Brain Trust have begun to abate their tall talk about planning, and to speak of experiment instead. Experiment it is—in a dingy and unclean laboratory, with cobwebs choking the microscopes, and every test-tube leaking. Such experiments are made by bulls in china shops, and by small boys turned loose in apple orchards. What, precisely, is the general idea underlying them in the present case? No one in Washington seems to know, and least of all the *Führer*. It remains, in fact, an unanswered question in the town whether he inclines toward the Left or toward the Right— which is to say, whether he is really for a Planned Economy or against it. One day the extreme revolutionaries seem to have the upper hand, and we are headed full tilt for communism, and the next day we beat a disorderly retreat to the Democratic platform of 1932. I dare say that most Americans would welcome any Planned Economy that showed the slightest sign of working, if only for the sake of getting rid of doubt and suspense, but how is the one we now hear of going to work so long as no two of its proponents agree as to where it is heading, or what it can accomplish, or what it is? How is it going to work so long as its devices are abandoned almost as fast as they are launched?

Failure of the NRA

The National Industrial Recovery Act and its attempts to impose labor and economic codes on business were criticized by both the Left and the Right. Daniel O. Hastings, a Republican senator from Delaware, wrote an article published in the October 13, 1934, issue of the magazine Today *in which he criticized the act and Roosevelt's policies in general.*

The turning over to the President, by a subservient Congress, of the powers which, under the Constitution, could only be exercised properly by Congress, upon the plea of the President that the emergency made it necessary, is of such vital importance to the nation that the voters must pass upon it. This is an issue that strikes at the very foundation of our government. The abuse of the power thus given emphasizes its danger, but makes a separate and distinct issue. Many Republicans in Congress voted to give the President these extraordinary powers, and they did it from a purely patriotic motive, but there are few, if any, who believe the powers given have been wisely used.

As an illustration, who could have foreseen what use would be made of the powers given in the National Industrial Recovery Act? Did anyone suppose that every little business of the nation was to be controlled, thereafter, by a bureau in Washington? Did anyone suppose he could not sell his services or his wares, thereafter, for an amount that was satisfactory to himself? Was it supposed that, thereafter, no one could go into business or extend his business without the consent of the President's representative? Was it believed that from this Act of a few pages the bureaus in Washington, by themselves, could write more than 10,000 pages of new laws, laws creating new crimes, and setting punishment by fine and imprisonment? The bureau administering this Act also has taken upon itself the right to levy a tax, to cover its expense, not only upon the person signing a code, but on all persons who come within the code definition. If the Democrats depend upon this Act, and its administration, as their outstanding accomplishment, they ought to be defeated.

These questions the advocates of the New Deal appear to overlook. They are hot for it, but they neglect to explain why, save on grounds so general that it is impossible to make head or tail of them. In late weeks some of them have forsaken the defensive for the offensive. . . . Their contention, in brief, is that all the opponents of the Brain Trust are simply morons with a congenital antipathy to brains. Obviously, they have failed to notice that what causes the Brain Trust to be suspect is not the belief that it has brains but the rapid growth of an unhappy conviction that it lacks them. If it has them, then why are they not functioning? And if they are functioning, then why can't the brethren sit down together quietly, and come to some sort of agreement as to what they are driving at? One of their original promises, as connoisseurs will recall, was to put down that anthropophagous competition between man and man and class and class which, according to their theory, was to blame for all the sorrows of mankind. To what extent has this been accomplished? Only to the extent of subsidizing one class at the cost of another. The first class, by the Brain Trust premises, consisted wholly of virtuous innocents (mainly, it appears, farmers) who had suffered cruelly at the hands of the New Economy—but actually it included also the whole vast rabble of chronic mendicants and incurable unemployables. The second class, by the same premises, consisted wholly of speculators and exploiters—but actually it included also every American who had worked hard in the good times, and saved his money against a rainy day.

Benefits of the New Deal

Where have the benefits of the New Deal, such as they are, really gone, and where do its burdens lie? Its benefits, obviously, have gone in the main, not to honest and industrious men caught in a universal misfortune, but to rogues and vagrants to whom a universal misfortune is only a new excuse for avoiding work. And its burdens lie, not upon the small group of brigands who flourished under Hoover, but upon the large body of good citizens who give a fair return for every dollar they earn, and ask only the right to pay their own way. This is all that the attempt to repeal and amend the competitive system has come to. If that system prospered scoundrels, then the New Deal prospers more of them, and worse ones. They were once, as the forerunners of the Brain Trust were fond of telling us, very few in numbers, and each had but one throat to cut. But their heirs and assigns have ten million votes, and they will still be passengers on the back of the American taxpayer long after the New Deal has ceased and desisted.

Its triumphs, it seems to me, have all been imaginary—save only the triumph, if it be one, of loading the public payroll with a vast and impudent camorra of magicians and astrologers, Chaldeans and soothsayers, and converting government into a public nuisance. Has it succored the wailing farmer? Nay, the farmer is still wailing, even as the horse-leech's daughter. Has there been any overhauling of the banking system, delivering it from crooks and fools and making it safe? All I can discover is that some deposits are guaranteed in some banks. As for the depositors who were "saved" by the Bank Holiday, they are still whistling for their money. But the Securities Act—surely that has achieved something? What it has accomplished is to hamper honest issues—and turn the thrifty over to wild-catters. The liberation of labor? Labor is still fighting for its most elementary rights. Speculation? It is still free to the insiders; only outsiders are barred. The national load of debt, public and private? It is larger than ever before, and still growing. Price fixing? It is now virtually official. But perhaps there has been going on, under all this, a real redistribution of the national income? Perhaps social justice has begun to flow at last, despite some unhappy phenomena on the surface? I seek an answer in the March returns of income tax. They show that the receipts from persons with incomes of more than $5,000 increased 23 per cent over 1933, and that those from persons with incomes of less than $5,000 decreased 13 per cent.

What the Marxians would call the dialectic of the New Deal is quite as silly as most of its overt measures. That dialectic is a feeble combination of worn-out platitudes and incredible hypotheses, and is as full of gross and manifest contradictions as the testimony at a murder trial. Whenever one of its prophets is pinned down to a categorical statement of it—as happened, for example, when Dr. Tugwell was haled before a Senate committee—he writhes like a deacon taken in crim. con., and must seek refuge in the doctrine that truth is a changing value, to be determined from time to time by trial and error. But trial and error is precisely the thing that these gaseous cerebrums were to save us from; if we must still endure it, then certainly it would be better to endure it at the hands of men with less "brains" and more sense. The real trial, of course, has been of the New Deal itself, and the real error has consisted in enduring it so long. It has cured none of the ills that the country was suffering from a year and a half ago, and it has multiplied the pains and penalties that went with them. Every American who helped to earn and amass what is left of the wealth of his country is worse off now than he was before, and every loafer and mendicant is more confirmed in his worthlessness.

The only real beneficiaries of the saturnalia of expropriation and waste are the gentlemen of the Brain Trust itself. Lifted out of their dismal classrooms, chicken-farms and law offices, they roll in the heady catnip of eminence and drink the fiery white mule of power. To them Utopia becomes a gorgeous reality, with a high-sounding title, a luxurious office and a good salary for every inmate, not to mention a staff of secretaries, messengers, press-agents, bibliographers and remembrancers, and the newspaper boys waiting in the ante-chamber. They have done well by themselves indeed—gloriously and gaudily well—at your expense and mine. As for the risk they take, they have nothing to lose but their "brains."

VIEWPOINT 5

"This act provides for controlled production. Without that, no price-lifting effort can possibly work."

The Agricultural Adjustment Act Will Help Farmers

Henry A. Wallace (1888-1965)

One of the main problems the Roosevelt administration faced during its first hundred days was the farm crisis. The American farmer did not share in the prosperity of the 1920s and was further hurt by the Great Depression. The prices farmers received for their crops fell drastically as the American economy worsened and foreign trade collapsed. Gross farm income fell from nearly $12 billion in 1929 to $5 billion in 1932. Many farmers were unable to meet mortgage payments and lost their farms. In some communities farmers banded together, halting distribution of their crops and physically resisting foreclosures and eviction sales, and there was much talk and worry about violent rebellion. In April 1933 the governor of Iowa declared martial law in several rural counties and deployed the National Guard to quell unrest.

President Franklin D. Roosevelt proposed and passed several legislative measures to deal with the economic crisis in rural America. The Emergency Farm Mortgage Act, passed in 1933, funded loans for farmers in immediate danger of losing their farms. More controversial was the Agricultural Adjustment Act

Excerpted from Henry A. Wallace, "Declaration of Interdependence," a speech broadcast May 13, 1933, and now part of *The Wallace Papers* at the Library of Congress.

(AAA), passed by Congress on May 10, 1933. The following view-point is taken from a May 13, 1933, radio address by Roosevelt's secretary of agriculture Henry A. Wallace, in which he explains and defends the principles of the AAA. The main idea behind the act was to raise farm prices by creating scarcity. The act allowed for the federal government to pay cash subsidies for farmers who would in return reduce production of seven basic commodities including cotton, wheat, and hogs. Funding for the act would be raised from a tax on processors of farm products. Wallace argues that cutting production is the key to rural economic improvement, and he calls for cooperation from the nation's farmers in implementing the law and cutting production.

Wallace, a former editor of an agriculture journal, was an important proponent of New Deal policies in the Roosevelt administration. He served as secretary of agriculture from 1933 to 1941, and was Roosevelt's vice president during his third term. Viewed as too liberal by some Democratic party leaders, he was replaced in 1944 by Harry S Truman.

The new Farm Act signed by President Roosevelt yesterday comprises twenty-six pages of legal document, but the essence of it can be stated simply. It has three main parts. The word "adjustment" covers all three.

First, the administration is empowered to adjust farm production to effective demand as a means of restoring the farmer's purchasing power. The secretary of agriculture is charged to administer this adjustment and to direct, at the same time, an effort to reduce those wastes of distribution which now cause food to pile up, unused, while people go hungry a hundred miles away.

Second is an accompanying authorization to refinance and readjust farm mortgage payments. . . .

In the third part of the act, the power for controlled inflation is delegated to the President, and this too signifies adjustment—adjustment of currency and credit to our changed needs. My own responsibility, however, as secretary of agriculture is solely with the first part of the act.

It should be made plain at the outset that the new Farm Act initiates a program for a general advance in buying power, an advance that must extend throughout America, lightening the way of the people in city and country alike. We must lift urban buying power as we lift farm prices. The Farm Act must not be considered an isolated advance in a restricted sector; it is an important part of a large-scale, coordinated attack on the whole problem of depression.

If enough people will join in the wide and swift adjustments that this act proposes, we can make it work. I say *if* because this act is not a hand-out measure. It does provide new governmental machinery which can be used by all who labor to grow and to bring us food and fabrics, to organize, to put their businesses in order, and to make their way together out of a wilderness of economic desolation and waste.

But the machinery will not work itself. The farmers and the distributors of foodstuffs must use it and make it work. The government can help map lines of march and can see that the interest of no one group is advanced out of line with the interest of all. But government officials cannot and will not go out and work for private businesses. A farm is a private business; so is a farmers' cooperative; and so are all the great links in the food-distributing chain. Government men cannot and will not go out and plow down old trails for agriculture or build for the distributing industries new roads out of the woods. The growers, the processors, the carriers and sellers of food must do that for themselves.

The Farm Bill

In a radio fireside chat on July 24, 1933, President Franklin D. Roosevelt provided this rationale for cutting agricultural production.

The Farm Act . . . is based on the fact that the purchasing power of nearly half our population depends on adequate prices for farm products. We have been producing more of some crops than we consume or can sell in a depressed world market. The cure is not to produce so much. Without our help the farmers cannot get together and cut production, and the Farm Bill gives them a method of bringing their production down to a reasonable level and of obtaining reasonable prices for their crops. I have clearly stated that this method is in a sense experimental, but so far as we have gone we have reason to believe that it will produce good results.

Following trade agreements, openly and democratically arrived at, with the consumer at all times represented and protected from gouging, these industries must work out their own salvation. They must put an end to cutthroat competition and wasteful disorder. The Emergency Adjustment Act makes it lawful and practical for them to get together and do so. It provides for a control of production to accord with actual need and for an orderly distribution of essential supplies.

In the end, we envision programs of planned land use, and we must turn our thought to this end immediately; for many thousands of refugees from urban pinch and hunger are turning, with little or no guidance, to the land. A tragic number of city families are reoccupying abandoned farms, farms on which born farmers, skilled, patient, and accustomed to doing with very little, were unable to make a go of it. In consequence of this backflow there are now 32 million people on the farms of the United States, the greatest number ever recorded in our history. Some of those who have returned to farming will find their place there, but most of them, I fear, will not.

I look to a day when men and women will be able to do in the country the work that they have been accustomed to do in the city; a day when we shall have more industrial workers out in the open where there is room to live. I look to a decentralization of industry; and hope that out of this Adjustment Act will come, in time, a resettlement of America. But in this respect we shall have to make haste slowly. We do not need any more farmers out in the country now. We do need more people there with some other means of livelihood, buying, close at hand, farm products; enriching and making more various the life of our open-country and village communities.

Reducing Production

In adjusting our production of basic foods and fabrics, our first need is to plant and send to market less wheat, less cotton, less corn, fewer hogs, and less of other basic crops whereof already we have towering surpluses, with no immediate prospect of clearance beyond the sea. The act authorizes the secretary of agriculture to apply excise taxes on the processing of these products and to pay the money thus derived to farmers who agree to enter upon programs of planned production, and who abide by that agreement. There are increasing possibilities that by trade agreements we may be able on certain crops or livestock products to arrive at a balanced abundance without levying a tax on the product at any point. In no case will taxes be levied on products purchased for the unemployed.

What it amounts to is an advance toward higher prices all along the line. Current proposals for government cooperation with industry are really at one with this Farm Act. Unless we can get reemployment going, lengthen payrolls, and shorten breadlines, no effort to lift prices can last very long. Our first effort as to agriculture will be to seek markets and to adjust production downward, with safe margins to provide enough food for all. This effort we will continue until such time as diminishing stocks raise prices to a point where the farmer's buying power will be as high as it was in the prewar years, 1909 to 1914.

The reason that we chose that period is because the prices farmers got for their crops in those years and the prices they paid for manufactured goods and urban services most nearly approached an equitable relationship. There was thus a balance between our major producing groups. At that time there was not the terrific disparity between rural and urban purchasing power which now exists and which is choking the life out of all forms of American business.

We do not propose to reduce agricultural production schedules to a strictly domestic basis. Our foreign trade has dwindled to a mere trickle; but we still have some foreign customers for farm products; we want to keep that trade, if possible, and to get more foreign trade, if we can. The immediate job, as I see it now, is to organize American agriculture to reduce its output to domestic need, plus that amount which we can export at a profit. . . .

Changing World Conditions

The first sharp downward adjustment is necessary because during the past years we have defiantly refused to face an overwhelming reality. In consequence, changed world conditions bear down on us so heavily as to threaten our national life. In the years immediately before the war, our agriculture was tending toward a domestic basis of production. The war rushed us out upon the markets of the world. Fifty million acres of Europe, not counting Russia, went out of cultivation. Food prices rose. A new surge of pioneers strode forth upon those high and dusty plains once called the Great American Desert and found that they could grow wheat there. Throughout the country, sod was broken. America entered the war. American farmers stepped out to serve the nation as American boys stepped up in answer to the call. Before the surge was over, we had put to the plow a vast new area. To replace the 50 million lost acres of Europe, America had added 30 million acres to its tilled domain and thrown its whole farm plant into high gear. . . .

The oversupplied situation began as a result of the war. As early as 1920 American agriculture was served notice that martial adventures must be paid for afterward, through the nose. The agricultural deflation was well under way by 1923; half of Montana's wheat farmers had by that time lost their farms. In 1929, the agricultural deflation became a plunge. Today, agriculture is twice as much deflated as general industry; and its prices are down 40 percent below the level of prices in general.

Ever since 1920, hundreds of thousands of farm families have had to do without civilized goods and services which in normal times they were glad and eager to buy. Since 1929, millions of farm people have had to patch their garments, store their cars and tractors, deprive their children of educational opportunities, and cease, as farmers, to improve their practices and their property. They have been forced to let their homes and other buildings stand bare and unpainted, eaten by time and the weather. They have been driven toward peasant, or less than peasant, standards; they have been forced to adopt frontier methods of bare sustenance at a time when in the old surging, unlimited sense of the word we have no longer a frontier.

When the farmer gets higher prices, he will start spending. He will have to. He needs things. He needs new shoes and clothing for all the family so that his children can go to school in any weather with dry feet, protected bodies, and a decent American feeling of equality and pride. . . .

To reorganize agriculture, cooperatively, democratically, so that the surplus lands on which men and women now are toiling, wasting their time, wearing out their lives to no good end shall be taken out of production—that is a tremendous task. The adjustment we seek calls, first of all, for a mental adjustment, a willing reversal of driving, pioneer opportunism and ungoverned laissez-faire. The ungoverned push of rugged individualism perhaps had an economic justification in the days when we had all the West to surge upon and conquer; but this country has filled up now and grown up. There are no more Indians to fight. No more land worth taking may be had for the grabbing. We must experience a change of mind and heart.

The frontiers that challenge us now are of the mind and spirit. We must blaze new trails in scientific accomplishment, in the peaceful arts and industries. Above all, we must blaze new trails in the direction of a controlled economy, common sense, and social decency. . . .

This Farm Act differs from the partway attacks on the problems that have been launched in the past. This act provides for controlled production. Without that, no price-lifting effort can possibly work; because if there is no control of acreage, the better price increases the next year's planting and the greater harvest wrecks the price. . . .

Our immediate job is to decide what products to concentrate on, what methods of production adjustment to employ on them, to determine to what extent marketing agreements can be useful, and to appraise the necessity for and rates of processing taxes.

To help us in these determinations, as rapidly as possible, we shall have here in Washington representatives of agriculture and representatives of the processing and distributing trades. These men and women will take part in commodity conferences, and in the light of their technical knowledge will suggest which of the several plans of attack will work best for different crops and regions. Bearing their recommendations in mind, we shall decide just what action to take and when to take it. As each decision is made, we shall get it out directly and publicly to the farmers affected and launch organization efforts throughout the nation.

As President Roosevelt indicated at Topeka last September, the right sort of farm and national relief should encourage and strengthen farmer cooperation. I believe we have in this new law the right sort of stimulus to that end.

Declaration of Interdependence

I want to say, finally, that unless, as we lift farm prices, we also unite to control production, this plan will not work for long. And the only way we can effectively control production for the long pull is for you farmers to organize, and stick, and do it yourselves. This act offers you promise of a balanced abundance, a shared prosperity, and a richer life. It will work if you will make it yours, and *make* it work.

I hope that you will come to feel in time, as I do now, that the rampageous individualist who signs up for adjustment and then tries to cheat is cheating not only the government but his neighbors. I hope that you will come to see in this act, as I do now, a Declaration of Interdependence; a recognition of our essential unity and of our absolute reliance one upon another.

VIEWPOINT 6

"We have 'bread lines knee-deep in wheat' and our principal effort is to reduce the supply of wheat."

The Agricultural Adjustment Act Has Not Helped Farmers

Norman Thomas (1884-1968)

The 1933 Agricultural Adjustment Act (AAA) sought to help economically strapped farmers by, among other measures, reducing crop production in order to boost prices. The federal government intervened in the nation's farms to an unprecedented degree in 1933, but with mixed success. Actions such as plowing under ten million acres of planted cotton and slaughtering six million piglets (which were processed and distributed to the unemployed) raised questions among both farmers and consumers about why such destructive actions were needed at a time Americans were going hungry. In 1934 more restrictive legislation such as the Bankhead Cotton Control Act was passed to set rigid production quotas for farmers, some of whom had defeated the goal of cutting production by farming their reduced acreage more intensively. However, the idea of restoring prosperity by cutting agriculture production was attacked from both the left and the right.

The following viewpoint is taken from an article by Norman Thomas, published in the May 1934 issue of *Current History*. Thomas, at one time a Presbyterian minister, was the Socialist party's candidate for president in all six elections between 1928

Excerpted from Norman Thomas, "Starve and Prosper!" Reprinted with permission from *Current History* magazine (May 1934), © 1934, Current History, Inc.

and 1948. In this viewpoint he attacks the idea of cutting agriculture production, arguing that such policies hurt American consumers and do not help poor farmers. He argues that attempts to force farmers to cut production are as ineffectual and counterproductive as were America's attempt to ban the sale and production of alcoholic beverages in the 1920s.

Thomas's attack on Roosevelt's farm policies broadens into a general criticism that summarizes his view of the New Deal—that it was doomed because it sought to tinker with the American capitalist system rather than replace it entirely with a new socialist one.

One of the ablest of the many able men associated with the Department of Agriculture is Professor M. L. Wilson. He first came to fame by his part in perfecting a wheat which would bring forth more abundantly. He next came to fame by his part in perfecting a law to bribe farmers, at the cost of a tax on consumers, not to plant so much wheat. Mr. Wilson's experience is a kind of symbol of the worst form of social insanity which our crazy world has yet seen. . . .

Fleeing from Abundance

In such a world no Dean Swift ever wrote so complete a satire on civilization as the honest and troubled men who wrote in the pedestrian language of law the Agricultural Adjustment Act. For thousands of generations, ever since the dim beginning of any sort of civilization, mankind has been struggling blindly, and only in recent years with vision and intelligence, against an inevitable scarcity. Pearl Buck's moving description of famine in a Chinese village, in her book *The Good Earth*, could with minor variations, have been told of villages round the world, all down the ages. It illustrates in an extreme form the problem of scarcity. To the ancestors of this generation it would have seemed that to make scarcity no longer inevitable would mean the dawn of the millennium. Our generation has instead, in this, the richest country in the world, fled from abundance. We do not know how to manage it, and therefore, by subsidized destruction, we return to familiar scarcity, in order to give our farmers prosperity. We have "bread lines knee-deep in wheat" and our principal effort is to reduce the supply of wheat.

It is not to be supposed that such obvious madness has gone unnoticed and unregretted even in a lunatic world. President Roosevelt frankly commended the Agricultural Adjustment Act to Congress as an experiment of uncertain worth only justified by the magnitude of the emergency. This has been the prevailing tone of the discussion both of the Agricultural Adjustment Act and more recently of the Bankhead bill for the compulsory regulation of the size of the cotton crop. Not once but repeatedly has Secretary Wallace, the most thoughtful member of the administration, deplored the necessity for curtailing production, a necessity which he finds inherent in our economic nationalism. To his powerful statement of the case in his now famous pamphlet, *America Must Choose*, we shall return later. . . .

Nearly a year of experimenting has completely vindicated those who from the beginning have argued that the administration's attempt to bribe farmers into voluntary cooperation for the reduction of crops would be progressively more and more of a failure. Under the AAA farmers who raise certain staple crops were paid to reduce acreage. They were paid for the acres they did not plant or, in the case of cotton, which they plowed under. There was a widespread but by no means universal acceptance of these contracts. I have seen some evidence from share-croppers that landlords evaded their contracts. Certainly the weather was favorable for a good cotton crop. There was an immense increase in the care with which the remaining acres were cultivated, and intensive cultivation was bound to make further gains in 1934. In the month of January this year I heard of one Southwestern city in which one single firm had increased its sales of fertilizer by more than 100 per cent, and this, I was told, was typical. The net result was that more cotton was ginned in 1933 than in 1932—13,043,110 500-pound bales, as against 13,001,508 in 1932. The farmers got paid for plowing their cotton under and then had a bigger crop!

Such a situation made it inevitable that the next experiment should be the Bankhead bill for the compulsory restriction of the number of bales any one farmer can market without paying a prohibitive tax. In this respect cotton is only a few jumps ahead of what must happen in the production of all great staples. In order to save farming we shall set up an immense bureaucratic machine over the farmers to tell them just how much they may produce. The decision will not be reached in the light of the needs of a world or even of America, but solely on an attempt to estimate the effective demand, at a price regarded by farmers as reasonable, or, in other words, by the vendibility of the crop under the price and profit system. That way lies disaster and nothing but disaster.

Enforcement Problems

In the first place, the attempt to enforce restricted production will be more difficult than the attempt to enforce prohibition. It runs foul of an instinct for production at least as deep as the desire for alcohol. The successful bootlegging of a crop will be profitable much as was the bootlegging of liquor. When the day comes, which Secretary Wallace regards as possible, when every cultivated field has to have its license tag, we may perhaps end the problem of unemployment by enlisting the unemployed in the enforcement army. Human ingenuity cannot devise tags or labels for identifying cotton or wheat, legitimately marketed and free from prohibitive tax, without inviting successful counterfeiting of such labels. In proportion to the initial success of this law in raising prices will the temptation to bootlegging be increased. It is possible that this lone single thing may ultimately break down the system, at great cost, however, to the whole community.

Explaining Farm Relief

The concept of paying farmers not to grow food struck many people as ludicrous. The following satirical explanation of the New Deal's farm programs by writer John Riddell was first published in Vanity Fair *in August 1933.*

In order to mix up the reader completely I should like to offer the following simple illustration of just what is meant by Farm Relief.

For example, let us say that Mr. A., a farmer, has just raised a parsnip. Nobody wants a parsnip, least of all Mr. A.; and so the Government steps in and offers Mr. A. five dollars if he will take his parsnip somewhere and get rid of it. Mr. A. gets ride of the parsnip and spends the five dollars for parsnip seeds, with which he raises one hundred more parsnips. He gets rid of these parsnips to the Government for five hundred dollars; and with this five hundred dollars he goes into the parsnip business on a large scale, raising millions of parsnips and getting rid of them to the Government at five dollars a parsnip. Thus Mr. A. is relieved because he raises parsnips, everybody else is relieved because he gets rid of them again, and the Government is relieved in time of all the money in the Treasury. This is known, roughly, as Farm Relief.

Meanwhile we shall have a growing list of evils. Practically, as is recognized in the Bankhead bill, the only way to reduce crops is on a percentage basis which begins by accepting the status quo and freezing it into eternal law. Each county and each farm must be given its percentage of the allotted crop. The desired price will be fixed more or less in the light of cost of production on the marginal farms. The best that one can expect a government bureau to do will be to rule out land that is clearly submarginal. It will be difficult to bring new land and new methods into use— that is, legally. The limit on production will be a premium on inefficiency. The farmer and the government bureaucracy between them will lose almost all interest in increasing the capacity of industrial workers to consume their cotton or their milk. They will be content, if the system works at all, with a guaranteed price for what they produce. . . .

It is the mixture of acreage reduction under the AAA with an abominable land system which the New Deal has not yet touched to which we owe the most disastrous results of acreage reduction. Inevitably, and in spite of any legislation, a system of paying landlords for not planting acres is bound to drive the tenant farmer off the land or reduce him to the level of a day laborer at outrageously low wages. This is precisely what is happening, especially to the share-croppers in the cotton and tobacco country. There are some 1,500,000 of these "forgotten men" whose economic and social conditions are, on the average, the worst I have seen anywhere in America. They own nothing. They are staked year by year by the landlord and get half the net value of the crop after the landlord has deducted his advances, which all too often are figured with a "crooked pencil," especially if the share-cropper has the added disadvantage of being a Negro. It must be added that illiterate whites fare little better. The cotton contract gave the share-croppers little more than the protection of pious words, and all the enforcement machinery is in the hands of the landlord class. The result is that thousands of share-croppers are being driven completely off the land or else deeper into peonage to the landlord.

So far, the major effort of the Department of Agriculture has been to whitewash the situation. The Bankhead bill gives the Secretary of Agriculture power to protect the share-croppers, but how is not specified, and it is difficult to see that much can be done under a land system which means peonage for thousands upon thousands of men. Even the government's laudable effort to put submarginal land back into forests will mean the displacement of thousands of farmers, mostly of the lowest economic status. Bad as their present condition is, it will become worse, unless there is definite provision to absorb them into industry.

Agriculture and Industry

Indeed, it is to the expansion of industry, rather than agriculture, that we must look to take care of men displaced by the coming of machinery to the help of agriculture. A decreasing number of agricultural workers scientifically trained can supply the food needs of a population which tends to become stationary. On the other hand, there is no near limit which can be set to the wants of men which industry can supply. In other words, there is no program for agriculture which is not bound up with industry. We are either going to accept the possibility of abundance in both agriculture and industry or we are going to try to curb industry and restore scarcity in both agriculture and industry. The present fear of machinery is on all fours with the desire to curb agricultural production.

Now it is easy enough to prove, as Walter Lippmann has recently done, that all along the line the fear of plenty is unwarranted. He is entirely right in saying that the use of labor-saving machinery makes a nation richer and not poorer as the comparative wealth of America abundantly testifies. Nevertheless, there is a problem of technological unemployment both in industry and agriculture, and it is not a problem which can take care of itself. Charles G. Ross, in the *St. Louis Post-Dispatch*, has convincingly proved that, if production were restored to the 1929 level, there would still be 4,000,000 unemployed. Machinery will be an unmixed blessing only when the time and rate of its introduction can be planned, not according to the inclination of this individual or that corporation for profit, but according to our ability to produce, distribute, and enjoy abundance, and to shorten working hours. This test cannot be imposed in a system ruled by the divine right of profit for the owners of property.

Under such a system we shall continue to have a further development of the course already begun, that is, a policy of subsidies for manufacturers and farmers who are politically powerful enough to demand it. Our experience with tariffs shows that groups never abandon subsidies voluntarily. Infant industries have never grown up beyond the need of tariffs. By the same token it is futile nonsense to assume that the attempt to make the farmers rich by restoring scarcity at the cost of a subsidy from the consumers is only an emergency measure lightly to be abandoned. It will scarcely be abandoned unless or until our effort to get rich by subsidizing each other breaks down as completely as the economy of the delectable island where very one made a living by taking in his neighbor's washing.

No, there is a better hope. It is the acceptance of the economy of abundance, and that requires us completely to supersede the price and profit system born of scarcity. Until we come to realize this basic fact, we must expect all manner of economic woes to which various political ills will be added. The ultimate political ill, of course, is international war to which a program of economic nationalism, no matter how it is dressed up, assuredly points. Along the way we shall have the varied and assorted ills of pork-barrel politics to which will be added an inevitable growth of a bureaucratic dictatorship which alone can enforce a comprehensive reduction in agricultural or industrial output.

That we do not immediately feel all these evils is due to a certain liberalism in President Roosevelt himself and to the unusual quality of Secretary Wallace and his principal advisers. Mr. Wallace himself has partially pointed the way out by his advocacy of economic internationalism or at least by a compromise which will give some measure of economic internationalism a chance. The weakness of his position is twofold:

1. Even on the basis of a national economy it is enough to make devils laugh to listen to an argument for the drastic reduction of the cotton crop or of milk reduction and then to consider that the children of share-croppers and of most of the textile workers do not have two sets of underclothes a year and that their wives have not enough sheets to go around. As for the milk situation, at a time when we are to be taxed for the production of milk, New York City is actually consuming about one-half of what has been estimated to be advisable for the health of its children. There is a great deal of expansion possible in agricultural consumption, to say nothing of industrial consumption, before we reach the limit of what our American fellow-citizens need as distinguished from what they can afford to buy.

2. The economic internationalism which Mr. Wallace advocates is more necessary yet harder to attain than he thinks. It is reason-

Artificial Props

The New Deal's agricultural programs came under attack from conservative as well as liberal sources. Mrs. George B. Simmons, a farmer's wife from Missouri who had written several articles criticizing the New Deal, spoke before the Women's National Republican Club. The address was reprinted in the August 12, 1935, issue of Vital Speeches of the Day.

The things being done by this Administration for us farmers never have made sense according to any principles of good farm management we have ever known, and my husband always managed to make something with his farming until this strange New Deal began to be shuffled out to us. We knew that there were enough figures to show that not over-production, but under-consumption was the trouble, that the chief obstacles to fair returns on our farming business were too-high costs of distribution, and the costs of what we had to buy, of industrial products, because industry was trying to maintain by more or less artificial means, prices both for labor and its output that were beyond our ability to pay. We did not see then, and we do not see now, how two wrongs can make a right, or any economic good to come ultimately from trying to put artificial props under Agriculture so it will imagine it is up where the artificial props of Industry are holding it. Both are bound to topple together, if this is continued.

ably clear that we cannot marry the kind of planned national economy toward which in a blind and stumbling way most nations are moving and a *laissez-faire* free trade between nations. Neither can we get a valid world economy on the basis of such bargaining between nations as may be furthered by giving the President power to raise or lower tariffs by 50 per cent. We shall have to come to some degree of world planning. And that is the hardest task before men.

It will be seen that I do not minimize the difficulties in the way of a successful practice of the economy of plenty. We owe a reluctant sympathy to the advocates and defenders of the AAA who have demanded, so far in vain, of their capitalist critics, "Tell us, what else can we do?". . .

The whole point is that our disintegrating capitalist nationalist system has no answer to the problem of agriculture, but only a choice between evils. Capitalism was born in an age of scarcity. Its incentives were the incentives of inevitable scarcity. Now that machinery enables us to have abundance, the day of a system born of scarcity is done. There is no royal road to plenty. That shared abundance which machinery has made the logical, not the only, basis for human well-being will not be realized save as we accept the philosophy and the organization of the cooperative commonwealth. The successful management of the machine age, with its necessary specialization and integration, requires plan. That plan must be for the common good. It cannot possibly be harmonized with the pursuit of profit as the reward of speculation or the ownership of property. It cannot be completely realized within the borders of any one nation. Men will go on trying arbitrarily to restore scarcity until they learn to accept a new social order based on the social ownership of the great means of production and their operation, according to plan, to the end that there may be abundance for all. . . .

In short, the conditions for achieving this new society are the conditions for achieving socialism, and he who objects to socialism is objecting to that acceptance of abundance to which increasingly the obvious follies and tragedies of a return to scarcity is compelling them to give the allegiance at least of their hopes.

CHAPTER 3

The New Deal and Its Critics

Chapter Preface

Despite election victories in Congress in 1934, by the spring of 1935, both President Roosevelt's programs and political coalition were showing signs of trouble. Within the space of a few weeks, the Supreme Court struck down as unconstitutional two key elements of Roosevelt's original New Deal (the National Industrial Recovery Act and the Agricultural Adjustment Act) on the grounds that they granted the federal government, especially the executive branch, powers not allowed under the U.S. Constitution. (The NIRA, an attempt to institute self-regulation by industries to limit competition and price-cutting, already had been criticized by many as a general failure in bringing about economic recovery.) Despite some positive signs, the economy was still in a depressed state compared to pre-1929 levels.

Roosevelt in the early part of his administration had attempted to unite business, labor, and other leaders in planning and implementing the New Deal. However, many business leaders and the wealthy became increasingly critical of what they viewed as the dangerously socialistic nature of Roosevelt's reforms. In August 1934 a group of conservative political and business leaders, including former Democratic party leader John J. Raskob, newspaper magnate William Randolph Hearst, and members of the industrialist Du Pont family, founded the American Liberty League. Over the next two years, the organization published and widely distributed pamphlets attacking the New Deal as socialistic and unconstitutional. Ironically, its efforts in the 1934 and 1936 elections are perceived by many historians to have helped rather than hurt Roosevelt.

A more significant challenge to Roosevelt came from the other side of the political spectrum, where some political figures attacked Roosevelt for not going far enough in altering America's economic and political system. Some of these leaders included elected officials from third parties, such as Minnesota governor Floyd B. Olson, a member of the Farmer-Labor party, and the brothers Robert and Phillip LaFollette, who were elected governor and senator from Wisconsin as members of the Progressive party, which called for more extensive economic reforms.

In addition to these politicians, three other strikingly disparate figures gained national prominence as critics of Roosevelt's New Deal. Charles Coughlin was a controversial Roman Catholic priest whose radio-broadcast sermons included political passages

144

attacking Roosevelt and advocating the nationalization of banks, utilities, and natural resources. Francis E. Townsend was a retired California physician who gained a large following with his plan for every person over sixty to receive a federal pension of $200 a month. Finally, Huey P. Long was a Democratic senator from Louisiana, who gained national attention with his "Share Our Wealth Program," and who before his 1935 assassination was considered a serious political rival to Roosevelt. The popularity of these three men increased the pressure on Roosevelt to expand his programs of reform and relief.

Partly in response to the pressures created by the popularity of these three figures, Franklin Roosevelt in June 1935 sent Congress five new pieces of "must" legislation. The proposals, which were passed after some changes by Congress, are called by some historians the "second" New Deal. They included the Revenue Tax Act, which increased income taxes on the wealthy and on corporations; the Banking Act of 1935, which gave the federal government additional control over the Federal Reserve System; and the Public Utility Holding Company Act, which placed power, water, and other utility companies under the regulation of the newly created Securities and Exchange Commission.

Two of the most important new measures were the National Labor Relations Act (or Wagner Act), and the Social Security Act. The Wagner Act restored the portions of the National Industrial Recovery Act that gave workers the right to collectively bargain and established the National Labor Relations Board to supervise union elections and investigate unfair labor practices by companies. The Social Security Act provided for the first time federal old-age pensions and unemployment insurance for Americans.

The Second New Deal proved popular with voters. Roosevelt won a landslide reelection over Republican Alf Landon. The laws passed in the summer of 1935, especially the Social Security Act, remain important New Deal legacies.

VIEWPOINT 1

"The theory of the Share Our Wealth Society is to have enough for all, but not to have one with so much that less than enough remains for the balance of the people."

Redistributing Wealth Can Help Americans Out of the Depression

Huey P. Long (1893-1935)

One of the most significant challenges to President Roosevelt during his first term came from Huey P. Long, a populist senator from Louisiana. Long had wielded near-dictatorial powers as governor of Louisiana and, with a hand-picked successor in the statehouse, continued to rule the state from his senatorial office in Washington. Long officially nominated Roosevelt for president at the 1932 Democratic convention. However, though an early supporter of the New Deal, Long began to criticize its inadequacies in alleviating what he viewed as America's fundamental problem—the maldistribution of wealth.

In 1934 and 1935 Long began to promote his own economic program, which he called Share Our Wealth. Long proposed heavy taxes that would limit an individual's annual income to one million dollars, with a family estate limit of five million. The resulting tax revenues would be used to guarantee all families a minimum annual income of twenty-five hundred dollars. Long was attacked by both Roosevelt supporters and opponents as a demagogue whose economic numbers did not add up, but he re-

From a letter of Huey P. Long, published in the *Congressional Record* 74th Congress, 2d Session, vol. 79, no. 107 (May 23, 1935): 8333-36.

mained highly popular with many Americans. Long launched a nationwide network of Share Our Wealth clubs and appeared to be positioning himself to run for president in 1936 or 1940. On September 8, 1935, however, his life and political career were cut short when he was assassinated by a relative of one of his Louisiana political enemies.

The following viewpoint is taken from a letter Long produced for his Share Our Wealth followers, which he inserted in the *Congressional Record* of May 23, 1935.

For 20 years I have been in the battle to provide that, so long as America has, or can produce, an abundance of the things which make life comfortable and happy, that none should own so much of the things which he does not need and cannot use as to deprive the balance of the people of a reasonable proportion of the necessities and conveniences of life. The whole line of my political thought has always been that America must face the time when the whole country would shoulder the obligation which it owes to every child born on earth—that is, a fair chance to life, liberty, and happiness.

Roosevelt's Promises

I had been in the United States Senate only a few days when I began my effort to make the battle for a distribution of wealth among all the people a national issue for the coming elections. On July 2, 1932, pursuant to a promise made, I heard Franklin Delano Roosevelt, accepting the nomination of the Democratic Party at the Chicago convention for President of the United States, use the following words:

> Throughout the Nation, men and women, forgotten in the political philosophy of the Government for the last years, look to us here for guidance and for a more equitable opportunity to share in the distribution of the national wealth.

It therefore seemed that all we had to do was to elect our candidate and that then my object in public life would be accomplished.

But a few nights before the Presidential election I listened to Mr. Herbert Hoover deliver his speech in Madison Square Garden, and he used these words:

> My conception of America is a land where men and women may walk in ordered liberty, where they may enjoy the advantages of wealth, not concentrated in the hands of a few, but dif-

fused through the lives of all.

So it seems that so popular had become the demand for a redistribution of wealth in America that Mr. Hoover had been compelled to somewhat yield to that for which Mr. Roosevelt had previously declared without reservation.

It is not out of place for me to say that the support which I brought to Mr. Roosevelt to secure his nomination and election as President—and without which it was hardly probable he would ever have been nominated—was on the assurances which I had that he would take the proper stand for the redistribution of wealth in the campaign. He did that much in the campaign; but after his election, what then? I need not tell you the story. We have not time to cry over our disappointments, over promises which others did not keep, and over pledges which were broken.

We have not a moment to lose.

Huey P. Long, senator from Louisiana, gained a national following during his Share Our Wealth campaign and was viewed by Franklin D. Roosevelt as a serious political rival.

It was after my disappointment over the Roosevelt policy, after he became President, that I saw the light. I soon began to understand that, regardless of what we had been promised, our only chance of securing the fulfillment of such pledges was to organize the men and the women of the United States so that they were a force capable of action, and capable of requiring such a policy from the lawmakers and from the President after they took office. That was the beginning of the Share Our Wealth Society movement. . . .

The Problem

It is impossible for the United States to preserve itself as a republic or as a democracy when 600 families own more of this Nation's wealth—in fact, twice as much—as all the balance of the people put together. Ninety-six per cent of our people live below the poverty line, while 4 per cent own 87 per cent of the wealth. America can have enough for all to live in comfort and still permit millionaires to own more than they can ever spend and to have more than they can ever use; but America cannot allow the multimillionaires and the billionaires, a mere handful of them, to own everything unless we are willing to inflict starvation upon 125,000,000 people.

We looked upon the year 1929 as the year when too much was produced for the people to consume. We were told, and we believed, that the farmers raised too much cotton and wool for the people to wear and too much food for the people to eat. Therefore, much of it went to waste, some rotted, and much of it was burned or thrown into the river or into the ocean. But, when we picked up the bulletin of the Department of Agriculture for that year 1929, we found that, according to the diet which they said everyone should eat in order to be healthy, multiplying it by 120,000,000, the number of people we had in 1929, had all of our people had the things which the Government said they should eat in order to live well, we did not have enough even in 1929 to feed the people. In fact, these statistics show that in some instances we had from one-third to one-half less than the people needed, particularly of milk, eggs, butter, and dried fruits.

But why in the year 1929 did it appear we had too much? Because the people could not buy the things they wanted to eat, and needed to eat. That showed the need for and duty of the Government then and there, to have forced a sharing of our wealth, and a redistribution, and Roosevelt was elected on the pledge to do that very thing.

But what was done? Cotton was plowed under the ground. Hogs and cattle were burned by the millions. The same was done to wheat and corn, and farmers were paid starvation money not to raise and not to plant because of the fact that we did not want so much because of people having no money with which to buy. Less and less was produced, when already there was less produced than the people needed if they ate what the Government said they needed to sustain life. God forgive those rulers who burned hogs, threw milk in the river, and plowed under cotton

149

while little children cried for meat and milk and something to put on their naked backs!

Historical Background

But the good God who placed this race on earth did not leave us without an understanding of how to meet such problems; nor did the Pilgrim fathers who landed at Plymouth in 1620 fail to set an example as to how a country and a nation of people should act under such circumstances, and our great statesmen like Thomas Jefferson, Daniel Webster, Abraham Lincoln, Theodore Roosevelt, and Ralph Waldo Emerson did not fail to explain the need and necessity for following the precedents and purposes, which are necessary, even in a land of abundance, if all the people are to share the fruits produced therein. God's law commanded that the wealth of the country should be redistributed ever so often, so that none should become too rich and none should become too poor; it commanded that debts should be canceled and released ever so often, so that the human race would not be loaded with a burden which it could never pay. When the Pilgrims landed at Plymouth in 1620, they established their law by compact, signed by everyone who was on board the *Mayflower*, and it provided that at the end of every 7 years the finances of their newly founded country would be readjusted and that all debts would be released and property redistributed, so that none should starve in the land of plenty, and none should have an abundance of more than he needed. These principles were preserved in the Declaration of Independence, signed in 1776, and in our Constitution. Our great statesmen, such men as James Madison, who wrote the Constitution of the United States, and Daniel Webster, its greatest exponent, admonished the generations of America to come that they must never forget to require the redistribution of wealth if they desired that their Republic should live.

And, now, what of America? Will we allow the political sports, the high heelers, the wiseacres, and those who ridicule us in our misery and poverty to keep us from organizing these societies in every hamlet so that they may bring back to life this law and custom of God and of this country? Is there a man or woman with a child born on the earth, or who expects ever to have a child born on earth, who is willing to have it raised under the present-day practices of piracy, where it comes into life burdened with debt, condemned to a system of slavery by which the sweat of its brow throughout its existence must go to satisfy the vanity and the luxury of a leisurely few, who can never be made to see that they are destroying the root and branch of the greatest country ever to have risen? Our country is calling; the laws of the Lord are calling; the graves of our forefathers would open today if their occupants could see the bloom and flower of their creation withering and dying because the greed of the financial masters of this country has starved and withheld from mankind those things produced by his own labor. To hell with the ridicule of the wise street-corner politician! Pay no attention to any newspaper or magazine that has sold its columns to perpetuate this crime against the people of America! Save this country! Save mankind! Who can be wrong in such a work, and who cares what consequences may come following the mandates of the Lord, of the Pilgrims, of Jefferson, Webster, and Lincoln? He who falls in this fight falls in the radiance of the future. Better to make this fight and lose than to be a party to a system that strangles humanity.

Wealth and Poverty

Senator George Norris of Nebraska, in an address delivered at the University of Nebraska on February 15, 1935, reprinted in Vital Speeches of the Day, *supported a proposed increase in the federal inheritance tax. He also decried concentrations of wealth amidst poverty.*

Is there anything unjust or unfair that men of great wealth should be prohibited from passing on intact great fortunes which would result in such injury to society? When we make one billionaire, we make millions of paupers. Whenever a man is put in that class, we create an army of hungry children, ragged mothers, and brokenhearted fathers. We drag down our civilization to a point where, eventually, it must fail. If we would have a united country, we must have a country of homes. We must bring comfort and pleasure to the fireside. We must establish the home as the unit and in it must be maintained the comforts and pleasures of life. This can only come about if we prevent the accumulation of all the property in the hands of a few. Such a condition would, in the end, bring about a form of human slavery more bitter, more aggravated, and more heinous than any which have ever afflicted humanity.

It took the genius of labor and the lives of all Americans to produce the wealth of this land. If any man, or 100 men, wind up with all that has been produced by 125,000,000 people, that does not mean that those 100 men produced the wealth of the country; it means that those 100 men stole, directly or indirectly, what 125,000,000 people produced. Let no one tell you that the money masters made this country. They did no such thing. Very few of them ever hewed the forest; very few ever hacked a crosstie; very few ever nailed a board; fewer of them ever laid a brick. Their fortunes came from manipulated finance, control of government, rigging of markets, the spider webs that have grabbed all businesses; they grab the fruits of the land, the conveniences and the luxuries that are intended for 125,000,000 people, and run their heelers to our meetings to set up the cry, "We earned it honestly." The Lord says they did no such thing. The voices of our forefathers say they did no such thing. In this land of abundance, they have no right to impose starvation, misery, and pestilence for the purpose of vaunting their own pride and greed. . . .

The debt structure alone has condemned the American people to bondage worse than the Egyptians ever forged upon the Israelites. Right now America's debts, public and private, are $262,000,000,000, and nearly all of it has been laid on the shoulders of those who have nothing. It is a debt of more than $2,000 to every man, woman, or child. They can never pay it. They never have paid such debts. No one expects them to pay it. But such is the new form of slavery imposed upon the civilization of America; and the street-corner sports and hired political tricksters, with the newspapers whom they have perverted, undertake to laugh to scorn the efforts of the people to throw off this yoke and bondage; but we were told to do so by the Lord, we were told to do so by the Pilgrim Fathers, we were guaranteed such should be done by our Declaration of Independence and by the Constitution of the United States.

The Share Our Wealth Program

Here is the whole sum and substance of the Share Our Wealth movement:

1. Every family to be furnished by the Government a homestead allowance, free of debt, of not less than one-third the average family wealth of the country, which means, at the lowest, that every family shall have the reasonable comforts of life up to a value of from $5,000 to $6,000. No person to have a fortune of more than 100 to 300 times the average family fortune, which means that the limit to fortunes is between $1,500,000 and $5,000,000, with annual capital levy taxes imposed on all above $1,000,000.

2. The yearly income of every family shall not be less than one-third of the average family income, which means that, according to the estimates of the statisticians of the United States Government and Wall Street, no family's annual income would be less than from $2,000 to $2,500. No yearly income shall be allowed to any person larger than from 100 to 300 times the size of the average family income, which means that no person would be allowed to earn in any year more than from $600,000 to $1,800,000, all to be subject to present income-tax laws.

3. To limit or regulate the hours of work to such an extent as to prevent overproduction; the most modern and efficient machinery would be encouraged, so that as much would be produced as

possible so as to satisfy all demands of the people, but to also allow the maximum time to the workers for recreation, convenience, education, and luxuries of life.

4. An old age pension to the persons over 60.

5. To balance agricultural production with what can be consumed according to the laws of God, which includes the preserving and storage of surplus commodities to be paid for and held by the Government for the emergencies when such are needed. Please bear in mind, however, that when the people of America have had money to buy things they needed, we have never had a surplus of any commodity. This plan of God does not call for destroying any of the things raised to eat or wear, nor does it countenance wholesale destruction of hogs, cattle, or milk.

6. To pay the veterans of our wars what we owe them and to care for their disabled.

7. Education and training for all children to be equal in opportunity in all schools, colleges, universities, and other institutions for training in the professions and vocations of life; to be regulated on the capacity of children to learn, and not upon the ability of parents to pay the costs. Training for life's work to be as much universal and thorough for all walks in life as has been the training in the arts of killing.

8. The raising of revenue and taxes for the support of this program to come from the reduction of swollen fortunes from the top, as well as for the support of public works to give employment whenever there may be any slackening necessary in private enterprise.

The Call for Support

I now ask those who read this circular to help us at once in this work of giving life and happiness to our people—not a starvation dole upon which someone may live in misery from week to week. Before this miserable system of wreckage has destroyed the life germ of respect and culture in our American people let us save what was here, merely by having none too poor and none too rich. The theory of the Share Our Wealth Society is to have enough for all, but not to have one with so much that less than enough remains for the balance of the people.

VIEWPOINT 2

"Confiscation of wealth may satisfy the vengeful in us. . . . But it is the path of national suicide."

Redistributing Wealth Would Not Help Americans Out of the Depression

David Lawrence (1888-1973)

Many of the proposals for helping America out of the Great Depression focused on the redistribution of wealth. Political leaders, including Louisiana senator Huey P. Long, Wisconsin senator Robert La Follette Jr., and Minnesota governor Floyd B. Olson argued that the Great Depression stemmed from policies of the 1920s that lowered taxes on the rich and concentrated wealth and economic power into fewer and fewer people. They challenged President Roosevelt from the left, calling for greater taxation on the wealthy. Conservatives opposed such measures, arguing that they would undermine America's capitalist economy. In 1935 Roosevelt proposed a Wealth Tax Act setting higher tax rates on the rich. The act met with strong opposition and was considerably weakened by Congress before becoming law.

In the following viewpoint, David Lawrence summarizes the conservative argument against wealth redistribution. Lawrence was founder and editor of *U.S. News*, a newspaper which eventually evolved into the newsmagazine *U.S. News & World Report*. He was also a frequent radio commentator. In 1934 his book *Beyond the New Deal*, from which this viewpoint is taken, was published.

Excerpted from David Lawrence, *Beyond the New Deal*. New York: McGraw-Hill, 1934.

Redistribution of wealth is an excellent catchphrase. It implies that he who hath not will receive a bounty. It also implies that to accomplish this we shall take away from him who hath and give it somehow to him who has failed, for one reason or another, to accumulate his rightful share.

But, if we are dealing with "redistribution of wealth" not as the slogan of politicians that promise the moon for votes, and if, instead, we are seriously examining the uneven distribution of worldly goods, we must find some way to retain all the incentive of the profit system—for otherwise the government credit will collapse through lack of revenues—and yet remove all the abuses which permit men to exploit their fellow men.

If the Lord had created men equal in brains and initiative, in physical stamina and social responsibility, we might have a different problem to consider. As it is the redistribution of wealth becomes a practical matter of today. Were we to start as Russia did by wiping the slate clean and confiscating all private property, the approach would be different. But proceeding on the assumption that we do not intend to appropriate private property in violation of the Federal Constitution, and that we want some modified form of capitalism or individualism which will abolish the abuses of the past and bring us back to a better standard of living than we enjoy today, then the question of method in the light of existing circumstances—not some theoretical future—becomes paramount.

Henry Ford's Example

I wonder how many people begrudge Henry Ford his success. Not many. He rose from a mechanic's bench to be the head of a billion dollar industry. He did not float public loans or stock issues. He steered clear of Wall Street. He did not exploit labor—he paid higher wages than his competitors. He made transportation at a price that came within the reach of the average man. He opened up by his low-priced automobile a vast inland territory. His life has been useful. Can he be accused of exploiting his fellow man? Can he be classed with the Wall Street bankers who are condemned for bringing on the panic of 1929? Of course not. He is America's best example today of real individualism.

There are tens of thousands of businessmen who have made smaller fortunes in precisely the same way as Henry Ford—honestly.

If we enforce the laws against fraud and dishonesty, if we prevent exploitation of human labor or sweatshop conditions or the payment of wages below a decent standard of living, we will have attained through government a social advance highly desirable. But there is no reason why such steps should require the destruction of the profit system. . . .

The latest official figures on income tax returns, which happen to be for the calendar year 1932, reveal some amazing facts. Whereas in 1928 there were more than 500 persons with incomes of a million dollars a year or over, there were in 1932 less than twenty-five individuals of that much wealth in the entire 120 million people.

"Come along. We're going to the Trans-Lux to hiss Roosevelt."

Roosevelt's New Deal policies were highly unpopular with the upper class, as this cartoon by New Yorker *cartoonist Peter Arno illustrates.*

Also, whereas there were 43,000 persons with incomes of $50,000 a year in 1928, there were in 1932 less than 8,000 such individuals. Mr. Roosevelt made redistribution of wealth one of the tenets of his speech of acceptance in Chicago and has indicated since he took office that he believes in the doctrine of redistribution. But the figures now show most all of it took place before Mr. Roosevelt was inaugurated.

The credit—and who will deny him this at least—must go, perforce, to Herbert Hoover. Popularly speaking, Mr. Hoover was responsible for the depression. Many millions of citizens voted that way. Hence he ought by the same token to be given credit for what has now become a major virtue—redistribution of wealth.

If the foregoing seems to be a political jest, then it will not be amiss to examine something far more serious—namely, the effect of the redistribution of wealth of 1932 and the more extensive drop in incomes which must have developed in 1933.

To those who never have had an income of $5,000 a year, such a sum seems wealth and riches enough for any man. The unattainable doubtless seems more precious than reality. So since to covet wealth often breeds class prejudice, it is not surprising that as the rich were toppled over in the depression they received scant sympathy. The conspicuous cases of greed and inordinate acquisition by dishonest and unethical means seemed somehow to color the thinking of the masses. Does a man dare even to speak of those who were honest but who lost fortunes, there is hurled at him an odd cynicism which refuses to believe that large incomes can be honestly earned except in the rarest cases.

It is unpopular nowadays even to speak a kind word for wealth. It is a sort of social evil, not to be mentioned except in phrases of bitter denunciation. To join the chorus has become a New Dealism—it is fashionable. And nothing seems to bring out the pied-piper-of-hamelin in us more than newfangled "isms."

Common People Who Pay

But who pays the piper? The wealthy? The rich? Not a bit of it. The common people pay. It is they who suffer when an economic system is upset. It is they who lose when leadership is overthrown and the spirit of enterprise is choked and incentive is abolished.

The sad truth will be confirmed by any social welfare worker who tries to raise funds for a hospital. Where are the rich of yesterday? Who can be found to give as generously as some who have been swept into oblivion and into the humiliating bankruptcies that have fastened their stigma on so-called homes of wealth from coast to coast? Where are the philanthropically inclined who gave ungrudgingly only two or three years ago to their colleges, their schools, to recreational centers for the poor, to the jobless in the first year or so of the depression when the holocaust had not yet engulfed all who once had wealth?

Education in America, a wonderful edifice which had been reared through the immortal gifts of countless benefactors, large and small, suffers today its greatest hour of distress. No longer is there substantial wealth in private hands for social betterment.

It might be said and with truth that not all rich people gave away money even in proportion to their wealth. Quite so. This was one of the injustices of a voluntary system of giving. But for every such inequality, there were thousands who gave till it hurt, yes, thousands who felt that the gift without the spirit of the giver was bare, that it was as blessed to give as to receive!

Giving will never again in this generation be America's greatest attribute. The people collectively used to average gifts of about two billion dollars a year to philanthropic causes. This will not come again because the government has taken over involuntarily the task of providing the social improvements which private philanthropy used to furnish. And the size of it will grow, thus increasing Federal and state and city taxation.

Long's Plan Impractical

Senator Huey Long's Share Our Wealth plan was attacked by many as simply unworkable. The following is taken from a speech by W. B. Bell, president of the American Cyanamid Company, delivered at the University of Virginia Institute of Public Affairs. The address appeared in Vital Speeches of the Day, *July 29, 1935.*

Let us . . . consider the program of Senator Huey Long. Senator Long proposes to give each of us a home worth a minimum of $5,000, together with all desired home comforts, by stripping those who have fortunes of more than $2,500,000 of all in excess of that sum. But this partial distribution of wealth works out much less per person than the plan which we have just considered. It would not yield the $5,000 home, with or without the comforts. Assuming the confiscation which Senator Long proposes, those of us who would benefit by the operation would hope to receive on the average, at most, about $135. Actually we would receive nothing of value. The assets distributed would have been rendered worthless. Furthermore, our industrial and economic system would not within the lifetime of any of those here present recover from such a blow to initiative, energy, thrift and ambition which alone accumulated or ever can accumulate the wealth which Senator Long proposes to confiscate. . . .

Huey Long's "Share the Wealth" plan is impracticable and won't work.

Perhaps it is after all a more logical scheme to levy taxes in order to get funds for social purposes. The burden then falls evenly on all classes. But will the people submit to increased taxation? Education will cost the middle classes of the American people many more hundreds of millions of dollars in the future than in the past. Already educational institutions, hitherto dependent on private gifts or aid from state governments, are at the Federal Treasury begging for help. And their pleas will increase as the profit system gets its solar plexus when the New Deal comes to fruition. What an irony of fate—the "brain trust" has given birth to its Frankenstein monster! . . .

Again we may ask: where are the rich? Many of them, of course, are in exile. They have taken their funds to other countries which, having gone through social readjustment, are ready to recognize the value of capital in the lifeblood of reconstruction. Other individuals have lost their wealth never to regain it. Men of fifty-five and sixty are rarely able to begin at the bottom and build again. They cannot look to the speculative channels that have made get-rich-quick-wallingfords in the past. The days of speculation may not be over but the opportunities for large wealth in short intervals as a substitute for the enterprise of annual earnings gradually accumulated may be said to be limited to invention and the accidents of gold discovery.

Here Comes That Tax Collector

So a new generation of wealth must grow up. It will take a long time to gather momentum especially in the face of restrictive laws which practically forbid new enterprise and strangle opportunities for the collection of those small amounts of capital which entrepreneurs have always needed to get a start on the road to fortune.

"Well, what difference does it make?" we may ask. The answer is that the American people have never really felt the lash of the tax collector. The Treasury has indicated its desire to make a door-to-door canvass to urge the filing of returns. It must have taxes. Suppose the people who believe the wealthy aren't paying their taxes should say: "Get it from the rich, soak them!" The tax collector may bring forth all these statistics to prove that there aren't any rich any more. But the prejudice will have been so deep-seated that the tax collector will be unconvincing.

The politicians in America, as in all democracies, always like to postpone or avoid or circumvent a disagreeable task. They have never told the American people that 97 per cent of our citizens have paid no taxes for many years to the Federal Treasury and that a sound system of taxation should have forced long before this a spreading of the tax burden in proportion to capacity to pay. There should never have been any exemptions. Even two dollars a year or less than four cents a week would have netted an enormous sum if collected at the source from every person capable of earning $260 a year. Surely four cents out of five dollars a week isn't a heavy tax. The labor unions collect dues by a check-off system. Why couldn't employers do likewise for Uncle Sam?

Had there been a consciousness of how the Federal Government must collect its revenues, there might not today be such calm indifference to the spending orgy at Washington. But unhappily there will be no such indifference when the government, hard pressed to meet the demands of the dole and social expenses of all kinds, will increase the tax rates to confiscatory levels in the higher brackets and to painful percentages in the middle-class groups. . . .

Radicals Still in Saddle

It will be argued that, of course, it is not intended to abolish the profit system—that this is but an academic theory. Then the practical question still confronts us—where is the money coming from to bear the cost of government in America and to carry on the great social institutions among which education has been our proudest boast?

Maybe wealth has learned its lesson. Maybe the political game has gone to an extreme and it is time to restore private initiative and to relax governmental control in accordance as individual initiative is reawakened to righteousness.

But among the casualties of the depression are many noble men and women who gave unstintingly of their profits and surpluses. Was the Business System wrong or the criminals who abused it? Today we are punishing the system as well as those who disregarded morals.

Unfortunately, we are beginning to punish the middle classes too for we are beginning to curtail education. We are already eliminating standards of living which a past generation had extended to every corner of the land. These downward readjustments are not difficult if they merely mean the elimination of luxury, if they simply deprive people of comforts and compel them to accept bare necessities. That is not the harm. The real damage is to the body and soul of millions of people who under a staggering burden seem to see ahead only a long, long trail of never-ending, never-diminishing taxes, a desperate, futile struggle to save a small surplus for the contingencies of life.

Wealth Necessary to Nation

To take from individuals their money, their wealth, is not to plunge them into poverty. There are conditions in which the penniless can laugh amid their tears. For they still have the wealth that faith gives, the wealth that springs from hope, the wealth that comes from honest records and unblemished character.

But if the tax collector bars the way and stands like the angel of death at the crossroads of human initiative and says: "Thou shalt not earn aught but a small tithe, thou shalt give to the tax collector now and till the end of thy years," would it be surprising to find that the so-called revolution of 1933 had resulted in a counter-revolution? There will then be a new group of radicals, a new army of rebels in the land. . . .

Confiscation of wealth may satisfy the vengeful in us. It may soothe a retaliatory spirit. But it is the path of national suicide. Revision of existing legislation, adopted in moments of ill-tempered and fanatical bitterness, is an essential step if we are to avoid the pitfalls that history so plainly records. There must always be the reward motive. To many people it is but another way to set goals of human ambition. For not all who achieve it are sensuous. Many are sensitive to the needs of their fellow citizens. When government kills the opportunity to earn, it sounds the death knell of the opportunity to serve.

VIEWPOINT 3

"Our social security program will be a vital force working against the recurrence of severe depressions in the future."

Social Security Will Benefit America

Frances Perkins (1880-1965)

On August 14, 1935, Franklin D. Roosevelt signed into law the Social Security Act. The act provided for state-administered, federally funded unemployment insurance and welfare benefits and federally funded and administered old age and survivors' pensions. Prior to the passage of this law only a few states provided old age pensions and only Wisconsin had laws on unemployment insurance.

A central figure in the enactment of the Social Security Act was Frances Perkins. Perkins, the first woman to serve in the cabinet of a U.S. president, was Franklin D. Roosevelt's secretary of labor from 1933 to 1945. Her previous career included teaching, social work, and service as New York state industrial commissioner and political adviser to then-governor Roosevelt. In 1934 Roosevelt appointed her to head a cabinet-level Committee on Economic Security, where the Social Security Act was largely written. The following viewpoint is taken from a radio speech Perkins gave on September 2, 1935, shortly after the Social Security Act was passed into law. It was reprinted in *Vital Speeches of the Day*. Perkins describes the act and its benefits for the American people.

Frances Perkins, from "The Social Security Act," a speech broadcast over the radio September 2, 1935. Reprinted in *Vital Speeches of the Day* 1: 792-94 (1935).

People who work for a living in the United States of America can join with all other good citizens on this forty-eighth anniversary of Labor Day in satisfaction that the Congress has passed the Social Security Act. This Act establishes unemployment insurance as a substitute for haphazard methods of assistance in periods when men and women willing and able to work are without jobs. It provides for old age pensions which mark great progress over the measures upon which we have hitherto depended in caring for those who have been unable to provide for the years when they no longer can work. It also provides security for dependent and crippled children, mothers, the indigent disabled and the blind.

Old people who are in need, unemployables, children, mothers and the sightless, will find systematic regular provisions for needs. The Act limits the Federal aid to not more than $15 per month for the individual, provided the State in which he resides appropriates a like amount. There is nothing to prevent a State from contributing more than $15 per month in special cases and there is no requirement to allow as much as $15 from either State or Federal funds when a particular case has some personal provision and needs less than the total allowed.

Following essentially the same procedure, the Act as passed provides for Federal assistance to the States in caring for the blind, a contribution by the State of up to $15 a month to be matched in turn by a like contribution by the Federal Government. The Act also contains provision for assistance to the States in providing payments to dependent children under sixteen years of age. There also is provision in the Act for cooperation with medical and health organizations charged with rehabilitation of physically handicapped children. The necessity for adequate service in the fields of public and maternal health and child welfare calls for the extension of these services to meet individual community needs.

Old-Age Benefits

Consider for a moment those portions of the Act which, while they will not be effective this present year, yet will exert a profound and far-reaching effect upon millions of citizens. I refer to the provision for a system of old-age benefits supported by the contributions of employer and employees, and to the section which sets up the initial machinery for unemployment insurance.

Old-age benefits in the form of monthly payments are to be paid to individuals who have worked and contributed to the insurance fund in direct proportion to the total wages earned by such individuals in the course of their employment subsequent to

1936. The minimum monthly payment is to be $10, the maximum $85. These payments will begin in the year 1942 and will be to those who have worked and contributed.

Because of difficulty of administration not all employments are covered in this plan at this time so that the law is not entirely complete in coverage, but it is sufficiently broad to cover all normally employed industrial workers.

As an example of the practical operation of the old-age benefit system, consider for a moment a typical young man of thirty-five years of age, and let us compute the benefits which will accrue to him. Assuming that his income will average $100 per month over the period of thirty years until he reaches the age of sixty-five, the benefit payments due him from the insurance fund will provide him with $42.50 per month for the remainder of his life. If he has been fortunate enough to have an income of $200 per month, his income will subsequently be $61.25 per month. In the event that death occurs prior to the age of sixty-five, 3½% of the total wages earned by him subsequent to 1936 will be returned to his dependents. If death occurs after the age of sixty-five, his dependents receive the same amount, less any benefits paid to him during his lifetime.

This vast system of old-age benefits requires contributions both by employer and employee, each to contribute 3% of the total wage paid to the employee. This tax, collected by the Bureau of Internal Revenue, will be graduated, ranging from 1% in 1937 to the maximum 3% in 1939 and thereafter. That is, on this man's average income of $100 a month he will pay to the usual fund $3 a month and his employer will also pay the same amount over his working years.

Unemployment Insurance

In conjunction with the system of old-age benefits, the Act recognizes that unemployment insurance is an integral part of any plan for the economic security of millions of gainfully employed workers. It provides for a plan of cooperative Federal-State action by which a State may enact an insurance system, compatible with Federal requirements and best suited to its individual needs.

The Federal Government attempts to promote and effectuate these State systems, by levying a uniform Federal pay-roll tax of 3% on employers employing eight or more workers, with the proviso that an employer who contributes to a State unemployment compensation system will receive a credit of 90% of this Federal tax. After 1937, additional credit is also allowable to any employer who, because of favorable employment experience or adequate reserves, is permitted by the State to reduce his payments.

In addition, the Act provides that after the current fiscal year the Federal Government allocate annually to the States $49,000,000 solely for the administration of their respective insurance systems, thus assuring that all money paid for State unemployment compensation will be reserved for the purpose of compensation to the worker. It has been necessary, at the present time, to eliminate essentially the same groups from participation under the unemployment insurance plan as in the old-age benefit plan, though it is possible that at some future time a more complete coverage will be formulated.

An Important Law

President Franklin D. Roosevelt signed the Social Security Act into law on August 14, 1935, at which time he released the statement excerpted here.

This social security measure gives at least some protection to thirty millions of our citizens who will reap direct benefits through unemployment compensation, through old-age pensions and through increased services for the protection of children and the prevention of ill health.

We can never insure one hundred percent of the population against one hundred percent of the hazards and vicissitudes of life, but we have tried to frame a law which will give some measure of protection to the average citizen and to his family against the loss of a job and against poverty-ridden old age.

This law, too, represents a cornerstone in a structure which is being built but is by no means complete. It is a structure intended to lessen the force of possible future depressions. It will act as a protection to future Administrations against the necessity of going deeply into debt to furnish relief to the needy. The law will flatten out the peaks and valleys of deflation and of inflation. It is, in short, a law that will take care of human needs and at the same time provide for the United States an economic structure of vastly greater soundness.

The State of New York, at the present time, has a system of unemployment compensation which might well illustrate the salient factors desired in such a plan; in the event of unemployment, the worker is paid 50% of his wages weekly for a period not exceeding 16 weeks in any 52 weeks. This payment begins within three weeks after the advent of actual unemployment. California, Washington, Utah and New Hampshire have passed unemployment insurance laws in recent months and Wisconsin's law is already in effect. Thirty-five States have old-age pension statutes and mothers' pension acts are in force in all but three States.

With the States rests now the responsibility of devising and enacting measures which will result in the maximum benefits to the

American workman in the field of unemployment compensation. I am confident that impending State action will not fail to take cognizance of this responsibility. The people of the different States favor the program designed to bring them greater security in the future and their legislatures will speedily pass appropriate laws so that all may help to promote the general welfare.

Federal legislation was framed in the thought that the attack upon the problems of insecurity should be a cooperative venture participated in by both the Federal and State Governments, preserving the benefits of local administration and national leadership. It was thought unwise to have the Federal Government decide all questions of policy and dictate completely what the States should do. Only very necessary minimum standards are included in the Federal measure leaving wide latitude to the States.

While the different State laws on unemployment insurance must make all contributions compulsory, the States, in addition to deciding how these contributions shall be levied, have freedom in determining their own waiting periods, benefit rates, maximum benefit periods and the like. Care should be taken that these laws do not contain benefit provisions in excess of collections. While unemployment varies greatly in different States, there is no certainty that States which have had less normal unemployment heretofore will in the future have a more favorable experience than the average for the country.

It is obvious that in the best interests of the worker, industry and society, there must be a certain uniformity of standards. It is obvious, too, that we must prevent the penalizing of competitive industry in any State which plans the early adoption of a sound system of unemployment insurance, and provide effective guarantees against the possibility of industry in one State having an advantage over that of another. This the uniform Federal tax does, as it costs the employer the same whether be pays the levy to the Federal Government or makes a contribution to a State unemployment insurance fund. The amount of the tax itself is a relative assurance that benefits will be standardized in all States, since under the law the entire collection must be spent on benefits to unemployed.

A Sound and Reasonable Plan

The social security measure looks primarily to the future and is only a part of the administration's plan to promote sound and stable economic life. We cannot think of it as disassociated from the Government's program to save the homes, the farms, the businesses and banks of the Nation, and especially must we consider it a companion measure to the Works Relief Act which does undertake to provide immediate increase in employment and corresponding stimulation to private industry by purchase of supplies.

While it is not anticipated as a complete remedy for the abnormal conditions confronting us at the present time, it is designed to afford protection for the individual against future major economic vicissitudes. It is a sound and reasonable plan and framed with due regard for the present state of economic recovery. It does not represent a complete solution of the problems of economic security, but it does represent a substantial, necessary beginning. It has been developed after careful and intelligent consideration of all the facts and all of the programs that have been suggested or applied anywhere.

Few legislative proposals have had as careful study, as thorough and conscientious deliberation, as that which went into the preparation of the social security programs. It is embodied in perhaps the most useful and fundamental single piece of Federal legislation in the interest of wage earners in the United States. As President Roosevelt said when he signed the measure: "If the Senate and House of Representatives in their long and arduous session had done nothing more than pass this bill, the session would be regarded as historic for all time."

This is truly legislation in the interest of the national welfare. We must recognize that if we are to maintain a healthy economy and thriving production, we need to maintain the standard of living of the lower income groups of our population who constitute ninety per cent of our purchasing power. The President's Committee on Economic Security, of which I had the honor to be chairman, in drawing up the plan, was convinced that its enactment into law would not only carry us a long way toward the goal of economic security for the individual, but also a long way toward the promotion and stabilization of mass purchasing power without which the present economic system cannot endure.

That this intimate connection between the maintenance of mass purchasing power through a system of protection of the individual against major economic hazards is not theoretical is evidenced by the fact that England has been able to withstand the effects of the world-wide depression, even though her prosperity depends so largely upon foreign trade. English economists agree with employers and workers that this ability to weather adverse conditions has been due in no small part to social insurance benefits and regular payments which have served to maintain necessary purchasing power.

Our social security program will be a vital force working against the recurrence of severe depressions in the future. We can, as the principle of sustained purchasing power in hard times makes itself felt in every shop, store and mill, grow old without being haunted by the spectre of a poverty-ridden old age or of being a burden on our children.

The costs of unemployment compensation and old-age insurance are not actually additional costs. In some degree they have long been borne by the people, but irregularly, the burden falling much more heavily on some than on others, and none of such provisions offering an orderly or systematic assurance to those in need. The years of depression have brought home to all of us that unemployment entails huge costs to government, industry and the public alike.

Unemployment insurance will within a short time considerably lighten the public burden of caring for those unemployed. It will materially reduce relief costs in future years. In essence, it is a method by which reserves are built up during periods of employment from which compensation is paid to the unemployed in periods when work is lacking.

The passage of this act with so few dissenting votes and with so much intelligent public support is deeply significant of the progress which the American people have made in thought in the social field and awareness of methods of using cooperation through government to overcome social hazards against which the individual alone is inadequate.

During the fifteen years I have been advocating such legislation as this I have learned that the American people want such security as the law provides. It will make this great Republic a better and a happier place in which to live—for us, our children and our children's children. It is a profound and sacred satisfaction to have had some part in securing this great boon to the people of our country.

VIEWPOINT 4

"How can recovery be promoted by additional expenditures from a Federal treasury already far in the red?"

The Administration's Social Security Proposal Will Harm America

John C. Gall (1901-1957)

One of the important New Deal measures of 1935 was the passage of the Social Security Act. Prior to this time the United States, unlike many countries in Europe and elsewhere, did not have a national system of old age pensions, unemployment insurance, or public relief. The Great Depression increased public demand for such relief and inspired a national movement, led by physician Francis Townsend, for old age pensions. Townsend's proposals for two-hundred-dollar monthly pensions financed by a national sales tax were deemed impractical by many, but the 1935 Social Security Act was in part a response to their popularity.

Not all people were united behind the 1935 Social Security Act. Among the opponents was John C. Gall, a labor lawyer and former Treasury official who worked many years for the National Association of Manufacturers, a business lobbying organization. In the following viewpoint Gall criticizes the proposed Social Security Act and its payroll taxes as impractical and costly to business. He also questions several assertions made by Frances Perkins, Roosevelt's secretary of labor, concerning the benefits of the proposed legislation. The viewpoint is taken from a radio address Gall made, later reprinted in *Vital Speeches of the Day*, June 17, 1935.

John C. Gall, "Will the Administration's Social Security Bill Promote Recovery?" a speech broadcast June 6, 1935. Reprinted in *Vital Speeches of the Day* 1: 610-13 (1935).

I approach a discussion of the subject of Social Security with full realization that the position of the manufacturer with respect to social legislation is easily misunderstood and as readily misinterpreted. Objection to the form of legislation, or to its timeliness, or to any of its details, is translated by many into opposition to its objective. But that is not the attitude of those for whom I am privileged to speak.

We agree at once that society must, as a matter of self-defense, care for all those persons who for one reason or another have become unwilling victims of any of the great hazards of life and who have no means of livelihood save that provided by society itself. We make no distinction in this respect between old age destitution and that arising from accident, ill health, or unemployment.

But the means by which this objective is to be accomplished, the political and social organizations which have the responsibility for providing the necessary assistance, and the extent of the assistance to be given are fundamental matters upon which we believe there not only can be, but is, great disagreement among people who, like ourselves, are sympathetic with the objective.

Will the Administration's Social Security Bill promote recovery? If I wished to indulge in the kind of wisecracking to which employers have been constantly subjected during the past two years, I should comment that *if this* bill will promote recovery it is the single exception which proves the rule. . . .

The Proposed Plan

For the purpose of our discussion, we shall have to assume that, broadly speaking, the Administration's proposal is for a measure embodying two groups of provisions, the one of a permanent character, the other temporary. The permanent features are a system of so-called unemployment insurance, more accurately described as "unemployment benefits"; a Federal contributory old-age pension provision; and provision for permanent entry of the Federal Government into the field of insurance through sale of old-age annuities. The features presumably intended to be temporary contemplate outright Federal appropriations to the several States to supplement State appropriations for relief of old-age dependency, aids to dependent children, maternal and child welfare, vocational rehabilitation, and public health services. The permanent features, except for the voluntary annuities to be sold, are to be supported by a special tax levy upon employers and employees. The annual appropriations by the Federal Government itself, for operation of the temporary provisions, will be approximately one hundred millions of dollars in the first year, and not less than two hundred millions per year in succeeding years until the permanent system becomes effective. These amounts take no account whatever of the additional State and local taxes and appropriations necessary to meet the minimum requirements for receipt of Federal appropriations.

The permanent old-age pension feature is to be supported through taxes on employers and employees subject to the Act. The unemployment benefit provisions do not represent a Federal system, but through the levy of a heavy payroll tax against employers, passage of State laws would be compelled in order that the employer's Federal tax might be remitted in proportion to his liability under State laws. The Federal Act does not require any levy whatever against employees who are ultimately supposed to benefit by the Act. The burdens levied under these permanent features begin almost at once, but no benefits are payable for several years to come.

The Harm of Government

Daniel O. Hastings, Republican senator from Delaware and one of the harshest critics of the New Deal, questioned Roosevelt's proposed Social Security program in a statement reprinted in the Congressional Digest *for March 1935.*

My fear is that when the Federal Government undertakes the job of social security, through direct taxation for that purpose, it has taken a step that can hardly be retraced. I fear it may end the progress of a great country and bring its people to the level of the average European. It will furnish delicious food and add great strength to the political demagogue. It will assist in driving worthy and courageous men from public life. It will discourage and defeat the American trait of thrift. It will go a long way toward destroying American initiative and courage. No man can determine with any degree of accuracy its cost upon the present or future generation. There is danger of our sympathy for its humane objectives overcoming our mature judgment.

That, briefly, is a broad outline of the so-called Social Security scheme. We are now asked whether it will promote recovery. The answer would seem too obvious to argue: How can recovery be promoted by additional expenditures from a Federal treasury already far in the red? How can recovery be promoted by the levy of new and additional taxes on employers and employees, when the effect is to withdraw from the channels of trade and commerce a substantial portion of the income normally spent for goods and services? How can real recovery, which means restoration of normal employment and payrolls, be promoted by discouraging employers from expanding employment and increasing payrolls? How can recovery be promoted by payroll taxes which directly induce the substitution of machinery for men? Let us not forget that employers pay men, not machines.

But let us see what some of the advocates of this bill have said of it as a recovery measure. The Secretary of Labor herself said, last November:

> Unemployment insurance alone is not a cure-all. It will not put men back to work and it does not eliminate the necessity for relief. Obviously, we need more than unemployment insurance. We need work programs and well conceived plans for economic rehabilitation. We need to revive the construction and other durable goods industries and to stimulate increased production by private industry.

Senator Pat Harrison, of Mississippi, in charge of the bill in the Senate, said on May 30th:

> At the outset I wish to impress upon you that it is not the purpose of unemployment compensation to meet the extraordinary situation with which we are now faced, for this emergency is being largely met by the public works program. The social security bill, on the other hand, looks to the future and seeks to provide ways and means for permanently dealing with the problem of unemployment in the years to come. . . .

These remarks related primarily to the unemployment compensation features of the measure. I presume no one will contend that the permanent old-age pension plan will promote recovery, since no benefits are to be paid under it until approximately 1942. Where, then, are the "recovery" features of the bill? In the mere appropriation of funds to the States under the temporary provisions of the Act? If so, and if that is a sound method of promoting recovery, why stop at one hundred million dollars, or even two hundred, per annum? Why not adopt the Townsend plan and purchase recovery even more quickly? Any argument that the mere distribution of public money promotes recovery is based on the fallacious proposition that consumer purchasing power can be produced and maintained by legislative fiat. The Secretary of Labor in April 1934 said that unemployment insurance "would have the important advantage of giving purchasing power to a small but steady market for the products of all our businesses and all our great industrial institutions. It would put a bottom to the fall of depression and unemployment as it has done in England."

England's Example

Well, let us see whether the English agree with her about that. The Royal Commission on Unemployment Insurance, appointed in 1930 after the British Unemployment Insurance system had completely broken down, reported after careful investigation, as follows:

> The effect of an insurance or a relief scheme upon the community's purchasing power varies. It is sometimes represented as an infallible remedy for unemployment, maintaining purchasing power under all circumstances and so providing a demand for unemployed labour. If the unemployment relieved is due to any causes . . . except general trade depression, there is no ground for this view. It overlooks the fact that the payment of unemployment benefit is merely a transfer of purchasing power to the beneficiaries from contributors and taxpayers who supply the Fund, and others who lend to the Government when the Fund is in debt. To the extent that it enables the unemployed to maintain their purchasing power without contributing currently to society's income, it reduces the resources and purchases of these others. The aggregate of purchases made, and therefore, it may be assumed, of employment given, is the same, the only difference is in the distribution of these purchases. . . .

What about foreign experience with compulsory unemployment insurance? It is obvious that Russia, Germany and Italy, operating under dictatorships, and with complete state control of industry and labor, offer no precedent unless the advocates of compulsory insurance wish to concede an analogy of political and economic conditions. There is much that we can learn from England, but even there the record is one of a complete breakdown of the insurance fund, and a resort to the public treasury. Their Act has been amended 25 times in the 24 years of its existence and is even now undergoing revision.

The Secretary of Labor in a radio address of February 25, 1935, said:

> It is not amiss to note here that social legislation in European countries, begun some 25 years ago, is still in a developmental state and has been subjected to numerous changes as experience and changing conditions dictated.

The question before us is not whether there is enough merit in compulsory social insurance to warrant our experimenting with it at the proper time. The question is whether we are warranted in experimenting in a time like this, when there is still widespread unemployment. Remember that no responsible advocate of unemployment insurance claims it will put a single unemployed man to work. On the other hand, official reports of the British Government show that certain types of unemployment are made chronic as a result of social insurance. All of you may not agree with Henry Ford but there is much common sense in his observation, made since the depression began, that:

> To regard present conditions as permanent and then to legislate

as if they were, is a serious mistake. It is the surest way to keep these wrong things with us. I would not insure unemployment; to me that looks like the surest way of establishing unemployment as a permanent evil. . . . In every case where it exists, unemployment insurance is simply taken out of industry's pay envelope in advance. The men can do that for themselves if they want to, as well as any government can do it. . . . Somebody has to earn everything that is paid. No amount of juggling can change that fact. There is no exempt class. Establish unemployment insurance and you simply remove the pressure toward abolishing unemployment. The people then accept unemployment as a not too serious fact. But it is useless to discuss that, because if you insure unemployment it is only a matter of time before the insurance collapses under the load of unemployment it creates.

In my opinion, the temporary provisions of the Social Security Bill should be segregated from the permanent features. Congress has already appropriated some five billions of dollars to be used by the President for relief of economic distress. Let the necessary amount be allocated from that fund to meet the requirements of destitution and dependency in the several States.

No Need for Haste

As to the permanent system contemplated by the bill enough has been said to indicate that it has no relation to recovery except, as many believe, to defer and retard it. As to those portions, there is no necessity for unseemly haste. The year 1936, after all, is not necessarily the millennium. Let us therefore proceed after mature study and consideration. Many problems have scarcely been touched by the studies so far made. It took the British two years to study a proposed revision after 20 years of experience.

These observations are, I believe, adequate to demonstrate the necessity for making haste slowly. This is particularly true in a country like ours where unemployment on a wide scale has been the exception and not the rule throughout our history; where natural resources abound; where new industries employing hundreds of thousands of people have developed and will continue to develop from year to year; and where many of our most serious social, political, and economic problems arise out of failure to balance the interests of industry and agriculture. It must be borne in mind that the agricultural population of Great Britain constitutes only about 8 per cent of the total. In this country our agricultural population is ¼ of our total. What will be the effect on them if they are left out of any system which may be adopted and yet are called upon to contribute to its support, both directly through taxation and indirectly through increased costs of the goods and services they must buy?

Must we institute a system, change it twenty-five times in the next twenty-five years as England has done, and at the end of that time find it necessary to constitute a commission to salvage the essentials of the system and restore the fund to solvency? Or shall we determine in advance what plan, if any, is best suited to our own people and our own standards?

Constitutional Questions

I regret that time does not permit me to discuss the serious constitutional questions involved in the Social Security Bill. The Associated Press informs us that the Secretary of Labor, upon leaving the White House on Tuesday, declared:

> The Social Security measure is not based on the interstate commerce clause, but rather on the Federal Government's taxing clause. We have consulted eminent lawyers on this legislation.

It would be interesting to know whether this legal advice was received from the same source that advised the Administration that the National Industrial Recovery Act was constitutional; that the Railway Pension Act was constitutional; that the Frazier-Lemke Act was constitutional; and that the removal of a member of the Federal Trade Commission was authorized by law,—as to all of which the Supreme Court held there was no constitutional warrant.

What a tragedy it would be for the Administration again to hold the promise to the ear and break it to the heart by forcing enactment of another law of doubtful constitutionality! That would promote, not social security, but a fresh wave of social insecurity.

Nor can I refrain from quoting what President Roosevelt as Governor of New York said on March 2, 1930:

> As a matter of fact and law, the governing rights of the States are all of those which have not been surrendered to the National Government by the constitution or its amendments. Wisely or unwisely, people know that under the Eighteenth Amendment Congress has been given the right to legislate on this particular subject, but this is not the case in the matter of a great number of other vital problems of government, such as the conduct of public utilities, of banks, of insurance, of business, of agriculture, of education, of social welfare, and of a dozen other important features. In these Washington must be encouraged to interfere.

That was sound law and sound policy in 1930. It is still good law and good policy in 1935.

May I conclude with the admonition of that great friend of young America, Edmund Burke:

> Better to be despised for too anxious apprehensions than ruined by too confident security.

VIEWPOINT 5

"Given the economic situation of 1932, the New Deal has been more helpful than harmful to Negroes."

The New Deal Has Aided Blacks

Robert C. Weaver (1907-)

The New Deal held a mixed record for black Americans, who were hit especially hard by the Great Depression. On one hand, many blacks benefited from the New Deal's relief and public employment programs. Blacks received a disproportionate share of the millions of jobs administered by the Works Progress Administration (WPA), for example. On the other hand, some New Deal programs perpetuated racial discrimination patterns and harmed blacks economically. The codes adopted by the National Recovery Administration, for instance, forced the shutdown of small black businesses and codified lower wages for blacks than for whites. Many black activists asserted that the tangible benefits for black Americans were few.

The following viewpoint is by Robert C. Weaver, an adviser on Negro Affairs for the Department of the Interior and one of several blacks appointed to important government posts in the Roosevelt administration. In an article first published in *Opportunity: Journal of Negro Life* in July 1935, Weaver defends the New Deal, arguing that its various programs have provided much assistance to blacks. He acknowledges difficulties in the execution of some New Deal programs but concludes that black Americans have in general benefited from them.

After Roosevelt's death Weaver taught at Columbia and New

From Robert C. Weaver, "The New Deal and the Negro: A Look at the Facts," *Opportunity: Journal of Negro Life* 13 (7): 200-203 (July 1935). Used with the permission of the National Urban League, Inc.

York universities and wrote several books, including *The Negro Ghetto*. In 1966 he became the first black American appointed to a U.S. presidential cabinet when Lyndon Johnson named him secretary of the Department of Housing and Urban Development.

It is impossible to discuss intelligently the New Deal and the Negro without considering the status of the Negro prior to the advent of the Recovery Program. The present economic position of the colored citizen was not created by recent legislation alone. Rather, it is the result of the impact of a new program upon an economic and social situation.

Much has been said recently about the occupational distribution of Negroes. Over a half of the gainfully employed colored Americans are concentrated in domestic service and farming. The workers in these two pursuits are the most casual and unstable in the modern economic world. This follows from the fact that neither of them requires any great capital outlay to buy necessary equipment. Thus when there is a decline in trade, the unemployment of workers in these fields does not necessitate idle plants, large depreciation costs, or mounting overhead charges. In such a situation, the employer has every incentive to dismiss his workers; thus, these two classes are fired early in a depression.

The domestic worker has loomed large among the unemployed since the beginning of the current trade decline. This situation has persisted throughout the depression and is reflected in the relief figures for urban communities where 20 per cent of the employables on relief were formerly attached to personal and domestic service. Among Negroes the relative number of domestics and servants on relief is even greater.

In selected cities, 43.4 per cent of the Negroes on relief May 1, 1934, were usually employed as domestics. The demand for servants is a derived one; it is dependent upon the income and employment of other persons in the community. Thus, domestics are among the last rehired in a period of recovery.

The new works program of the Federal Government will attack this problem of the domestic worker from two angles. Insofar as it accelerates recovery by restoring incomes, it will tend to increase the demand for servants. More important, however, will be its creation of direct employment opportunities for all occupational classes of those on relief.

Although it is regrettable that the economic depression has led to the unemployment of so many Negroes and has threatened the

177

creation of a large segment of the Negro population as a chronic relief load, one is forced to admit that Federal relief has been a godsend to the unemployed. The number of unemployed in this country was growing in 1933. According to the statistics of the American Federation of Labor, the number of unemployed increased from 3,216,000 in January 1930 to 13,689,000 in March 1933. In November 1934 the number was about 10,500,000 and although there are no comparable current data available, estimates indicate that current unemployment is less than that of last November. Local relief monies were shrinking; and need and starvation were facing those unable to find an opportunity to work. A Federal relief program was the only possible aid in this situation. Insofar as the Negro was greatly victimized by the economic developments, he was in a position to benefit from a program which provided adequate funds for relief.

The harsh living conditions faced by many black sharecroppers and migrant agricultural workers in the South are depicted in this 1939 photograph of a Missouri roadside camp.

It is admitted that there were many abuses under the relief setup. Such situations should be brought to light and fought. In the case of Negroes, these abuses undoubtedly existed and do exist. We should extend every effort to uncover and correct them. We can admit that we have gained from the relief program and still fight to receive greater and more equitable benefits from it.

The recent depression has been extremely severe in its effects upon the South. The rural Negro—poor before the period of trade decline—was rendered even more needy after 1929. Many tenants found it impossible to obtain a contract for a crop, and scores of Negro farm owners lost their properties. The displacement of Negro tenants (as was the case for whites) began before, and grew throughout the depression. Thus, at the time of the announcement of the New Deal, there were many families without arrangements for a crop—an appreciable number without shelter. The following summary of conditions in one county of a southern state will serve as an illustration. In Greene County, North Carolina (where the population in 1930 was 18,656 divided almost equally between whites and Negroes) the FERA [Federal Emergency Relief Administration] survey reported data as of January 1934 relative to the period of displacement of families. This material shows that for this county, displacement of tenants was most severe in 1931-1932.

The Negro Farmer

The problems facing the Negro farmer of the South are not new. They have been accentuated by the crop reduction program. They are, for the most part, problems of a system and their resistance to reform is as old as the system. This was well illustrated by the abuses in the administration of the Federal feed, seed, and fertilizer laws in 1928-1929. These abuses were of the same nature as those which confront the AAA [Agricultural Adjustment Administration] in its dealings with Negro tenants.

The southern farm tenant is in such a position that he cannot receive any appreciable gains from a program until steps are taken to change his position of absolute economic dependence upon the landlord. Until some effective measure for rehabilitating him is discovered, there is no hope. The new program for land utilization, rural rehabilitation, and spreading land ownership may be able to effect such a change. Insofar as it takes a step in that direction, it will be advantageous to the Negro farmer. The degree to which it aids him will depend upon the temper of its administration and the extent to which it is able to break away from the *status quo.*

In listing some of the gains which have accrued to Negroes under the New Deal, there will be a discussion of three lines of activity: housing, employment, and emergency education. These are chosen for discussion because each is significant in itself, and all represent a definite break from the *status quo* in governmental activity, method, and policy. They do not give a complete picture; but rather, supply interesting examples of what is, and can be, done for Negroes.

The Housing Division of the Federal Emergency Administration of Public Works has planned 60 Federal housing projects to be under construction by December 31, 1935. Of these, 28 are to be developed in Negro slum areas and will be tenanted predominantly or wholly by Negroes. Eight additional projects will provide for an appreciable degree of Negro occupancy. These 36 projects will afford approximately 74,664 rooms and should offer accommodations for about 23,000 low income colored families. The estimated total cost of these housing developments will be $64,428,000, and they represent about 29 per cent of the funds devoted to Federal slum clearance developments under the present allotments.

A Fair Chance

Interior secretary Harold L. Ickes appointed a number of blacks to his department and was one of the chief New Deal supporters of black civil rights. His address to the twenty-seventh annual convention of the National Association for the Advancement of Colored People (NAACP) was printed in the organization's journal The Crisis *in August 1936.*

Negroes are demanding that the ideals and principles upon which the Nation was founded shall be translated into action, and made to apply to themselves as well as to other citizens. They are not asking the Government to coddle them nor to direct their activities, but they do want the Government to assure them a fair chance and an equal opportunity in their desire to attain a fuller life.

Your Government at the present time is not insensitive to this plea, for it comports with its own conception of its responsibility. It is attempting to build a new social order and to set up higher ideals for all of its citizens. In helping the common man to achieve a life that is more worthwhile, this Administration is seeking the greatest good for the greatest number of the people.

Projects in Negro areas have been announced in seven cities: Atlanta, Cleveland, Detroit, Indianapolis, Montgomery, Chicago, and Nashville. These will cost about $33,232,000 and will contain about 20,000 rooms. Two of these projects, the University development at Atlanta, and the Thurman Street development in Montgomery, are under construction. These are among the earliest Federal housing projects to be initiated by the PWA [Public Works Administration].

After a series of conferences and a period of experience under the PWA, it was decided to include a clause in PWA housing contracts requiring the payment to Negro mechanics of a given percentage of the payroll going to skilled workers. The first project to be affected by such a contractual clause was the Techwood development in Atlanta, Georgia. On this project, most of the labor employed on demolition was composed of unskilled Negro workers. About 90 per cent of the unskilled workers employed laying the foundation for the Techwood project were Negroes, and, for the first two-month construction period, February and March, 12.7 per cent of the wages paid skilled workers was earned by Negro artisans. . . .

Under the educational program of the FERA, out of a total of 17,879 teachers employed in 13 southern states, 5,476 or 30.6 per cent were Negro. Out of a total of 570,794 enrolled in emergency classes, 217,000 or 38 per cent were Negro. Out of a total of $886,300 expended in a month (either February or March 1935) for the program, Negroes received $231,320 or 26.1 per cent. These southern states in which 26.1 per cent of all emergency salaries were paid to Negro teachers, ordinarily allot only 11.7 per cent of all public school salaries to Negro teachers. The situation may be summarized as follows: Six of the 13 states are spending for Negro salaries a proportion of their emergency education funds larger than the percentage of Negroes in those states. The area as a whole is spending for Negro salaries a proportion of its funds slightly in excess of the percentage of Negroes in the population. This development is an example of Government activity breaking away from the *status quo* in race relations.

There is one Government expenditure in education in reference to which there has been general agreement that equity has been established. That is the FERA college scholarship program. Each college or university not operated for profit, received $20 monthly per student as aid for 12 per cent of its college enrollment. Negro and white institutions have benefited alike under this program.

The New Deal

In the execution of some phases of the Recovery Program, there have been difficulties, and the maximum results have not been received by the Negroes. But, given the economic situation of 1932, the New Deal has been more helpful than harmful to Negroes. We had unemployment in 1932. Jobs were being lost by Negroes, and they were in need. Many would have starved had there been no Federal relief program. As undesirable as is the large relief load among Negroes, the FERA has meant much to them. In most of the New Deal setups, there has been some Negro representation by competent Negroes. The Department of the Interior and the PWA have appointed some fifteen Negroes to jobs of responsibility which pay good salaries. These persons have secretarial and clerical staffs attached to their offices. In addition to these new jobs, there are the colored messengers, who number around 100, and the elevator operators for the Government buildings, of whom there are several hundred. This is not, of course, adequate representation; but it represents a step in the desired direction and is greater recognition than has been given Negroes in the Federal Government during the last 20 years. Or again, in the Nashville housing project, a Negro architectural firm is a consultant; for the Southwest Side housing project in Chicago, a Negro is an associate architect. One of the proposed projects will have two Negro principal architects, a Negro consultant architect, and a technical staff of about six Negro technicians. In other cities competent colored architects will be used to design housing projects.

This analysis is intended to indicate some advantages accruing to the Negro under the Recovery Program, and to point out that the New Deal, insofar as it represents an extension of governmental activity into the economic sphere, is a departure which can do much to reach the Negro citizens. In many instances it has availed itself of these opportunities. An intelligent appraisal of its operation is necessary to assure greater benefits to colored citizens.

VIEWPOINT 6

"On every hand the New Deal has used slogans for the same raw deal [for Negro workers]."

The New Deal Has Not Aided Blacks

John Davis (1905-1973)

One of the major political shifts of the 1930s occurred among black Americans. Traditionally supportive of the Republican party since the Civil War, in 1936 almost three out of four black voters supported President Roosevelt. Roosevelt's economic relief and public employment programs had provided work and relief for many blacks. Administration officials such as Harold L. Ickes and Harry Hopkins appointed blacks to high government posts and advocated racial integration. First Lady Eleanor Roosevelt was a strong public supporter of black civil rights. All these factors contributed to black political support.

The New Deal, however, also received much harsh criticism from black intellectuals. They argued that many of its programs did little to directly counter the segregation and discrimination black Americans still faced. One of the New Deal's critics was black lawyer and writer John Davis. Davis organized the Joint Committee on National Recovery in 1933 to combat what it viewed as unfair and discriminatory practices permitted by the National Recovery Administration. The NRA was established in 1935 to draw up industry codes that set national standards for production, wages, and prices. Many of these codes preserved racially discriminatory business practices. Davis's organization

John Davis, "A Black Inventory of the New Deal," *Crisis* 42: 141-45 (1935).

filed briefs and conducted public hearings in a mostly futile attempt to persuade the NRA to change these practices. In the following viewpoint, taken from a 1935 article in *The Crisis*, Davis argues that many of the programs of the New Deal were actually harmful to black Americans.

It is highly important for the Negro citizen of America to take inventory of the gains and losses which have come to him under the "New Deal." The Roosevelt administration has now had two years in which to unfold itself. Its portents are reasonably clear to anyone who seriously studies the varied activities of its recovery program. We can now state with reasonable certainty what the "New Deal" means for the Negro.

At once the most striking and irrefutable indication of the effect of the New Deal on the Negro can be gleaned from relief figures furnished by the government itself. In October, 1933, six months after the present administration took office, 2,117,000 Negroes were in families receiving relief in the United States. These represented 17.8 per cent of the total Negro population as of the 1930 census. In January, 1935, after nearly two years of *recovery measures*, 3,500,000 Negroes were in families receiving relief, or 29 per cent of our 1930 population. Certainly only a slight portion of the large increase in the number of impoverished Negro families can be explained away by the charitable, on the grounds that relief administration has become more humane. As a matter of fact federal relief officials themselves admit that grave abuses exist in the administration of rural relief to Negroes. And this is reliably borne out by the disproportionate increase in the number of urban Negro families on relief to the number of rural Negro families on relief. Thus the increase in the number of Negroes in relief families is an accurate indication of the deepening of the economic crisis for black America.

The National Recovery Administration

The promise of NRA to bring higher wages and increased employment to industrial workers has glimmered away. In the code-making process occupational and geographical differentials at first were used as devices to exclude from the operation of minimum wages and maximum hours the bulk of the Negro workers. Later, clauses basing code wage rates on the previously existing wage differential between Negro and white workers tended to continue the inferior status of the Negro. For the particular firms, for whom none of these devices served as an effective means of keeping down Negro wages, there is an easy way out through the securing of an exemption specifically relating to the *Negro* worker in the plant. Such exemptions are becoming more numerous as time goes on. Thus from the beginning relatively few Negro workers were even theoretically covered by NRA labor provisions.

Discrimination in New Deal Programs

Sociologist Guy Johnson of the University of North Carolina wrote an article for Social Forces *(October 1934). It detailed the racial obstacles blacks faced in the American South, which the New Deal had done little to change.*

Even in the administration of federal relief, the Civil Works program, the A.A.A. [Agricultural Adjustment Administration], etc., there has been, particularly in the lower South, a tendency to perpetuate the existing inequalities. Negro tenants received pitifully little of the crop reduction money last fall. Landlords quite generally took charge of the checks and applied them to back debts of the tenants. Furthermore, many landlords are known to have "understandings" with local relief administrators to prevent the "demoralization" of their Negro labor, and it is reported that some go as far as to charge to their tenants' accounts all food and other supplies furnished by the relief office. The director of relief in a southern seaboard city remarked not long ago, "I don't like this fixing of a wage scale for work relief. Why, the niggers in this town are getting so spoiled working on these relief jobs at thirty cents an hour that they won't work on the docks for fifty cents a day like they did last year." In allotting C.W.A. [Civil Works Administration] jobs, re-employment offices throughout the South ignored the Negro skilled worker almost as effectively as if he did not exist. In one tobacco center, for example, 13 per cent of the white C.W.A. workers received the skilled rates of pay, while only 1.2 per cent of the Negro workers received such pay. In another industrial city, 15 per cent of the whites on C.W.A. pay rolls received skilled rates, but not one Negro did so. If skilled Negroes worked, they worked at the unskilled rates.

But employers did not have to rely on the code-making process. The Negro worker not already discriminated against through code provisions had many other gauntlets to run. The question of importance to him as to all workers was, "as a result of all of NRA's maneuvers will I be able to buy more?" The answer has been "No." A worker cannot eat a wage rate. To determine what this wage rate means to him we must determine a number of other factors. Thus rates for longshoremen seem relatively high.

But when we realize that the average amount of work a long-shoreman receives during the year is from ten to fifteen weeks, the wage rate loses much of its significance. When we add to that fact the increase in the cost of living—as high as 40 per cent in many cases—the wage rate becomes even more chimerical. For other groups of industrial workers increases in cost of living, coupled with the part time and irregular nature of the work, make the results of NRA negligible. In highly mechanized industries speed-up and stretch-out nullify the promised result of NRA to bring increased employment through shorter hours. For the workers are now producing more in their shorter work periods than in the longer periods before NRA. There is less employment. The first sufferer from fewer jobs is the Negro worker. Finally the complete break-down of compliance machinery in the South has cancelled the last minute advantage to Negro workers which NRA's enthusiasts may have claimed.

The Agricultural Adjustment Administration

The Agricultural Adjustment Administration has used cruder methods in enforcing poverty on the Negro farm population. It has made violations of the rights of tenants under crop reduction contracts easy; it has rendered enforcement of these rights impossible. The reduction of the acreage under cultivation through the government rental agreement rendered unnecessary large numbers of tenants and farm laborers. Although the contract with the government provided that the land owner should not reduce the number of his tenants, he did so. The federal courts have now refused to allow tenants to enjoin such evictions. Faced with this Dred Scott decision against farm tenants, the AAA has remained discreetly silent. Farm laborers are now jobless by the hundreds of thousands, the conservative government estimate of the decline in agricultural employment for the year 1934 alone being a quarter of a million. The larger portion of these are unskilled Negro agricultural workers—now without income and unable to secure work or relief.

But the unemployment and tenant evictions occasioned by the crop reduction policies of the AAA is not all. For the tenants and sharecroppers who were retained on the plantations the government's agricultural program meant reduced income. Wholesale fraud on tenants in the payment of parity checks occurred. Tenants complaining to the Department of Agriculture in Washington have their letters referred back to the locality in which they live and trouble of serious nature often results. Even when this does not happen, the tenant fails to get his check. The remainder of the land he tills on shares with his landlord brings him only the most meagre necessities during the crop season varying from three to five months. The rest of the period for him and his family is one of "root hog or die."

The past year has seen an extension of poverty even to the small percentage (a little more than 20 per cent) of Negro farmers who own their own land. For them compulsory reduction of acreage for cotton and tobacco crops, with the quantum of such reduction controlled and regulated by local boards on which they have no representation, has meant drastic reduction of their already low income. Wholesale confiscation of the income of the Negro cotton and tobacco farmer is being made by prejudiced local boards in the South under the very nose of the federal government. In the wake of such confiscation has come a tremendous increase in land tenantry as a result of foreclosures on Negro-owned farm properties.

Nor has the vast public works program, designed to give increased employment to workers in the building trades, been free from prejudice. State officials in the South are in many cases in open rebellion against the ruling of PWA [Public Works Administration] that the same wage scales must be paid to Negro and white labor. Compliance with this paper ruling is enforced in only rare cases. The majority of the instances of violation of this rule are unremedied. Only unskilled work is given Negroes on public works projects in most instances. And even here discrimination in employment is notorious. Such is bound to be the case when we realize that there are only a handful of investigators available to seek enforcement.

Public Works Employment

Recently a move has been made by Negro officials in the administration to effect larger employment of Negro skilled and unskilled workers on public works projects by specifying that failure of a contractor to pay a certain percentage of his payroll to Negro artisans will be evidence of racial discrimination. Without doubting the good intentions of the sponsors of this ingenious scheme, it must nevertheless be pointed out that it fails to meet the problem in a number of vital particulars. It has yet to face a test in the courts, even if one is willing to suppose that PWA high officials will bring it to a test. Percentages thus far experimented with are far too low and the number of such experiments far too few to make an effective dent in the unemployment conditions of Negro construction industry workers. Moreover the scheme gives aid and comfort to employer-advocates of strike-breaking and the open shop; and, while offering, perhaps, some temporary relief to a few hundred Negro workers, it establishes a dangerous precedent which throws back the labor movement and the organization of Negro workers to a considerable degree. The scheme, whatever its Negro sponsors may hope to the contrary, becomes therefore only another excuse for their white superiors maintaining a "do-nothing" policy with regard to discrimination against Negroes in the Public Works Administration.

No Relief from Racism

Future United Nations diplomat and Nobel prize winner Ralph J. Bunche was a political science professor at Howard University in Washington, D.C., when he wrote a critical evaluation of the New Deal for the January 1936 issue of Journal of Negro Education.

Striking at no fundamental social conditions, the New Deal at best can only fix the disadvantages, the differentials, the discriminations, under which the Negro population has labored all along. The traditional racial stereotypes,—which have been inherited from the master-slave tradition and which have been employed by the ruling class of large land-holders in the South and Industrialists in the North to give effective expression to their determination to keep the Negro in a servile condition and as a profitable labor supply,—remain, and are indeed, often heightened by the New Deal.

The Negro has no pleasanter outlook in the long-term social planning ventures of the new administration. Planning for subsistence homesteads for industrially stranded workers has been muddled enough even without consideration of the problem of integrating Negroes into such plans. Subsistence Homesteads projects are overburdened with profiteering prices for the homesteads and foredoomed to failure by the lack of planning for adequate and permanent incomes for prospective homesteaders.

In callous disregard of the interdiction in the Constitution of the United States against use of federal funds for projects which discriminate against applicants solely on the ground of color, subsistence homesteads have been planned on a strictly "lily-white" basis. The more than 200 Negro applicants for the first project at Arthurdale, West Virginia, were not even considered, Mr. Bushrod Grimes (then in charge of the project) announcing that the project was to be open only to "native white stock." As far north as Dayton, Ohio, where state laws prohibit any type of segregation against Negroes, the federal government has extended its "lily-white" policy. Recently it has established two Jim-Crow projects for Negroes. Thus the new administration seeks in its program of social planning to perpetuate ghettoes of Negroes for fifty years to come.

An even more blatant example of this policy of "lily-white" reconstruction is apparent in the planning of the model town of

Norris, Tennessee, by the Tennessee Valley Authority. This town of 450 model homes is intended for the permanent workers on Norris Dam. The homes are rented by the federal government, which at all times maintains title to the land and dwellings and has complete control of the town management. Yet officials at TVA openly admit that no Negroes are allowed at Norris.

TVA has other objectionable features. While Negro employment now approaches an equitable proportion of total employment, the payroll of Negro workers remains disproportionately lower than that of whites. While the government has maintained a trade school to train workers on the project, no Negro trainees have been admitted. Nor have any meaningful plans matured for the future of the several thousand Negro workers who in another year or so will be left without employment, following completion of work on the dams being built by TVA.

None of the officials of TVA seems to have the remotest idea of how Negroes in the Tennessee Valley will be able to buy the cheap electricity which TVA is designed to produce. They admit that standards of living of the Negro population are low, that the introduction of industry into the Valley is at present only a nebulous dream, that even if this eventuates there is no assurance that Negro employment will result. The fairest summary that can be made of TVA is that for a year or so it has furnished bread to a few thousand Negro workers. Beyond that everything is conjecture which is most unpleasant because of the utter planlessness of those in charge of the project.

Recovery legislation of the present session of Congress reveals the same fatal flaws which have been noted in the operation of previous recovery ventures. Thus, for example, instead of genuine unemployment insurance we have the leaders of the administration proposing to exclude from their plans domestic and agricultural workers, in which classes are to be found 15 out of every 23 Negro workers. On every hand the New Deal has used slogans for the same raw deal.

The sharpening of the crisis for Negroes has not found them unresponsive. Two years of increasing hardship has seen strange movement among the masses. In Chicago, New York, Washington and Baltimore the struggle for jobs has given rise to action on the part of a number of groups seeking to boycott white employers who refuse to employ Negroes. "Don't Buy Where You Can't Work" campaigns are springing up everywhere. . . . And proposals for a 49th State are being seriously considered by various groups.

Interracial Approaches

In sharp contrast with these strictly racial approaches to the problem have been a number of interracial approaches. Increasing numbers of unemployed groups have been organized under radical leadership and have picketed relief stations for bread. Sharecroppers unions, under Socialist leadership in Arkansas, have shaken America into a consciousness of the growing resentment of southern farm tenants and the joint determination of the Negro and white tenants to do something about their intolerable condition.

In every major strike in this country Negro union members have fought with their white fellow workers in a struggle for economic survival. The bodies of ten Negro strikers killed in such strike struggles offer mute testimony to this fact. Even the vicious policies of the leaders of the A. F. of L. [American Federation of Labor] in discrimination against Negro workers is breaking down under the pressure for solidarity from the ranks of whites.

This heightening of spirit among all elements of black America and the seriousness of the crisis for them make doubly necessary the consideration of the social and economic condition of the Negro at this time. It was a realization of these conditions which gave rise to the proposals to hold a national conference on the economic status of Negroes under the New Deal at Howard University in Washington, D.C., on May 18, 19 and 20. At this conference, sponsored by the Social Science Division of Howard University and the Joint Committee on National Recovery, a candid and intelligent survey of the social and economic condition of the Negro will be made. Unlike most conferences it will not be a talk-fest. For months nationally known economists and other technicians have been working on papers to be presented. Unlike other conferences it will not be a one-sided affair. Ample opportunity will be afforded for high government officials to present their views of the "New Deal." Others not connected with the government, including representatives of radical political parties, will also appear to present their conclusions. Not the least important phase will be the appearance on the platform of Negro workers and farmers themselves to offer their own experience under the New Deal. Out of such a conference can and will come a clear-cut analysis of the problems faced by Negroes and the nation.

But a word of caution ought to be expressed with regard to this significant conference. In the final analysis it cannot and does not claim to be representative of the mass opinion of Negro citizens in America. All it can claim for itself is that it will bring together on a non-representative basis well informed Negro and white technicians to discuss the momentous problem it has chosen as its topic. It can furnish a base for action for any organization which chooses to avail itself of the information developed by it. It cannot act itself.

Thus looking beyond such a conference one cannot fail to hope that it will furnish impetus to a national expression of black America demanding a tolerable solution to the economic evils which it suffers. Perhaps it is not too much to hope that public opinion may be moulded by this conference to such an extent that already existing church, civic, fraternal, professional and trade union organizations will see the necessity for concerted effort in forging a mighty arm of protest against injustice suffered by the Negro. It is not necessary that such organizations agree on every issue. On the problem of relief of Negroes from poverty there is little room for disagreement. The important thing is that throughout America as never before Negroes awake to the need for a unity of action on vital economic problems which perplex us.

Such a hope is not lacking in foundation upon solid ground. Such an instance as the All India Congress of British India furnishes an example of what repressed groups can do to better their social and economic status. Perhaps a *"National Negro Congress"* of delegates from thousands of Negro organizations (and white organizations willing to recognize their unity of interest) will furnish a vehicle for channeling public opinion of black America. One thing is certain: the Negro may stand still but the depression will not. And unless there is concerted action of Negroes throughout the nation the next two years will bring even greater misery to the millions of underprivileged Negro toilers in the nation.

VIEWPOINT 7

"The time has come now when with the use of machinery and efficiency we can produce with a 30-hour week more than we can sell at home and abroad."

A Thirty-Hour Week Will Help Unemployed Americans

Hugo L. Black (1886-1971)

Hugo L. Black is best known for his long tenure on the U.S. Supreme Court. Appointed by Franklin D. Roosevelt in 1937, he served until 1971. Prior to his appointment, however, Black was a senator from Alabama and a key liberal supporter of Roosevelt's New Deal. Some of his ideas were more liberal than Roosevelt's.

One such idea that was heavily debated during the New Deal was shortening the work week. Black was a sponsor of a federal law setting a national standard of a thirty-hour work week for factories producing articles for interstate commerce. In the following viewpoint, taken from a speech before Congress in 1933 and reprinted in the *Congressional Record* of April 3, 1933, Black argues that limiting the number of hours a person can work could reduce unemployment by spreading work around to more people. Black's bill passed the Senate, but, lacking Roosevelt's strong support, did not pass the House. However, the issue of regulating labor's hours remained an important one, and in 1938 the Fair Labor Standards Act set minimum wage rates and established the present forty-hour work week.

From Hugo L. Black, "For a Thirty-Hour Work Week," *Congressional Record*, 73d Congress, 2d Session (April 3, 1933): 1115, 1127.

Now, at this very time, with more than 12,000,000 people help-less and hopeless in the grip of unemployment, starvation, hunger, misery, and want, we find people in every State of this Nation, men and women, sitting there with the constant whir of machinery dinning into their ears, working from 10 to 16 hours a day in order to earn a mere pittance to keep themselves from starving to death.

Do you tell me that this problem is not national? Do you tell me that the time has not come for bold and courageous action if we are to meet it?

"Oh," they say, "you will breed idleness." No; we do not breed idleness. Throughout all the years the excuse for machinery has been that it would relieve human beings from the drudgery and slavery of long hours of constant toil. That relief has been promised them since the advent of the machine. The time has come now when with the use of machinery and efficiency we can produce with a 30-hour week more than we can sell at home and abroad.

What do we find? We find that instead of the advantages of im-proved machinery going to consumers and the men who work, it has gone to increase the tolls of those who own the plants; and they have built them and overbuilt them until they find them-selves crucified on their cross of greed and unable to sell their product because they have robbed the laborer of the ability to purchase.

Mr. President, they tell us that this proposal will breed idleness. Well, what is the difference? Are not 12,000,000 wholly idle to-day? Are they not idle without hope? Do they not have despair in their hearts and fear that those whom they love will not be able to live because of the lack of food? Have we not taken away from them the security that comes from honest work and honest toil and an honest job? And are we not at the same time destroying our unemployed people by permitting others to work long hours and depriving them of the legitimate opportunities of leisure which should be theirs?

I do not subscribe to this doctrine, this propaganda which has been industriously circulated mainly by the writings of people who were never compelled to listen to the whir of machinery 12 or 13 hours a day, who never went down into the recesses of the earth to dig coal, but who have talked about the "exaltation" of constant, laborious drudgery. I have never heard, in that beautiful story that appears in Holy Writ, that anybody was excluded from the Garden of Eden because of the fact that work was a blessing and not a curse.

I welcome the coming of earned leisure to people when I think of the minds dwarfed by constant toil, when I think of the intellects that perhaps might have soared to great heights in the thought and genius of this Nation that have been deprived of their opportunity by reason of the fact that they must sit and listen to the grinding whir of machinery hour after hour until their energy is sapped, their life practically is taken, and the very blood is drained from their faces. I think, what may we have lost in some of those people? . . .

Reducing the Work Week

William Green, president of the American Federation of Labor, spoke on behalf of the thirty-hour work week in testimony reprinted in the Congressional Digest, *April 1935.*

The opposition to 30 hours follows historical precedent. People who oppose the 30-hour week on the claim that a reduction in hours of work will mean a great decrease in the volume of production, are repeating arguments which were made one hundred years ago against the establishment of the 10-hour day, and fifty years ago against the 8-hour day. These arguments were made and are now made on the assumption of a static society—an assumption which is false, as a glance at history will show. For more than a hundred years there has been a movement in this country for a shorter work week. The fight for the 30-hour week is the present phase of this century-old movement.

I do not anticipate leisure with any apprehension or any horror. I welcome it. I am glad that the day has come when, in our land that we love, we can, if we are bold enough and courageous enough, give to the men who toil that which is theirs—the benefit of that leisure which comes from machinery and efficiency. Where should it go? Where is it going today? It is not going to the 12,000,000 men who are unemployed. It is not even going to the people who are working 16 hours a day. No, Mr. President; the avarice and greed of commerce has seen to that. Now that their spokesmen see the time coming when there is an enlightened public sentiment all over this land, manifested in the Senate, manifested in the House, manifested in the White House, manifested in the Supreme Court—when they see that the time is ripe for recognizing the fact that people, human beings, are the things that need to be protected in this country—no wonder they come forward at this late hour and say, "If you will just let us alone, we will reduce the hours of labor."

Mr. President, I am not willing to depend upon them now. They come too late. Quick action is imperative. I introduced this bill in the belief that, if passed, it will mark a milestone in the way of human progress. I believe it will immediately put millions to work. I hope that it may be passed, and may establish throughout this country a normal working day of 6 hours. If we can produce what we need in that time, why work any more? Do people love laborious work so much? Those who have written about the great glories of tiring and wearisome labor have usually done so from a safe place occupied by them where they knew they would never be dependent upon their hands to earn their daily bread.

Mr. President, I speak here today for the 12,000,000 who have lost their jobs. I speak for 25,000,000 more who have partially lost their jobs. I speak for the whole 48,000,000 who are walking the streets today not knowing whether they will have a job tomorrow or not. I speak for the unorganized millions who must support the unemployed with billions of taxes. And then you tell me that Congress, which has the right to regulate interstate commerce, has no power to say that these poisoned goods shall not infest the currents and streams of interstate commerce, destroying the commerce itself, sapping the lifeblood of the individuals and the Nation! You tell me that Congress is here with hands held out impotently, saying, "We would like to do this, but the Constitution is in the way"!

That Constitution was never written to be an obstacle to human progress. It has never been so held. It is expansive; it is elastic to meet conditions as they are. I do not believe that that great document, which was written in order to protect human liberty and human government, can be safely interposed in order to block this great forward movement upon which America is bound to embark.

No Square Deal

My friends, in conclusion let me say this:

I do not know what your action will be with reference to this bill; but mark my words: All over this Nation the people are watching Congress, and the people know that they have not been getting a square deal. Up in that little town in New Jersey that was testified about, where 40 per cent of the people are working, some of them 16 hours per day, as these jobless people see the overwork forced upon the others we cannot take out of their minds the fact that there is something wrong. We cannot sit here and continue to pour out the money and credit of the United States to sustain failing business enterprises and at the same time ignore the men and women upon whom the safety of this Republic depends. When enough of them are out of jobs, and when enough of them lose hope, when they see legislation fail to pass that they knew would relieve conditions, do not be deceived. The people are the same in every age and in every country—patient, long-suffering, kind, you may say—but the kindness is taken out of the human heart when its owner sees the factory working 12, 13, 14, 15, 16 hours a day, with underpaid labor, as the unemployed hold out their hands in distress in order to get the very necessities of life for themselves and their children.

I present this bill as a real step forward on the part of the people of this country. It is not a complete remedy for existing conditions. We shall have to go farther, and we might just as well recognize the fact.

VIEWPOINT 8

"The immediate effect of a 30-hour bill would be a huge increase in unemployment."

A Thirty-Hour Week Will Not Help Unemployed Americans

Malcolm Muir (1885-1979)

One measure proposed to improve the conditions of working people and reduce unemployment was to limit work to thirty hours a week. Many in the business community strongly criticized the idea, embodied in bills sponsored by Senator Hugo L. Black of Alabama. Among the critics was Malcolm Muir, president of McGraw-Hill Publishing Company, a publisher of scientific and technical journals as well as *Business Week*, a magazine Muir founded in 1929. Muir was also an administrator and member of the National Recovery Administration Industrial Advisory Board from July 1933 to January 1934, during which time he helped develop and organize codes for labor and prices for businesses and industries. In the following viewpoint, taken from a radio address given January 31, 1935, and reprinted in *Vital Speeches of the Day*, February 11, 1935, Muir argues that the thirty-hour week would weaken the economy and would not improve the welfare of Americans.

Malcolm Muir, "National Dangers of the Thirty-Hour Week," a speech broadcast January 31, 1935. Reprinted in *Vital Speeches of the Day* 1 (February 11, 1935): 319-20.

The thirty-hour week was never passed. However, debates over the issue helped pave the way for the 1938 Fair Labor Standards Act, which established minimum wage rates and the forty-hour week. Muir left McGraw-Hill in 1937 to become editor and president of *Newsweek* magazine, a position he held until 1959.

———————————

There has been introduced in Congress an extraordinary bill. You probably have heard something about it already and I think you are going to hear a great deal more about it because it would so vitally affect the lives of every man and woman.

It is called the Black-Connery Bill. This bill proposes that it be the law of this country that those working in office, shop, or factory shall not be allowed to work more than six hours in one day or more than five days in one week. It further provides that wages shall not be reduced from whatever they are today for the longer week's work. Of course such an idea has a great appeal. I suppose the majority of those who work wish that they did not have to work as hard or as long, as at present. Obviously if the working hours of each person are cut it will take more people to get the same amount of work done. This should mean more jobs and the idea that we can make more jobs which will put a great many of the unemployed back in factories, stores, and shops without cutting the wages of those now employed, has a very strong appeal.

Of course, we would like to see the millions of people who want work get it and we would like to see the great expense of supporting them out of taxes reduced but the great question is, will the Black-Connery Bill accomplish that purpose.

Shortening Work Days

In the back of the minds of those who are past forty is the recollection that the hours of work for the average man and woman have been getting shorter and shorter. There is no question but that this has been a good thing. We remember when the twelve hour day was not uncommon. Then came the ten hour day and then from perhaps 1900-1920 there gradually came the eight hour day.

All this has been good, on the whole. The twelve hour day was I suppose a holdover from the habits of the farm and the hand workshop and the general life of an earlier day. It is one thing to do the work around the farm from daybreak to dark because unless it is haying or harvest or ploughing time, the pace is moderate and the jobs are widely varied. There are long seasons, as in winter, when there isn't so much to be done. It is quite another thing to stand on an automobile assembly line making the same motions, so many to the minute, hour after hour for twelve hours, or even ten. Eight we find, is reasonable limit. And the same thing applies to the girl at the high-powered sewing machine in the clothing factory, or the bank clerk running an electric adding machine at top speed. We found, as the modern machine developed that we had to reduce our working hours, for human reasons. And, of course, the machines increased our ability to make things so rapidly that the amount of goods we made increased even though we didn't work so long.

Well, why not go further? Why not cut hours from 40 a week, which probably is something like the average today, down to thirty ? That is what people are asking. Like the old New England Yankees, we might answer a question with a question, and ask, "Well, why not 20 ? Why not 10? In fact, why work at all?"

Let us look at this question of work and wages and everyone's prosperity. I think we shall have shorter hours of work as time goes on. I think we may reach the 30-hour week in time. But for Congress to pass a law that would disrupt all business and change our working and living habits overnight is not the way to do it. We shall get there just as slowly, or just as swiftly as machinery and manufacturing skill improve in one industry after another—and no more swiftly or no more slowly. Any attempt to do it by law will be a disaster of proportions so serious I hate to think about it.

Why do I say that? Well, let us get down to simple principles. No one works for money wages. We all work for the things money will buy. We have to have food and shelter and clothing, and after we get those things, we want an automobile, and a radio, and an electric refrigerator and tickets for the movies. With money we can always get those things, so we say we are working for money. But when we stop to think, we see that isn't so. We work to get *things*.

Now, what would happen if Congress should pass a law cutting down the hours of work by one-fourth, with no pay cut? It is the same thing as raising wages one-third. It is the same thing to the manufacturer, surely, for he will have to hire one-third more men to turn out the same amount of goods.

It is certainly the same thing to you for it is just a simple way of saying that the price of everything you have to buy will be increased considerably. I am not going to give you a lot of statistics—statistics should be seen and not heard—but I believe they show conclusively just what your common sense will tell you—that with the price of everything increased considerably, everybody would find out that he was no better off—was worse off, in fact. That is what I meant when I said, we don't work for money, really. We work for *things*. Any plan which makes it impossible for us to buy so many things as we do now is no benefit; it is a step backward.

Hurting Workers

Neil Carothers, a professor of economics at Lehigh University in Bethlehem, Pennsylvania, spoke against a proposed thirty-hour work week in Senate testimony reprinted in April 1935 in the Congressional Digest.

The real objective of the 30-hour week is to create by law a special advantage for a special minority group of workers. It would be at the expense of the consumer, all other laborers and of the standard of living of the country. Just incidentally, it will injure the workers themselves in the end. The monopoly will exist for a time, at the expense of the country, but it will collapse. The excessive costs engendered will inevitably react on manufacturers in interstate trade. They will be hurt by local and foreign competition.

The industries themselves will be driven to frantic efforts to substitute machines for men, and will succeed in many lines. In the end many of the beneficiaries of such a law will join the ranks of the unemployed. This writer's sympathies are with the unorganized, overworked and poorly paid. He would like to see definite measures to aid the poor devil who washes dishes in a restaurant 60 hours a week, the scrubwoman on her knees, the overworked bookkeeper, the man who works with a pick all day long. He has no sympathy for legislation for the benefit of a special class, or for a Senate that passes it.

If someone will improve the present tools and machinery so that a man can produce in six hours as much as he does now in eight, why, then, we can pay him one-third more, and maybe cut the price to you of the goods he makes. Now do not be deceived by the fact that this sounds very simple. It is simple, but it actually represents what has happened over the course of the years. As the labor cost of making an article has come down through the invention and the improvement of machinery and methods, prices have come down, wages have increased, hours have been shortened, and everybody has been better off. Walk through a 10-cent store and see the amazing things you can buy for a dime, and try to remember what your grandfather paid for similar articles. Then ask yourself if you believe all these things can be made so much more cheaply that everybody who makes them can have a one-third boost in wages, on one day's notice, or even on a year's notice and still make these things to sell for a dime.

Do you think automobiles can suddenly be made a third to a quarter cheaper? Or do you think, as I do, that the result of the

Black-Connery Bill would be to increase the price of cars so that a great number of people would suddenly discover they could not afford to buy one? That would mean that fewer cars would be made, which would mean that soon more people would be out of work, as the same effect was felt in other industries. We should be much worse off than when we started.

Farmers

Of course, there is one very big group of our people who would be hard hit by any such law. I mean the farmers. They wouldn't get any shorter hours, and the price of everything they buy would be boosted right away. Since they would have no more money to buy with, they would simply have to buy fewer things. And that would further increase unemployment. Much of such recovery as we have had so far has been due to the fact that the prices the farmer gets for the things he raises have been boosted so that he has been able to buy more of the things city people make, and that has created a great many jobs. The farm prices, as you know, were seriously below the prices of manufactured goods. The dislocation was part of the cause of the depression. Well, the Black-Connery Bill would do a great deal to put us right back into that mudhole again. Unless the government raised farm prices to match. And of course, every one of us would pay for that through increased prices of food.

It is plain enough to anyone who will think about it even a little that the amount of money each one of us receives for our work is not really the measure of our prosperity. During the Alaska gold rush reports came back that workmen were getting paid $25 a day. So they were, but they paid $100 for a pair of shoes, $15 a day for board; $25 for a quart of strawberries. You can raise everybody's wages, if you raise prices at the same time. But you can't do this quickly in any other way.

Now, up to this point, I have tried not to be alarming. But there is something that has to be said, and we might as well face it. Passage of the Black-Connery Bill would have not only bad effects over the long range of time, but it would bring down upon our heads an immediate and appalling disaster. I know those are strong words, and I know exactly what they mean. But I repeat, an immediate and appalling disaster. Business can adapt itself to the most difficult, the most outrageous circumstances, and it has done so again and again in the past.

But one thing business cannot do—never has done, and never will.

It cannot change abruptly. Faced with a law ordering an increase in labor costs of one-third immediately, most small businesses and all but a few of the biggest corporations would have to shut down. They have no reserves left to meet such an enormous increase in cost. Reserves have long since been used up in the depression. True, business would make some kind of a new beginning, some day. But the first, the immediate effect of a 30-hour bill would be a huge increase in unemployment. There are now millions of jobless. I should expect the Black-Connery Bill to double their number, very quickly.

Now don't get the idea that this would be done out of deliberation, or as a kind of employers' strike of protest, or anything like that. When the factory shuts down, it is the boss who loses money, hand over fist. And he wants to keep going, and make profits. But it would simply be impossible under the 30-hour bill. He would have to raise his prices immediately and you would stop buying. We are all just getting ready to buy again, after doing without things for these few past years. We are tempted by bargains, or we have decided we can at last risk spending a little money for something we have wanted. Now jack up prices suddenly, and we will stop buying again.

An Economic Shock

It would be a profound shock to the the country—and the country, on the eve of what I confidently believe to be a revival, can't stand another shock. Therefore, do not consider the 30-hour week bill as a matter of interest only to wage earners in shops and factories. It will slow up all recovery and lower, not improve, the living standards of every man, woman, and child in this country.

No, we do not want the 30-hour week just yet, whether we are employers or workers. And it concerns you so directly that it behooves you to convince yourself that you do not want it, and then make your conviction known. Make no mistake, this pleasant-sounding plan would only rob you and your families of any chance of again enjoying prosperity and happiness.

CHAPTER 4

Twilight of the New Deal

Chapter Preface

In the 1936 elections Franklin D. Roosevelt defeated his Republican opponent, Kansas governor Alf Landon, receiving 523 electoral votes and more than 27 million popular votes—the highest vote totals of any presidential candidate up to that time. In addition to traditional Democratic voters including Southerners, Catholics, and urban voters, Roosevelt had created a New Deal coalition of blacks, Mexican-Americans, organized labor, intellectuals, and other people who supported and benefited from his new programs. The coalition also elected additional Democrats to the House and Senate. The landslide electoral victory seemed to promise great new achievements (or an executive dictatorship, depending on one's view) for the New Deal.

Roosevelt's political success reflected his economic success in helping the country recover from the Great Depression. National income had risen from $40.2 billion in 1933 to $64.7 billion in 1936. Farm income and average weekly wages of workers had risen, and four to five million fewer people were unemployed. However, seven million people remained jobless and the Great Depression was far from over, a fact Roosevelt acknowledged in his second inaugural address:

> I see millions of families trying to live on incomes so meager that the pall of family disaster hangs over them day by day. . . .
>
> I see millions lacking the means to buy the products of farm and factory and by their poverty denying work and productiveness to many other millions.
>
> I see one-third of a nation ill-housed, ill-clad, ill-nourished.
>
> It is not in despair that I paint you that picture. I paint it for you in hope—because the Nation, seeing and understanding the injustice in it, proposes to paint it out. . . . The test of our progress is not whether we add more to the abundance of those who have much; it is whether we provide enough for those who have too little.

Although Roosevelt's second term would have less impact than his first, his second term had some significant achievements. A National Housing Act set up loans for low-income housing in 1937. Enforcement of antitrust laws was increased, marking in some respects a reversal of early New Deal priorities. The 1938 Fair Labor Standards Act abolished child labor and established minimum wages and maximum hours for industrial workers.

However, Roosevelt's second term was marked with defeats and setbacks as well. He began his term with a call to increase the size of the Supreme Court. Many people, including New Deal supporters, viewed this call as a power grab and an effort to force the Supreme Court to stop overturning New Deal legislation. Roosevelt's defeat on this measure damaged his relations with Congress and his popularity. Another setback was a severe economic recession that began in the fall of 1937 and continued through most of 1938. The recession renewed debate as to whether the New Deal was helping or hurting America's efforts to rebound from the Great Depression.

The 1938 congressional elections resulted in a political setback for the New Deal as both Republicans and conservative Democrats gained or retained seats in Congress, and greatly dampened the political urge for reform. After 1938 Roosevelt's and the nation's attention turned increasingly from domestic to foreign issues as war threatened in Europe.

VIEWPOINT 1

"Neither [Congress] nor the Chief Executive can afford to weaken or destroy great reforms which, during the past five years, have been effected on behalf of the American people."

The New Deal Must Be Extended

Franklin D. Roosevelt (1882-1945)

Franklin D. Roosevelt, campaigning on the accomplishments of his first term, won the election of 1936, which also resulted in large Democratic majorities in both houses of Congress. However, his second term was not as productive. An ill-fated attempt to enlarge the Supreme Court in order to appoint more justices sympathetic to the New Deal was widely attacked as an executive power grab. The congressional defeat of this proposal cost him political momentum and clout over Congress, which was exacerbated by conflicts with many conservative Democrats from the South who increasingly voiced their misgivings over the New Deal. Criticisms of the New Deal picked up in 1937 when the U.S. economy suffered a sharp recession that was blamed by some on New Deal policies.

The following viewpoint is taken from one of Roosevelt's fireside chats to the nation. It was broadcast on April 14, 1938, several months into the recession. Roosevelt defends the record of the New Deal and states that Americans are better off than in the early years of the Depression. He also calls for further spending in government employment and relief programs. Many of the pro-

Adapted from Franklin D. Roosevelt's radio speech, "Fireside Chat on Economic Conditions," April 14, 1938.

grams and expenditures Roosevelt proposed in this address eventually passed into law. However, Roosevelt's efforts to unseat conservative Democratic senators in the 1938 elections failed, and the midterm elections saw substantial Republican gains. The New Deal as a source of new domestic legislation was essentially over.

Five years ago we faced a very serious problem of economic and social recovery. For four and a half years that recovery proceeded apace. It is only in the past seven months that it has received a visible setback.

And it is only within the past two months, as we have waited patiently to see whether the forces of business itself would counteract it, that it has become apparent that government itself can no longer safely fail to take aggressive government steps to meet it.

This recession has not returned us to the disasters and suffering of the beginning of 1933. Your money in the bank is safe; farmers are no longer in deep distress and have greater purchasing power; dangers of security speculation have been minimized; national income is almost 50 per cent higher than in 1932; and government has an established and accepted responsibility for relief.

But I know that many of you have lost your jobs or have seen your friends or members of your families lose their jobs, and I do not propose that the government shall pretend not to see these things. I know that the effect of our present difficulties has been uneven; that they have affected some groups and some localities seriously, but that they have been scarcely felt in others. But I conceive the first duty of government is to protect the economic welfare of all the people in all sections and in all groups. I said in my message opening the last session of Congress that if private enterprise did not provide jobs this spring, government would take up the slack—that I would not let the people down. We have all learned the lesson that government cannot afford to wait until it has lost the power to act.

A Message to Congress

Therefore, I have sent a message of far-reaching importance to the Congress. I want to read to you tonight certain passages from that message, and to talk with you about them.

In that message I analyzed the causes of the collapse of 1929 in these words: "overspeculation in and overproduction of practically every article or instrument used by man . . . millions of people had been put to work, but the products of their hands had exceeded the purchasing power of their pocketbooks. . . . Under the inexorable law of supply and demand, supplies so overran demand which would pay that production was compelled to stop. Unemployment and closed factories resulted. Hence the tragic years from 1929 to 1933."

I pointed out to the Congress that the national income—not the Government's income, but the total of the income of all the individual citizens and families of the United States—every farmer, every worker, every banker, every professional man and every person who lived on income derived from investments—that national income amounted, in the year 1929, to eighty-one billion dollars. By 1932 this had fallen to thirty-eight billion dollars. Gradually, and up to a few months ago, it had risen to a total of sixty-eight billion dollars—a pretty good come-back from the low point.

I then said this to the Congress:

> But the very vigor of the recovery in both durable goods and consumers' goods brought into the picture early in 1937 certain highly undesirable practices, which were in large part responsible for the economic decline which began in the later months of that year. Again production outran the ability to buy.
>
> There were many reasons for this overproduction. One was fear—fear of war abroad, fear of inflation, fear of nationwide strikes. None of these fears has been borne out.
>
> . . . Production in many important lines of goods outran the ability of the public to purchase them. For example, through the winter and spring of 1937 cotton factories in hundreds of cases were running on a three-shift basis, piling up cotton goods in the factory and in the hands of middle men and retailers. For example, also, automobile manufacturers not only turned out a normal increase of finished cars, but encouraged the normal increase to run into abnormal figures, using every known method to push their sales. This meant, of course, that the steel mills of the Nation ran on a twenty-four hour basis, and the tire companies and cotton factories speeded up to meet the same type of abnormally stimulated demand. The buying power of the Nation lagged behind.
>
> Thus by the autumn of 1937 the Nation again had stocks on hand which the consuming public could not buy because the purchasing power of the consuming public had not kept pace with the production.
>
> During the same period . . . the prices of many vital products had risen faster than was warranted. . . . In the case of many commodities the price to the consumer was raised well above the inflationary boom prices of 1929. In many lines of goods and materials, prices got so high that buyers and builders ceased to buy or to build.

. . . The economic process of getting out the raw materials, putting them through the manufacturing and finishing processes, selling them to the retailers, selling them to the consumer, and finally using them got completely out of balance.

. . . The laying off of workers came upon us last autumn and has been continuing at such a pace ever since that all of us, Government and banking and business and workers, and those faced with destitution, recognize the need for action.

All of this I said to the Congress today and I repeat it to you, the people of the country tonight.

I went on to point out to the Senate and the House of Representatives that all the energies of government and business must

be directed to increasing the national income, to putting more people into private jobs, to giving security and a feeling of security to all people in all walks of life.

Thinking About All of You

I am constantly thinking of all our people—unemployed and employed alike—of their human problems of food and clothing and homes and education and health and old age. You and I agree that security is our greatest need; the chance to work, the opportunity of making a reasonable profit in our business— whether it be a very small business or a larger one—the possibility of selling our farm products for enough money for our families to live on decently. I know these are the things that decide the well-being of all our people.

Therefore, I am determined to do all in my power to help you attain that security, and because I know that the people themselves have a deep conviction that secure prosperity of that kind cannot be a lasting one except on a basis of business fair dealing and a basis where all from top to bottom share in prosperity, I repeated to the Congress today that neither it nor the Chief Executive can afford

to weaken or destroy great reforms which, during the past five years, have been effected on behalf of the American people. In our rehabilitation of the banking structure and of agriculture, in our provisions for adequate and cheaper credit for all types of business, in our acceptance of national responsibility for unemployment relief, in our strengthening of the credit of State and local government, in our encouragement of housing, slum clearance and home ownership, in our supervision of stock exchanges and public utility holding companies and the issuance of new securities, in our provision for social security, the electorate of America wants no backward steps taken.

We have recognized the right of labor to free organization, to collective bargaining; and machinery for the handling of labor relations is now in existence. The principles are established even though we can all admit that, through the evolution of time, administration and practices can be improved. Such improvement can come about most quickly and most peacefully through sincere efforts to understand and assist on the part of labor leaders and employers alike.

The never-ceasing evolution of human society will doubtless bring forth new problems which will require new adjustments. Our immediate task is to consolidate and maintain the gains achieved.

In this situation there is no reason and no occasion for any American to allow his fears to be aroused or his energy and enterprise to be paralyzed by doubt or uncertainty.

I came to the conclusion that the present-day problem calls for action both by the Government and by the people, that we suffer primarily from a failure of consumer demand because of lack of buying power. It is up to us to create an economic upturn.

> How and where can and should the Government help to start an upward spiral?

I went on to propose three groups of measures and I will summarize the recommendations.

Measures for Recovery

First, I asked for certain appropriations which are intended to keep the Government expenditures for work relief and similar purposes during the coming fiscal year at the same rate of expenditures as at present. That includes additional money for the Works Progress Administration; additional funds for the Farm Security Administration; additional allotments for the National Youth Administration, and more money for the Civilian Conservation Corps, in order that it can maintain the existing number of camps now in operation. . . .

Second, I told the Congress that the Administration proposes to make additional bank reserves available for the credit needs of the country. About one billion four hundred million dollars of gold now in the Treasury will be used to pay these additional expenses of the Government, and three-quarters of a billion dollars of additional credit will be made available to the banks by reducing the reserves now required by the Federal Reserve Board.

These two steps, taking care of relief needs and adding to bank credits, are in our judgment insufficient by themselves to start the Nation on a sustained upward movement.

Therefore, I came to the third kind of Government action which I consider to be vital. I said to the Congress:

> You and I cannot afford to equip ourselves with two rounds of ammunition where three rounds are necessary. It we stop at relief and credit, we may find ourselves without ammunition before the enemy is routed. If we are fully equipped with the third round of ammunition, we stand to win the battle against adversity.

The third proposal is to make definite additions to the purchasing power of the Nation by providing new work over and above the continuing of the old work.

First, to enable the United States Housing Authority to undertake the immediate construction of about three hundred million dollars of additional slum clearance projects.

Second, to renew a public works program by starting as quickly as possible about one billion dollars worth of needed permanent public improvements in states, counties and cities.

Third, to add one hundred million dollars to the estimate for federal aid highways in excess of the amount I recommended in January.

Fourth, to add thirty-seven million dollars over and above the former estimate of sixty-three million dollars for flood control and reclamation.

A Plea for Support

President Roosevelt went on the airwaves on June 24, 1938, asking for voters to support liberal candidates in the upcoming party primaries. His attempt to gain more support for additional New Deal programs largely failed.

It is because you are not satisfied, and I am not satisfied, with the progress we have made in finally solving our business and agricultural and social problems that I believe the great majority of you want your own Government to keep on trying to solve them. In simple frankness and in simple honesty, I need all the help I can get—and I see signs of getting more help in the future from many who have fought against progress with tooth and nail.

Fifth, to add twenty-five million dollars additional for federal buildings in various parts of the country.

In recommending this program I am thinking not only of the immediate economic needs of the people of the Nation, but also of their personal liberties—the most precious possession of all Americans. I am thinking of our democracy and of the recent trend in other parts of the world away from the democratic ideal.

Democracy has disappeared in several other great nations—not because the people of those nations disliked democracy, but because they had grown tired of unemployment and insecurity, of seeing their children hungry while they sat helpless in the face of government confusion and government weakness through lack of leadership in government. Finally, in desperation, they chose to sacrifice liberty in the hope of getting something to eat. We in America know that our own democratic institutions can be preserved and made to work. But in order to preserve them we need to act together, to meet the problems of the Nation boldly, and to prove that the practical operation of democratic government is equal to the task of protecting the security of the people.

Not only our future economic soundness but the very soundness of our democratic institutions depends on the determination of our Government to give employment to idle men. The people of America are in agreement in defending their liberties at any cost, and the first line of that defense lies in the protection of economic security. Your Government, seeking to protect democracy, must prove that Government is stronger than the forces of business depression. . . .

We are a rich Nation; we can afford to pay for security and prosperity without having to sacrifice our liberties in the bargain.

In the first century of our republic we were short of capital, short of workers and short of industrial production; but we were rich in free land, free timber and free mineral wealth. The Federal Government rightly assumed the duty of promoting business and relieving depression by giving subsidies of land and other resources.

Thus, from our earliest days we have had a tradition of substantial government help to our system of private enterprise. But today the government no longer has vast tracts of rich land to give away and we have discovered that we must spend large sums to conserve our land from further erosion and our forests from further depletion. The situation is also very different from the old days, because now we have plenty of capital, banks and insurance companies loaded with idle money; plenty of industrial productive capacity and several millions of workers looking for jobs. It is following tradition as well as necessity, if Government strives to put idle money and idle men to work, to increase our public wealth and to build up the health and strength of the people—and to help our system of private enterprise to function.

It is going to cost something to get out of this recession this way, but the profit of getting out of it will pay for the cost several times over. Lost working time is lost money. Every day that a workman is unemployed, or a machine is unused, or a business organization is marking time, is a loss to the Nation. Because of idle men and idle machines this Nation lost one hundred billion dollars between 1929 and the spring of 1933. This year you, the people of this country, are making about twelve billion dollars less than last year.

If you think back to the experiences of the early years of this Administration you will remember the doubts and fears expressed about the rising expenses of Government. But to the surprise of the doubters, as we proceeded to carry on the program which included Public Works and Work Relief, the country grew richer instead of poorer.

It is worthwhile to remember that the annual national people's income was thirty billion dollars more in 1937 than in 1932. It is true that the national debt increased sixteen billion dollars, but remember that in this increase must be included several billion dollars worth of assets which eventually will reduce that debt and that many billion dollars of permanent public improvements—schools, roads, bridges, tunnels, public buildings, parks and a host of other things—meet your eye in every one of the thirty-one hundred counties in the United States.

No doubt you will be told that the Government spending program of the past five years did not cause the increase in our national income. They will tell you that business revived because of private spending and investment. That is true in part, for the Government spent only a small part of the total. But Government spending acted as a trigger to set off private activity. That is why the total addition to our national production and national income has been so much greater than the contribution of the Government itself. . . .

Necessary Debt

You may get all kinds of impressions in regard to the total cost of this new program, or in regard to the amount that will be added to the net national debt.

It is a big program. Last autumn in a sincere effort to bring Government expenditures and Government income into closer balance, the Budget I worked out called for sharp decreases in Government spending.

In the light of present conditions those estimates were far too low. This new program adds two billion and sixty-two million dollars to direct Treasury expenditures and another nine hundred and fifty million dollars to Government loans—and the latter sum, because they are loans, will come back to the Treasury in the future.

The net effect on the debt of the Government is this: between now and July first, 1939—fifteen months away—the Treasury will have to raise less than a billion and a half dollars of new money.

Such an addition to the net debt of the United States need not give concern to any citizen, for it will return to the people of the United States many times over in increased buying power and eventually in much greater Government tax receipts because of the increase in the citizen income. . . .

Finally I should like to say a personal word to you.

I never forget that I live in a house owned by all the American people and that I have been given their trust. . . .

In these great problems of government I try not to forget that what really counts at the bottom of it all, is that the men and women willing to work can have a decent job to take care of themselves and their homes and their children adequately; that the farmer, the factory worker, the storekeeper, the gas station man, the manufacturer, the merchant—big and small—the banker who takes pride in the help he gives to the building of his community, that all these can be sure of a reasonable profit and safety for the savings they earn—not today nor tomorrow alone, but as far ahead as they can see.

VIEWPOINT 2

"The New Deal program has created a vast number of new problems of government. . . . More problems have been created than solved."

The New Deal Must Be Limited

Robert A. Taft (1889-1953)

Robert A. Taft, a lawyer, state representative, and son of former president William H. Taft, was elected Republican senator of Ohio in 1938 and served in the Senate until his death. Taft's 1938 victory over a Democratic incumbent was one of several defeats for Roosevelt and the Democratic party, which saw its once-commanding majorities in the House and Senate shrink. While Republican and conservative efforts failed to roll back or repeal New Deal programs, they did succeed in limiting the amount of significant new domestic legislation passed after 1938.

The following viewpoint is taken from a July 14, 1939, address delivered at the Institute of Public Affairs at the University of Virginia. Taft argues that the New Deal endangers the economy by promoting government interference in private business and by creating large budget deficits.

Adapted from Robert A. Taft, "New Problems of Government," an address to the University of Virginia's Institute of Public Affairs, July 14, 1939, and reprinted in *A Republican Program* (1939): 21-34.

The New Deal program has created a vast number of new problems of government. Every activity creates a new problem, and usually an interesting one. Some are well administered; some are hopelessly inefficient; all are experimental and subject to a continual change of policy. Little public attention is paid to them. Few men even in Congress have a comprehensive idea of the countless activities of government. A good many more problems have been created than solved.

But there are two great problems whose solution, in my opinion, is essential if the nation is to survive. I wish to suggest what those problems are, and how the Republicans propose to meet them.

Unemployment

The first and most important problem is that of unemployment. The question is how we can encourage again in the United States the tremendous volume of private enterprise which existed in the twenties. Our national income is still far below that of 1928, although there are 10 million more people today among whom it must be divided. If we could get back to the business activity of those days, we should have a $90 billion income, 40 percent larger than we have today. Any such increase would take up the greater part of the present unemployment. Unless it can be cured, we may have to admit that the whole American system of democratic government is a failure. The people may well have reason to turn to some other system under which men at least can secure work.

Whatever else has resulted from the great increase in government activity . . . it has certainly had the effect of checking private enterprise completely. This country was built up by the constant establishment of new business and the expansion of old businesses. In every city and every village throughout the country, men were constantly starting out on their own initiative to improve on the enterprises of others, or develop a new product. They put a few men to work. If successful, they expanded to employ ten or a hundred or thousands. If unsuccessful, they passed from the picture without need of government subsidy.

New methods of production were found, and small industries expanded into large industries. Men were willing to spend their time and their money in order that they might provide more completely for themselves and their family in their old age, in order that they might rise above the average standard of living and enjoy a little more luxury or a little more power. In the last six years this process has come to an end because of government regulation and the development of a tax system which penalizes hard work and success. We must and can resume the progress which returned us to prosperity after every depression, but it can only be done by a radical change in government policy.

The policy of fixing the prices of basic commodities has been frequently attempted in history, and has always failed in the end, usually resulting in lower prices for those whom it attempted to benefit. I believe that most of the laws attempting to regulate prices and wages should be repealed, although I believe in a minimum wage law to protect unorganized employees against oppression where the right of collective bargaining cannot be made effective. Laws attempting to dictate the amount of production and the method of operating agriculture and business should be repealed. Those resulting from some definite abuse should be confined to the cure of that abuse.

Seven Lean Years

New York governor Thomas E. Dewey, who was nominated for president by the Republican party in 1944 and 1948, vigorously attacks the record of the New Deal in a speech made in Louisville, Kentucky, on May 11, 1940.

Let us consider the New Deal record. Let us take its seven years and compare them with the preceding seven years—Republican years. . . .

Here are the results of the comparison. First among the items is national income.

National Income: Down. From $70 billion average in the Republican years to $62 billion in the New Deal years.

The next item is farm income.

Farm Income: (Including all government payments) *Down.* From $9 billion in the Republican years to $7.5 billion in the New Deal years.

And then some more:

Agricultural Exports: Down. From $1.5 billion to less than three-quarters of a billion dollars a year.

Farm Prices: Down. Nearly 20 per cent.

Industrial Wages and Salaries: Down. From $21 billion to $16.5 billion.

Dividend Payments: Down. From $4.5 billion to $3 billion.

New Capital Invested: Down. From $4 billion to less than one billion.

New Building: Down. More than 50 per cent.

There is not much of a campaign document for the New Deal in those figures.

The SEC [Securities and Exchange Commission] should confine itself to the prevention of fraud in the sale of securities. The NLRB [National Labor Relations Board] should confine itself to seeing that the employees of each employer obtain, through collective bargaining, what they themselves really desire.

The limitation of farm production and the making of unsound loans on crops for the sole purpose of maintaining prices should come to an end.

Government competition with private industry should be confined to is present limits, and assurance given that it will not be expanded into other fields.

The government should gradually withdraw from the business of lending money and leave that function to private capital under proper regulation.

Encouraging Private Industry

The whole tax system should be reformed to put a premium on expansion of industry and the risking of private money in the development of new and old enterprises.

The capital gains tax should be substantially modified, so that such risks as result in profit may not be subjected to high surtaxes.

Above all, the laws must be administered with a constant effort to encourage the development of private industry. There must be a real sympathy with its success, a real desire to relieve it from unnecessary harassment and discouragement. There must be a recognition of the fact that the making of profits is not a crime; that the average businessman, making a success in his own business, is an essential cog in the national machine, and ought to be encouraged, as long as it does not cost the taxpayer any money.

I am convinced that we can restore prosperity. We have come out of every past depression by the recovery of private industry. The American people are the same people they were in the twenties. They have the same ingenuity and courage and determination. Human nature is the same now as it was then. There are just as many wants unsatisfied, or more. There are just as many economic and scientific frontiers as there ever were. After all, it is fifty years since we had any physical frontiers, and most of that time we have been a prosperous nation. It can be done, but it cannot be done by government regulation of agriculture and commerce and industry.

The Problem of Budget Deficits

The other new problem which must be solved is that of adjusting our expenses to our income. How can we maintain the humanitarian measures I have described within a tax system that does not completely bog down the industrial machine? If anything is certain, it is that a continuation of the present policy of reckless expenditure, without regard to taxes, can only lead to bankruptcy, repudiation, and a breakdown of our entire economic life. No government has ever continued a deficit policy without ultimate repudiation. Sooner or later the time comes when the burden of debt is so great that the people refuse to meet the expense of the interest. The temptation to pay in paper money becomes politically irresistible. Leading as it must to inflated prices, it wipes out the savings of the people and bears down most heavily on the groups with fixed income, to the benefit only of successful speculators. If we ever reach the point which Germany reached after the World War, it is doubtful if we could ever reestablish a system based on thrift and saving and investment of funds in private enterprise. The American system as we know it would not survive.

People say that the budget cannot be balanced, but of course it can be if a courageous government determines that it shall be. Expenses can be reduced; taxes can be increased. Probably a combination of both will be necessary. The people must face the fact that if we are going to give government help to the more unfortunate families, through relief, pensions, insurance, housing, and medical assistance, that help will have to be supplied by those who do not require it themselves. It cannot come from the rich, because if we confiscate all the incomes over $10,000 a year, we would only get $7 billion, and the total tax bill today is already $18 billion. It can only come from the two-thirds who are not underprivileged—from the average prudent and successful workman.

The only people who can support men and women who do not work are those who are working. Obviously the humanitarian measures must be administered as economically as possible. Pensions cannot be carelessly increased, as the Congress has just increased the old-age pension from $30 to $40, unless a majority of the people are willing to pay the taxes necessary to pay the increase. I was shocked by the fact that Wednesday a dozen senators voted a pension which would cost the people $5 billion without the slightest suggestion of any way in which the money could possibly be raised. There must be an utter repudiation of that point of view.

Furthermore, these laws should be administered so that the recipients of government assistance are not placed in a better position through that assistance than the other workmen with private jobs, who have saved their own money and have to provide the taxes. There has been too much tendency on the part of each department to look only at its own job, and try to please its wards by a liberal administration in its particular field. The man who lives in government housing should not be better off than the man who has built his own home out of his own savings. The man who gets an old-age pension should not be better off than he who has spent his life in making provision for his own old age. In short, measures to assist the lower-income groups must be administered with just as much consideration for the middle-income groups,

The Forgotten Man

Wendell Willkie, a utilities executive, was the surprise choice for the Republican presidential nomination in 1940. In his June 28 speech accepting the nomination, he argues that the New Deal has not helped the average American.

When the present administration came to power in 1933, we heard a lot about the forgotten man. The Government, we were told, must care for those who had no other means of support. With this proposition all of us agreed. And we still hold firmly to the principle that those whom private industry cannot support must be supported by government agency, whether federal or state.

But I want to ask anyone in this audience who is, or has been, on relief whether the support that the Government gives him is enough. Is it enough for the free and able-bodied American to be given a few scraps of cash or credit with which to keep himself and his children just this side of starvation and nakedness? Is that what the forgotten man wanted us to remember?

What that man wanted us to remember was his chance—his right—to take part in our great American adventure.

But this administration never remembered that. It launched a vitriolic and well-planned attack against those very industries in which the forgotten man wanted a chance.

who have to do the paying, as for the lower-income groups.

The budget can be balanced. Economy can be secured even in relief without decreasing its efficiency. If administration were returned to the localities, with full discretion to administer both work relief and direct relief in the manner best suited to local conditions, the federal government would pay less, even though it supplied two-thirds of the entire cost. There would be far more equal treatment of those on relief; more liberal treatment for direct relief clients than today. Housing can be cheaper, and there does not need to be the large subsidy required by the present program. . . .

The Need to Economize

It is no easy task to economize. It cannot be done effectively over the opposition of the Executive, for many federal policies can be changed only by affirmative legislation, which the Executive can block. For instance, until the relief policy is completely changed, we must go on voting the appropriations required by the present WPA [Works Progress Administration] system. Economy cannot be secured piecemeal, for each project has its appeal, and often a very attractive appeal. Some leadership must develop a plan for balancing the budget within two years and hold

Congress to it.

This is the proper function of the Executive, but if the Executive will not do it, Congress will have to create a budget committee of its own. The findings of such a committee can only be carried through with a strong leadership for economy, backed by a majority of the members in both houses of Congress. I feel confident that expenses can be reduced by several billions of dollars; that a tax system can produce the necessary income in a way that will not destroy the very income which is to provide the taxes. It can be done, but it cannot be done by neglecting the fundamental principles of common sense.

VIEWPOINT 3

"In the past three and a half years more progress has been made in providing security . . . than during the whole history of the nation."

The Federal Government Has Improved Relief Programs for the Poor

Harry Hopkins (1890-1946)

Harry Hopkins was one of Franklin D. Roosevelt's closest aides, both during Roosevelt's New York governorship and in the White House. As administrative head of the Federal Emergency Relief Administration (1933-34), the Civil Works Administration (1933-34), and the Work Projects Administration (1935-40), Hopkins distributed more than $10 billion in relief and public jobs and was a key figure in the unprecedented involvement of the federal government in economic relief. He later served Roosevelt as secretary of commerce and as an adviser during World War II.

The following viewpoint is taken from a 1936 book Hopkins wrote titled *Spend to Save*. Hopkins describes how the federal government relief programs took shape under his direction, and he defends their goals and accomplishments. He argues that the government has the responsibility to provide employment in times of economic hardship.

Excerpts from *Spend to Save* by Harry Hopkins are reprinted by permission of W.W. Norton and Company, Inc. Copyright © 1936 by W. W. Norton and Company, Inc.

When under the Federal Emergency Relief Act of May 12th, the Federal Emergency Relief Administration came into existence on May 22, 1933, it assumed two responsibilities. One of them was financial. Congress had made available to it $500,000,000 to be spent cooperatively with the states in taking care of the unemployed. In the next four years of the relief administration, Congress was to increase its trust with larger sums to a total of more than $6,000,000,000 for the relief of unemployment. I believe it can be truthfully said that none of this has ever clung to the hands of any official who has had a part in spending it. . . .

I have said that Congress charged the relief administration with two responsibilities. The second was the care of eighteen million persons. Four million destitute American families looked to us for their very existence.

We can make less cheerful account of the way we have met this second charge upon us. It is curious that among the almost innumerable criticisms we have experienced, the one most truthful allegation is never made except by the families who depend upon us. We have never given adequate relief. We can only say that out of every dollar entrusted to us for the lessening of their distress, the maximum amount humanly possible was put into their hands.

Three Governmental Groups

Our immediate task was to set up machinery for this job. Federal participation in emergency relief brought many significant changes in relief practices. In general three governmental groups were involved in the administration of relief: the Federal government, the state governments, and the local governments. The bulk of the work of administering relief rested in the local governments. The investigation of relief clients, the determination of need, the administration of work relief projects, and innumerable activities connected with the disbursement of funds to the people in need were all conducted by local officials of the local relief administrations. Contrary to a popular misconception, the Federal government did not directly administer relief in the localities. Local governments in their relief activities were supervised by the state emergency relief administrations, and in turn the state administrations were subject to a minimum of Federal regulations. These regulations were essential to assure relatively uniform standards and honest administration of the funds. Thus the emergency relief program has been primarily a local relief program, operated by local relief officials, but financed largely by Federal funds. We decided that all sums should be spent only through public agencies. There existed a large army of professional social workers and of public spirited citizens who, as paid or as volunteer workers, had been struggling with this overwhelming burden of dependency before the relief administration opened its doors. We felt that if these persons were to help administer public relief, they should come upon the public payroll and be paid commensurately with other public servants.

Over and above these persons in the states there had to be chosen some outstanding man for state administrator who would have a well-knit organization under him. We have found that long experience at public or social work did not necessarily qualify a man for such untried responsibilities.

From the beginning we strove to make methods of emergency relief differ deeply from practices of local poor relief, which still held a heavy hand over many local agencies. Under the philosophy of this ancient practice, the applicant was in some way morally deficient. He must be made to feel his pauperism. Every help which was given him was to be given in a way to intensify his sense of shame. Usually he was forced to plead his destitution in an offensively dreary room. We asked for the establishment of respectable light quarters conveniently placed in the neighborhoods of those who had to use them. We tried to have the applicant received by an intelligent and sympathetic human being who did not, in his own mind, put a stigma upon the unfortunate person before him. We tried to see that relief officials were people who understood that the predicament of the worker without a job is an economic predicament not of his own making; that his religion, race or party is irrelevant. His need was the only thing that had to be established. . . .

Hard Decisions

Probably the worst decisions that we have had to make, and those of the most far-reaching importance, have been those which have determined or affected the adequacy of relief. Each decision had finally to rest with the judgment of a handful of men whose opinion might be no better than that of several others who would have come to a different conclusion. Although for each family it might entail the expense of no more than a few cents, or more than a few dollars, it ran into millions.

Should we pay the rent? There was never a clearcut decision on this. Sometimes we did and sometimes we did not. For a lack of full acceptance of that responsibility thousands of landlords have taken a loss, and millions of families have seen themselves moved from the hill to the hollow; consecutively from good quarters to bad, from bad into worse.

Should we pay hospital bills? This we decided in the negative and hospitals have been overburdened with the weight of sickness and dependency which fell upon them. We paid for medicine and sometimes for the doctor.

Should we place in institutions those dependents of a family who most obviously belonged there? We decided against this also and families already unsettled with want and strain were further demoralized by the burden.

The federal Works Progress Administration (WPA), which operated from 1935 to 1943, employed more than eight million Americans at an average monthly wage of $54.33.

AP/Wide World Photos

We made such decisions because the first thing for which our money had to go was food to keep people alive. In more places than could be believed, families had been asked to live on two dollars a month. In spite of the fact that we were able to raise relief from such a sum to at least fifteen dollars, and that we have probably left behind us a basic minimum unprecedented in many communities, we must admit that our prevalent standard had no margin of safety, even after nutrition advisers had educated women as to how to get the maximum nourishment from the food which was allowed them. There have been families who have had less than they wanted to eat and little that they liked. . . .

During these early months, the attitude of the American community was undergoing a deep change. By no means all the comfortable citizens who watched their fellows go hungry had been indifferent to their misery. Frustrated by lack of means of aiding them, they had been forced into helplessness. A new spirit now took hold of them. Capable leaders assumed larger tasks. Men and women who had never been in public work in their lives left homes and offices to help. An entirely new group of public servants were enlisting, were being drafted, and being trained. A new standard of public decency was being set. . . .

As a nation we were beginning to acknowledge that our economic distress was no overnight disaster which would recede some fine morning like the waters of a flood. Direct relief might do to tide over a few months or a year, or even longer. But millions had already been out of a job for several years. In addition to want, the unemployed were confronting a still further destructive force, that of worklessness. This feeling became articulate in many quarters, but most particularly among the unemployed themselves. Letters came, delegations arrived, protesting against the indignity of public charity. Men who had never in their lives asked for, or accepted, a cent of alms refused to believe that the situation had gone into permanent reverse. It made no difference to them in what pretty words the unattractive fact of their dependency was dressed. It was charity and they didn't like it. They were accustomed to making a return for their livelihood. It was a habit they liked, and from which they chiefly drew their self-respect. The family of a man working on a Works Progress Administration project looks down its nose at neighbors who take their relief straight. We can talk all we want to about some coming civilization in which work will be outmoded, and in which we shall enjoy a state of being rather than one of action, but contemporary sentiment is still against "a man who gets something for nothing." Those who voluntarily take something for nothing are put in jail. Those who are forced to accept charity, no matter how unwillingly, are first pitied, then disdained.

As we are educated further into the ways and means of social security we should be able to remove this cloud from the man who has no other choice than to be a pensioner. In our own anxiety to achieve a work program I think we as an administration have perhaps overemphasized the undesirability of relief, inasmuch as we have not been able to remove from hundreds of thousands of people the inescapability of accepting it. . . .

America has spent the last few years in the counting house. Only a few will say we have been counting out our money only. We have counted our national wealth and our national income. We have counted our poverty, and I have tried here to give a part of the new audit. We have measured our will and our intelligence. From our inventory we have emerged, as a nation, with the conviction that there is no need for any American to be destitute, to be illiterate, to be reduced by the bondage of these things into either political or economic impotence.

The Rights of Americans

We are sometimes accused of stirring up class hatreds when we say such things. On the contrary, I believe that under national scrutiny all Americans are revealed as Americans, with rights as well as obligations; that there is coming out of our new knowledge of who Americans are and how they live a reunion of forces which had flown so far apart that they no longer knew each other.

The ways by which more and more people can have their rightful share of the national income I shall leave to the experts, the legislators, and to forces of labor who are intent on bringing this about. If we had no other reason for it than to keep the system going, ways would have to be figured out by which the worker could buy back his full share of the goods he helped to put through the mill of national business. There is, however, another way of looking at it. One may believe that the human being should come first, and the serviceability of the economic system in which he functions should be estimated by the number of persons who share in its rewards. There is reason to think that the present system is capable of giving to all its workers those things which are now the expectations of a comparative few: a warm, decent place to live in; a liberal diet; suitable clothes; travel, vacations, automobiles, radios, and college educations for those who want them. Even one who does not pretend to be an expert on the subject can see a few fairly obvious means by which we can approach the problem of redistribution. Wages must be raised and hours lowered. Unfair profits will have to be translated into lower unit price. Some three million persons over sixty years of age should be taken out of the labor market. Most of them are there not because they want to be, but from dire necessity. Compulsory school age, with some exceptions, probably should be raised, and young boys removed from competition with their fathers.

Until the time comes, if it ever does, when industry and business can absorb all able-bodied workers—and that time seems to grow more distant with improvements in management and technology—we shall have with us large numbers of unemployed. Intelligent people have long since left behind them the notion that under fullest recovery, and even with improved purchasing power, the unemployed will disappear as dramatically as they made their appearance after 1929.

Even if they did so disappear, there would still remain with us the people who cannot work, or should not, and who have no one to support them; the too old, the too young, mothers with small children, the sick and crippled. These people cannot be left to fumble their way along alone; to be sent from one vacillating agency to another, given something one month and not the next, with almost nothing in the present and, so far as they know, nothing at all in the future. For them a security program is the only answer. In the past three and a half years more progress has been made in providing security for them than during the whole history of the nation. The Social Security Board has been set up; appropriations have been made, public education has begun, but most important, over one million unemployable persons are already receiving its benefits. We need only to refine, extend and consolidate gains that have been made in order to provide minimum security for all of them.

The Works Progress Administration

In its May 20, 1940, issue, The New Republic, *a liberal magazine, published an editorial evaluating Roosevelt's second term. The magazine praised many aspects of the New Deal, including public employment programs such as the Works Progress Administration.*

The WPA was established in January, 1935. The shortcomings of the WPA have been greatly overstressed, but they are insignificant beside the gigantic fact that it has given jobs and sustenance to a minimum of 1,400,000 and a maximum of 3,300,000 persons for five years. Its work projects have added immeasurably to the national wealth; in some regions the school, health and recreation facilities it has called into existence have fairly revolutionized communal life. It must also be remembered that, as its permanent technique for dealing with the relief problem, the New Deal has been simultaneously developing its programs for unemployment insurance, old-age pensions, assistance to mothers, dependent children and the handicapped.

Many who wanted the continuance of Federal relief by grants in aid to states, contended that if you gave unemployable people back to the care of the states, they would be neglected. In some places, even widely, this has proved to be true. States should never pass them on to the niggardly and degrading practices of county and township poor relief. Federal aid, I believe, should be given through the Social Security Board which, with similar state and local boards, should pass this benefit as a pension without stigma to those who need it. If this is to be done, it is equally clear that the Social Security Board must be given power to regulate standards of administration in states and cities. Too small a benefit will not serve the purpose of a pension. Political control of the manner in which it is administered would destroy it. An adequate civil service made up of permanent employees is absolutely essential to the success of any pension system.

Assurance as to the source of such large sums is of paramount importance. At the present time, because it makes initial expenditures, the local community determines the amount of pensions. As I have said before, local funds in the main come from a tax on real estate. For an enlarging program of inevitably increasing outgo, the real estate tax is too thin a reed to lean upon. We should at once consider coordination of tax methods to assure a fair and equitable distribution of the tax base.

There will remain, however, as the responsibility of government, a standing army of able-bodied workers who have no jobs. Probably for years to come it will be an army of substantial size. It will be flexible, increasing and decreasing with seasons, with changes in production habits and industrial geography, but chiefly, until we have vanquished it, changing with cyclical unemployment. If we keep it in training so that only by sickness or old age will its members lapse into unemployability, it can be a reserve drawn upon by private undertakings at any time they need new labor and are willing to pay the going wage for it. Private businesses or industries, however, cannot be asked to keep upon their payrolls large numbers of workers whom they cannot use.

What is the outlook for these unemployed? First, workers must have unemployment insurance. This is part of any social security program. An insurance benefit, however, will not tide a man through an indefinite period of unemployment. Nor will it take care of the annual net increase of over 400,000 workers who come of age each year, and the other young who have never had jobs. It will not take care of the casual laborer, the agricultural or the household worker. The Social Security Act potentially covers only about half the workers in the nation. One of the first necessities is to see if it cannot be given greater coverage.

To me, the only possible solution for those who cannot be absorbed by long-time or large-scale public works is a work program. I believe we must continue such a program until other forces produce a very substantial increase in the volume of employment. Some people would like to turn the unemployed back to the communities. Others advocate restoration of Federal relief. They would permit local governments to share the cost, but they would give local governments complete discretion as to the size and the character of the benefit. What we might expect of such a benefit, how large it would be and in what manner administered has already been indicated to us by the fate of many unemployables who have already suffered from it.

Behind their arguments is a natural desire to make unemployment relief cheaper. There is widespread feeling that by some mysterious means an unemployed person will not eat so much or require such warm clothes if his relief is given by the local community as if it were given through a Federal plan in cooperation with states or municipalities. Granted that direct relief is cheaper, the nation will get no return on its money if it goes back to direct relief. We shall go through the gesture of keeping people alive. For all its tremendous natural wealth, the American people are the greatest resource of the country. So far men and women, with few exceptions, have found no substitute for useful work to keep themselves sound of body and mind. In other words, work conserves them as a national asset, and lack of work lets them sink into a national liability. . . .

We are beginning to wonder if it is not presumptuous to take for granted that some people should have much, and some should have nothing; that some people are less important than others and should die earlier; that the children of the comfortable should be taller and fatter, as a matter of right, than the children of the poor.

The Children of the Poor

It finally whittles itself down, I suppose, to a matter of the children, since we ourselves are not likely to see all those ends accomplished toward which we strive. Suppose we place two grown men beside each other. One has been given all the privileges of his time, and has made good use of them; the other has never had a glimpse of privilege. The first is healthy; the second sick from neglect. If we were told that one was going to be abandoned, and the other encouraged to carry on, which one should we choose to keep? In a democracy, no matter how conspicuously we fail to operate upon the principle, we don't admit that one man has more right to live than another. Yet realistically, it would be easy to say which is the more useful member of society.

Put two children in their place. Upon one child privilege has only started to take effect. Neglect of the other has scarcely begun. How shall the choice be made between them, and who will dare to be the chooser?

VIEWPOINT 4

"Relief in a good part of the United States is crumbling under the impact of the recession."

The Federal Government Has Failed to Adequately Provide for the Poor

Samuel Lubell (1911-1987) and Walter Everett (dates unknown)

The recession of 1937-38 was in some respects as severe as the early years of the Great Depression. Unemployment rose by four million people, and the work relief rolls of the Works Progress Administration swelled by 500 percent. The following viewpoint is by journalists Samuel Lubell and Walter Everett, who investigated the state of relief programs and reported the findings in the August 20, 1938, issue of *The Nation* magazine. Lubell and Everett describe exhausted relief programs in many communities that were unable to adequately provide for the welfare of the poor. They criticize the New Deal for not going far enough in providing relief and recognizing that unemployment may be a permanent, not a temporary, problem.

Samuel Lubell and Walter Everett, "The Breakdown of Relief," *The Nation*, August 20, 1938, © 1938, The Nation Company, Inc. Reprinted with permission.

Relief in a good part of the United States is crumbling under the impact of the recession like a town rocked by a series of earthquakes. In some cities relief agencies have already slammed their doors against thousands in dire need. Akron's reliefers must keep body and soul together on twelve cents a person for a day's food. Cleveland's poor are still begging from door to door and foraging in garbage cans. Detroit's jobless sick must trust to God or nature if their illnesses require any but the cheapest drugs. Evictions have became a daily routine in Chicago. Distress and suffering are spreading like the plague.

For five weeks we have been touring industrial cities in western Pennsylvania, Ohio, Indiana, Michigan, and Illinois—places where the recession hit the hardest. Everywhere unemployment is almost as great as during the blackest days of the depression, and relief loads are even heavier. One out of every six families in Pittsburgh either is receiving direct relief or is on the WPA [Work Projects Administration]; one out of five in Chicago; one out of four in Akron; more than one out of four in Detroit; one out of three in Cleveland; one out of two in Flint. Most of the cities and some of the states have plunged neck-deep into debt to provide even miserable handouts. Many communities are on the brink of default. Virtually none have funds to last longer than the next few months.

Cutbacks in Relief

Food, clothing, and shelter budgets for families receiving direct relief have been lopped so drastically and so generally that it is impossible to measure the results in human suffering. After the first few days of traveling through "dole slums," we came to expect that children six, seven, and eight years old would have legs as spindly as the starving Armenians for whom we used to contribute our pennies. Regional WPA officials estimate that in Ohio, Indiana, Michigan, and Illinois budgets have been slashed on the average 20 to 50 per cent. And that cut has been made since the start of the recession, when "economy" had already lowered relief standards below the level of adequacy set by private charities.

Wilfred S. Reynolds, director of the Council of Social Agencies in Chicago, estimates the city's standard relief budget to be 15 per cent below his agency's definition of adequacy. In the last six months that already inadequate budget has been reduced by something like half. Even now, with fresh funds appropriated by the special session of the legislature in May, there is no allotment for electricity or gas. Food allotments have been maintained at "par," but those getting aid must do their purchasing in daily dribbles, for ice is not included. Medical care is furnished "when required," half-rent "when necessary." The "when required" generally means in an emergency; the "when necessary" could be translated "when evicted."

The stark implications of the Depression were chronicled and preserved by photographers, including Dorothea Lange, who shot this poignant image. Lange gained fame in the 1930s with her series of photographs of poor agricultural workers and their families.

Chicago, like many other cities, has adopted the intriguing policy of letting rent payments run behind until the landlord's patience is exhausted and the family evicted. Only when the client comes into the district office with a court order to move in forty-eight hours will relief authorities give him a month's rent for a new flat. Housing conditions of relief families are indescribable. Some landlords refuse to rent to persons without a job. Those who accept them generally offer lodgings that no regular rent-payer would take. Joel D. Hunter, head of Chicago's United Charities, told us of one house into which sixteen Negro families had moved. Separated by beaverboards, sixty persons lived in that one-family dwelling, some of the smaller children sleeping in wardrobe drawers.

Leo Hart, an organizer for the Steel Workers' Organizing Committee in South Chicago, said hardly a day passed without some union member being put out on the street. As many nonunionists must be behind in rent. Hart took us to see Louis Carillo, a steel worker, who had been evicted a week before with his eight children. The Carillos had found temporary lodgings in a friend's home. We entered through a smelly alley and a yard formed of cinder dumpings and rubbish. The Illinois Central tracks ran beside the house; across the tracks was a bookie establishment. Carillo's furniture was still in the truck. In the driver's seat, sprawled over two pillows, without sheets, was one of the Carillo children. That driver's seat was the boy's bed at night.

Carillo is a Mexican who came to Chicago in 1924. We found him wearing a battered hat, soiled shirt, torn trousers, and suspenders with one snapper gone. He hadn't shaved for two days, and the graying tips of his whiskers stood out against his dark skin. He spoke with an accent. "I jus' found myself a shack. I'll move later today. I bin stayin' here as long as I could get away with it. This my first time bin evicted. My girl got sick in 1936—her lungs," he went on. "We took her to the hospital. It did her good! Then, they told me they didn't have enough money to keep her. We had to take her home. It was cold in our house. She got worse." Carillo's thirteen-year-old daughter was spared the ordeal of the eviction, though. She died last May.

It is a mistake to think that the Illinois legislature solved Chicago's relief ills. It is even more of an error to speak of the relief crises of cities like Cleveland, Toledo, Dayton, and Columbus in the past tense. The law passed by the Ohio Assembly will go about as far in meeting the relief problems of these and other Ohio cities as a cup of coffee and a flop for the night would go in making a new man out of a panhandler. These cities already are several million dollars in red. All the new law does is allow them to go deeper into debt by mortgaging tax receipts for the next three years. When we left Cleveland late in June enough money had been scraped together for food orders for ten days. Last week a relief worker whom we had befriended there wrote us in Chicago. "Things remain in the same general state as in June. The city has borrowed some money from the bankers. Four-day orders are being issued but only for the most urgent cases. The others beg and forage as they did in the spring."

Relief Administrator Frank E. Bubna described conditions in Cleveland as "about the same as in the worst part of the depression, if anything a little worse." Cleveland's movie houses are crowded; its ball park is packed. But for weeks the authorities were unable even to provide milk for needy children, and the WPA's supplies of skimmed milk, dried beans, flour, and vegetables were all the poor had to eat. It was the Federal Surplus Commodities Corporation that made good Mayor Harold Burton's promise that "no one will starve." The WPA has stretched its definition of "employable" so that every man who can so much as hold a tool and sign a time-sheet has been certified. WPA rolls have leaped from 20,000 last fall to almost 75,000 in mid-July. Only about 18,000 families are on direct relief, fewer than the city has cared for at any other time since the crash. Cleveland's total industrial pay roll has been estimated as around $2,600,000 a week. The WPA is spending upward of $1,250,000 weekly....

Roosevelt's Failures

Norman Thomas, running for president as the Socialist candidate, attacked Roosevelt's record on relief in a 1936 campaign speech.

[Some people claim Roosevelt] has helped most of the workers, including the unemployed, and he has made it easier to organize them. Yes, as compared with Hoover, yet how little has been done.

Help for the unemployed? More than ten million still in the sorrowful ranks of men, workless and unwanted. Not the 3½ million Roosevelt promised to put to work at relief jobs, but some 2 million. And those at wages as low at $19 a month in certain regions. Relief shot through with politics. An insecurity, not a security, law which puts the burden of unemployment insurance on the workers as consumers and gives the bosses a premium on increasing technological unemployment. No program of new housing to aid employment and end slums.

Unemployment and relief obviously are permanent problems. But still state legislatures won't admit it. The Ohio General Assembly, dominated by the rural members, has persistently refused to allot relief funds for more than six months in advance. Rural prejudices have been fanned by Governor Martin L. Davey and a powerful business lobby, the Inter-Organization Conference. Ohio's cities can solve their relief problems only by obtaining the power to raise funds through taxes. The sole purpose of the Inter-Organization Conference has been to defeat any and all tax proposals. Since 1935, when the conference was set up, no new tax laws have been enacted. The Illinois Manufacturers' Association, which has fought relief appropriations as consistently, seems animated by the same type of reasoning. At a conference called by Governor Henry Horner to discuss the need for a special session last spring, a representative of the association heatedly argued: "We can't keep feeding these bums forever."

Nine years of depression and widespread unemployment, five years of relief administration by government agencies, and still there isn't a city in this entire area that has anything resembling a sound relief policy! The mental bankruptcy of public officials is evidenced by their frantic "purges." Cleveland hired a private agency to make "credit investigations" of sample relief clients at $3 a head, only to net "savings" that weren't sufficient to meet the investigators' bills. In Cincinnati relief authorities abruptly dropped all clients and had them reapply. Perhaps they hoped some of the needy would lose the address of relief headquarters in the shuffle.

Illinois is administering its relief program in truly medieval fashion through townships. The townships raise their own funds, set their own standards. There are more than 1,400 of them—townships and standards. Relief taxes are levied on real property, which means that the richer townships can do without state assistance, while the poorer communities, where the need is greatest, collect so little that even with state aid essential items have to be restricted.

Illinois, Michigan, and Ohio have no income tax. Instead of financing their relief programs in this way, they have resorted to sales taxes—levies which take their toll even out of relief checks.

Failed Programs

Millions of dollars are being spent on relief—expenditures have soared to a new high and still are mounting—but to no one's satisfaction: not to those on relief, who are getting barely enough to keep alive; not to officials administering relief, who are powerless to stop the deterioration, physical, mental, and moral, that is going on among relief clients; not to the taxpayer, who wonders where it will all end and what lasting good is being accomplished. And all because the country refuses to recognize that relief is a permanent problem, that bare subsistence handouts cannot take the place of rehabilitation.

VIEWPOINT 5

"It is not only perilous if we do not start soon to approach a balanced budget, but it will be disastrous."

Government Spending Should Be Reduced

Harry F. Byrd (1887-1966)

The recession of 1937-38 compelled President Roosevelt to increase federal spending for relief and economic stimulus. Such policies were increasingly opposed by many who viewed the recession as the result of too much government interference and excessive federal budget deficits. Conflicts over the necessity of federal spending existed both within and without the Roosevelt administration.

The following viewpoint is taken from a December 10, 1938, speech by Harry F. Byrd delivered before the Massachusetts Federation of Taxpayers. Byrd, a former governor of Virginia, entered the U.S. Senate in 1933 as a supporter of Franklin D. Roosevelt. However, within a few years he became one of the leaders of conservative Democratic opposition to the New Deal. In the following speech he attacks what he viewed as wasteful government spending, arguing that balancing the budget should be a top government priority. Among his targets for criticism is Marriner S. Eccles, the head of the Federal Reserve System and an advocate of helping the economy with government spending.

Throughout his long Senate career, Byrd maintained his opposition to increasing the size, spending, and power of the federal government. He resigned his seat in 1965 and was replaced by his son, Harry F. Byrd, Jr.

From Harry F. Byrd, "National Financial Preparedness: The Brain-trusters Should Go Home," a speech delivered to the Massachusetts Federation of Taxpayers Associations, Boston, December 10, 1938. Reprinted in *Vital Speeches of the Day* 5 (January 15, 1939): 219-22.

It is a particular honor and a particular pleasure for a Virginian to be permitted to address this distinguished gathering of Massachusetts citizens. I am delighted to come here as the guest of the Massachusetts Federation of Taxpayers, whose constructive work is well known to me. Today nothing is more important than to bring to the citizens of our nation a true understanding of the complex administration of our governments and baptize ourselves afresh in the pure principles of representative democracy. . . .

The sacred responsibility of preserving representative democracy rests upon the shoulders of American citizens because here it has flowered to the fullest perfection in freedom and in our progress and our development. Preserve it not only for ourselves and Americans who came after us, but as an inspiration and encouragement to the depressed peoples in other lands who seek the blessings of the freedom we enjoy here.

Democracy must be made efficient. Democracy must be made effective to meet conditions and new problems, but this, and all of this, can be accomplished within the framework of our constitutional government, and preserve as a continuing vital force the fundamental principles which are just as valid today as ever before. . . .

For the past several years we have had at Washington much loose talk and loose thinking of a new liberalism which will sweep away the clouds of depression; wave a magic wand of legislative panaceas for our ills and give a substitute for those time-old virtues of thrift, frugality, self-reliance and industry that have made our country great and given to us a progress, a freedom, a happiness, a contentment that has never before been enjoyed by any great nation. From my own personal observation in the Senate of the United States, a modern liberal is tested and judged in proportion as to how liberal he is willing to be with other people's money. If a senator votes to squander the people's money for every fantastic spending scheme devised in the human mind, he is a great liberal. If a senator acts to safe-guard the public treasury, to spend the taxpayers' money judiciously, and only for necessary and useful functions, he is proclaimed a "reactionary," "an economic royalist," and more recently a "copperhead."

Calling names never solved a problem or offered a solution for difficulties. For myself, how I am classified in the public life of America is of little concern to me. I am a Democrat. I have voted my convictions and owe my allegiance to my constituents of Virginia and to my oath as a senator of the United States. I intend to take orders from no man, no matter how powerful he may be. I prefer to be a "Yes, but, Senator" to a "Yes, Yes, Senator.". . .

Today the time has come to analyze, to appraise the good as well as the bad, and to pass judgment on the vast legislation adopted by the National Congress in the past six years. Our last election indicates very clearly that the American people intend to do this very thing, and are doing it. In this analysis let us remember that the real test of a law—the real worth of legislation—is in practical administration and effect upon all the millions of our citizens, and that a principle enacted into a law—a just and fair principle—is often defeated by the maladministration of its operation.

"Nonsense, if it gets too deep, you can easily pull me out."

With much important legislation enacted in this period, I can heartily agree. I have been in accord with the foreign policies of our government. I have supported Secretary Cordell Hull in his efforts to regain our foreign trade and to repair some of the damage of the Hawley-Smoot Tariff Bill signed by President Hoover. I have supported adequate national defense and will continue to do so unless national defense is used merely as a means of pump priming and public spending. I favored control of the New York Stock Exchange and will vote for greater control to eliminate existing abuses. I am opposed to monopolies that operate to throttle competition and fix prices. I applaud the remarkably fine work done in the reorganization of the banking system. As a member of a Special Committee of the Finance Committee to consider a revision of the social security legislation, I will support measures to reform and strengthen and make workable a social security program within the ability of our citizenship to support. Social security, in one form or another, is here to stay.

In surveying recent legislation, remember that private enterprise is the foundation stone on which our Republic is founded. Private enterprise, and not the government, must provide employment for our citizens. Private enterprise is the motor that provides the taxes for our government to operate. If taxes become confiscatory, if governmental regimentation becomes too oppressive, if governmental competition becomes too destructive, then private enterprise can neither pay the taxes nor give employment to the workers. Remember too that the character of our individual citizen is our most valuable national possession, and the character of many can and will be injured, if not destroyed, by unrestricted and profligate public relief, as character comes from self-help and industry and not from idleness and thriftlessness. The very immensity of our relief expenditures has made impractical the confinement of relief to those actually in need—an obligation that all of us recognize must be met in the fullest measure—with the result that millions of able-bodied citizens rely upon the government for support and have ceased to exert their effort for self-help and to obtain private employment.

A grant to the states by the Federal government is not a gift. Nothing would curb the wanton extravagance in our Federal government more than a recognition of this very simple and elementary principle. Actually every grant from the Federal government in the past five years has in fact been a mortgage, and a first mortgage, on the property of every citizen in each of the 48 states. In this confederation of states—United States of America—the parent government has no money except such as is derived from the states by taxation. It has no security on which to borrow except the property of the citizens of the 48 states, so instead of a grant being a gift, the states are given a mortgage to pay with accrued interest, and the bureaucrats at Washington take a toll for top-heavy administrative cost, which, in some instances, as I have shown on the floor of the Senate, has equaled a full 33 per cent of the sum expended.

A Wasteful Government

As one who for three years has been investigating our federal expenditures as Chairman of the Select Committee on Investigation of Executive Agencies of the Government, I assert that we have at Washington today the most costly, the most wasteful and most bureaucratic form of government this Republic has ever known or any other nation has been afflicted with.

For nine years we have spent more than our income for recovery and relief. Our deficit for the current fiscal year will be the largest in peace-time history. For recovery and relief we have spent $27,000,000,000 since the depression began. In addition, we have borrowed and loaned $8,000,000,000 more to citizens and corporations, much of which, I predict, will never be repaid to our government. Our debt in 1932 was $16,000,000,000, with no contingent liabilities. On July 1, next, we will owe at least $41,000,000,000 in direct debt and will have a contingent liability, which is not listed on the financial statements of the government and of which no government official has made announcement. This liability is just as much an obligation as the reported debt. Thirty government corporations have been organized with authority to issue bonds, debentures and notes to the amount of $16,229,325,000. These obligations when issued are guaranteed in full for principal and interest by the government of the United States, but I repeat are not included in the debt you find reported in the Treasury statements. With much difficulty, I have ascertained that on June 1, last, bonds, debentures and notes had been issued by these corporations, over three-fourths having been sold to the public to the amount of $7,940,462,000, so that our actual debt on July 1, next, will approach $50,000,000,000. . . .

Our situation today, in brief, is this:

We have trebled the public debt in five years. This debt is now an average of over $1,000,000,000 for each state, and the interest before this debt is paid will be more than the debt itself. The federal appropriations in this current year are the largest in peace-time history. Our tax collections for the year ending last July were the largest. Yet in the present fiscal year our deficit will be the largest peace-time deficit. In the ninth consecutive year of great deficits, we are farther away—and I say this advisedly—farther away from a balanced budget than at any time since the depression began.

The Federal government alone is spending $23,000 every minute of every day and every night including Sunday, and of this $11,500 is being added each minute to the public debt.

Coincident with the rise in the federal debt and increase in federal taxation have come similar increases in the burdens of the states and localities. The Federal government has demanded the same prodigality of spending by the other governmental units of our Republic, and the sovereign state of Georgia has only recently been publicly reprimanded because that state was reluctant to amend its constitution to issue state bonds and abandon its wise and frugal policy of pay-as-you-go.

This current year, the fiscal year of 1939, the expenditures of all governments in America will be more than $20,000,000,000, or about one-third of the total gross income of this nation, and this $20,000,000,000 is more than twice the value of all products that come from the soil and under the ground, all the products of the farm; including livestock, the products of the forest and the products of the mines. How long can a Republic exist spending one-third of its gross income and twice the value of the new wealth that comes from the soil? . . .

A Perilous Situation

We are facing a perilous situation and what can be done about it? Can we expect any leadership from the present administration for economy and retrenchment? As one who has fought for five years for prudent spending at Washington, I say no. As a Democrat I say it with sorrow, as my party is in power, but the Republican party cannot escape responsibility for their share in the present orgy of spending. Mr. Hoover added the first five billions to the public debt and a majority of the Republican members in the Senate have voted for the huge appropriation bills.

Government Spending

Wendell Willkie, Roosevelt's third Republican opponent for president, attacks government spending in his June 28, 1940, speech accepting the Republican nomination.

The New Deal believes, as frequently declared, that the spending of vast sums by the government is a virtue in itself. They tell us that government spending insures recovery. Where is the recovery?

The New Deal stands for doing what has to be done by spending as much money as possible. I propose to do it by spending as little money as possible. This is one great issue in domestic policy and I propose in this campaign to make it clear.

So long as the economic philosophy of such men as Chairman [Marriner] Eccles of the Federal Reserve Board dominates the fiscal policies of the present administration, no leadership from those in high places in Washington to restore the country to a sane budget policy can be hoped for. Mr. Eccles, one of the sponsors of the discredited undivided profits tax, repealed by public demand, believes that government spending should be regulated not by the needs in the functions of government, but for the purpose of promoting prosperity by spending borrowed money. The more you borrow and spend, the more prosperous you are; the more taxes you pay, the more prosperous you are, says Mr. Eccles. This incredible statement was made by the head of our National Banking system in New York last week and indicates to what depths of false reasoning we have sunk in the crack-pot legislative ideas of those holding important public positions. "It is perilous," says Mr. Eccles, "to reduce public spending," and to adopt sound principles of financing after nine years of fiscal insanity. I say it is not only perilous if we do not start soon to approach a balanced budget, but it will be disastrous. What about the hardships and distress we will suffer when the pay day comes and our sweat and toil must pay for this reckless waste, not only to repay the principal of the debt, but for the interest.

If federal spending is a prop for prosperity, what will happen when the prop is withdrawn, as some day must be done because not even the richest nation in the world can continue indefinitely to violate the basic principles of sound finance. We have primed the pump with borrowed money for five years. The result has been a tragic failure. Our unemployment today, as just announced by the government, is over 10,500,000, or 3,000,000 more than a year ago, and not so many less than when the depression began.

Mr. Eccles further said in New York that the recession that began in the fall of 1937 was caused by reduced public spending. The actual records contradict this statement. For the year beginning July 1, 1937, all governments—local, state and national— spent $18,415,000,000, and for the previous year $17,516,000,000. So we spent more and not less. Mr. Eccles said again that taxes in America were 17½ per cent of the national income and 20 per cent in England, and cited this as one of the reasons why the business index in England is now 118 per cent of the 1929 level and in the United States 75 per cent. He omitted to say that England is on a pay-as-you-go basis and that while our tax collections this year are 17½ per cent of our income, our actual expenditures for all governments totalled 30 per cent, or 10 per cent more than in England. Following this line of reasoning, then our prosperity should be greater than England's prosperity, but Mr. Eccles says it is not.

To my way of thinking, Mr. Eccles paid a tribute in this comparison to pay-as-you-go financing. If Great Britain can reduce her public debt per capita, as she has done, for the past five years, and have a relatively higher prosperity than we have, then a pay-as-you-go plan in this country may bring to us the advantages that Great Britain now apparently enjoys.

Under the pay-as-you-go plan England has reduced her per capita taxation 5 per cent as compared to the levies of 1928. Our Federal government has increased the per capita taxation in the same period by 22 per cent and is paying by taxation only one dollar out of each two dollars expended. . . .

The vast federal spending is entrenched in every nook and corner of America. Actually one out of every 80 men, women and children in the United States is now on the regular payroll, as more than one million and a half are regularly employed by the

Federal government in its various activities. In addition, there are more than one million federal pensioners, and to this must be added the millions receiving federal relief and subsidies of one kind or another. To dismantle and reduce this gigantic bureaucracy is a task of overwhelming proportions, but the reward is the preservation of sound government and to prevent inflation and keep our country secure for our children and those to follow.

Let me suggest a program:

First thoroughly reorganize the Federal government for simplification, retrenchment and economy, and I propose to introduce such legislation.

With equal emphasis I submit there should be a cancellation of the existing authority of 30 federal borrowing corporations which now have power to add $8,000,000,000 to the public debt; and that such corporations, about which so little is known, should function through the budget, allowing Congress to approve or reject future expenditures. This action would preclude at least a portion of the enormous public debt now impending.

Cutting Government Spending

Inescapable in this program is the fact that, exclusive of relief, 30 per cent of the total expended by the government today is for activities new to the government in the last five years (the Greenbelts, and tree belts, and other such dispensable activities). Let these be reduced to the minimum and great sums can be saved without impairing the necessary functions of government.

This program would embrace a thorough, honest purge of relief rolls eliminating all undeserving, and reducing relief costs by stopping all expenditures in excess of providing for those in need; and this can only be done by requiring localities to bear a portion of the burden, thereby directing local interest to reform in the relief program. Elimination of unnecessary relief costs is vital to the preservation of the character of the American people.

It is a fact that 33 states take from the Federal government for relief (exclusive of grants and subsidies) more than they pay into the Treasury from which they draw. Virginia and Massachusetts are among the 15 states in all the nation with relief drafts on the Federal government of less than they contribute in revenue.

Reasonable taxation is one of the best assurances of business prosperity. The essence of our Democracy is the conducting of our government within the ability of our people to pay.

Government efficiently and economically operated is our best protection against the undermining of democracy.

National financial preparedness would be the objective of this program. Financial preparedness is the greatest bulwark of national defense, and it is the greatest guarantee for national security.

Viewpoint 6

"We ultimately found that only the government . . . was able by its lending and spending to . . . bring about the upturn that we have since had."

Government Spending Will Help the Economy

Marriner S. Eccles (1890-1977)

Marriner S. Eccles was a Utah bank president and business executive who first gained national prominence in February 1933 when he testified during congressional hearings on how the country could climb out of the Great Depression. Influenced by the ideas of American economist William T. Foster and British economist John Maynard Keynes, Eccles advocated greater government spending to promote consumer demand and stimulate the economy. Such ideas countered the conventional economic wisdom of the time. Franklin D. Roosevelt appointed Eccles assistant secretary of the treasury in 1934. From 1936 to 1948 Eccles headed the Federal Reserve System, the central banking system of the United States.

Roosevelt's own commitment to stimulating the economy by federal government spending was countered by his private and public support of a federal balanced budget, a goal shared by many in his own administration. An advocate of balanced budgets in many of his public speeches, Roosevelt began to order cuts in spending in New Deal programs in 1937. The recession that began in the fall of that year intensified debate within the Roosevelt administration as to whether a balanced budget or in-

Marriner S. Eccles, "Government Spending Is Sound," a radio address reprinted in *Vital Speeches of the Day* 5 (February 15, 1939): 273-274.

creased government spending should be the priority. In early 1938 Roosevelt agreed with such advisers as Eccles, Harry Hopkins, and Thomas Corcoran and called for a new $5 billion spending program. In the following viewpoint, taken from a radio address given on February 15, 1939, Eccles defends the concept of greater government spending to help the economy.

At the outset, I want to clear away some of the more glaring misconceptions of my views. I *do not* believe in government spending at any time for spending's sake. I *do* believe in government deficit-spending in depression periods as a supplement and stimulant to private spending, using only the man power, materials and money that otherwise would be idle, and using them only in a way that avoids competition with private enterprise. I believe that inefficiency and waste should be eliminated. Government should get the maximum of value for the money it spends, recognizing the size and inherent difficulties of the unemployment and relief problem—the objective always being a maximum of private employment. I abhor politics and favoritism in any phase of government expenditures. I am as anxious as anyone to see the Federal budget balanced. In my judgment this cannot be accomplished until the national income is higher than it will be this year. I do not believe it can be done at this time either by reducing government expenditures or by increasing Federal taxes, particularly those that bear most heavily upon consumption. I believe that the only way the budget can be brought into balance is through increased Federal revenue from an increased national income.

I am just as much against inflation as I am against deflation. However, we do not want to stay in a perpetual deflation because of fear of inflation. Inflation can and should be prevented, and this can be done by giving adequate powers to the Treasury and the Federal Reserve System. I do not see how it would be possible to have a dangerous general inflation so long as we have a large amount of idle men and unused resources. Long before inflation could develop, we would have a volume of business activity that would increase the national income to a point where the budget could easily be balanced. I do not believe, and I have never said, that the Federal debt should continue to grow indefinitely and no part of it ever paid. I do believe that it cannot safely be reduced except when national income is high and when private debt is expanding. Reduction of government debt at such a time would tend to counteract any trend toward inflation that might develop, just as expansion of the government debt during depression tends to offset deflationary developments.

I realize that government spending is not a cure-all or a remedy for all of our problems or for special conditions that may be retarding private employment and investment. Everything should be done to bring about a prompt solution of these problems. In the meantime, I can see no practical alternative except to sustain purchasing power through public employment until private employment substantially increases.

Opposition Views

The viewpoint which I have outlined relative to the need for government spending is strongly opposed by Senator [Harry F.] Byrd, by most of the press, and by many of the bankers and large business interests of the country today. Most of them still demand, as they did at the bottom of the depression in 1932, that government expenditures be cut and that the Federal budget be brought into balance in order to re-establish confidence. Only in this way, they believe, will jobs be provided in private enterprise.

I quite understand why so many of our bankers and businessmen have this viewpoint, for I did also until about 1929. I knew from experience that private investment had led the way out of past depressions without government spending.

In the face of fundamental changes that have come over our economy—changes that I think many of our businessmen and bankers either have not fully perceived or fully appraised—I can no longer bring myself to believe that the nation can risk stopping its support to the unemployed in the hope or expectation that, upon doing so, private enterprise will move forward on any scale sufficient to give them jobs.

To discuss these fundamental changes adequately, would take more time than I have on the air. I can only remind you that we are no longer a nation with rapidly expanding markets at home and abroad, as we were through most of our history. We are no longer pushing our frontiers westward and opening up vast new territories to settlement. We no longer have great incoming tides of immigration. The day has passed when millions can follow Horace Greeley's advice and go West when they fail to find employment or opportunity in the populous eastern centers. The era of railroad expansion has come to an end.

We no longer have expanding foreign markets. We are now a creditor and not a debtor nation, as we were before the war. We are no longer willing to lend billions of dollars abroad, as we did in the '20's, to enable foreigners to absorb American products.

The rapid growth of the automobile and related industries, which were important factors in the expansion of the '20's, has been greatly slowed down. There are not immediate visible vast markets awaiting production by existing industry. Nor does new invention and new industry, which I should especially like to see encouraged and stimulated, hold out prospects for enough investment and employment to absorb great numbers of the unemployed at this time.

Government Unlike an Individual

If I felt that the government were risking a dangerous inflation, or that it could not afford the expenditures, because of the size of the national debt, I would not advocate a continuance of the present stimulus—on the basis of a deficit. I do not share these fears. I do not agree with those who believe, as Senator Byrd does, that the government is like an individual in its fiscal affairs and, therefore, should not spend more than its income, but should always balance its budget and keep out of debt.

I do not scorn the old precepts of thrift and frugality, as the Senator has said. One of the most familiar of these time-honored sayings is: "Neither a borrower nor a lender be." Admirable as these maxims are for the individual, they cannot be applied realistically to business or to the nation. If there were no borrowing or lending in the business world, there would be no business except by the primitive methods of barter. Borrowing and lending means creating debt. We have never had a period of prosperity without an expansion of debt. Conversely, we have never had a period of deflation without a contraction of debt.

I would like to see more equities and fewer debt forms in our economy, but it operates now very largely by the process of debts being created and extinguished. To recognize that debt expands with prosperity, which we all favor, does not mean that one is in favor of debt, but only that under our system we cannot have the prosperity which we all want without the debts which we all dislike.

It is beyond dispute, I think, that as debt contracts or expands, business activity rises and falls and that national income increases or decreases in relatively greater volume. Thus, from 1929 to 1933, total debts, both public and private, contracted by 14 per cent. Yet at the same time national income fell by more than 50 per cent. As a result, the private debt structure, even though contracted, was so large in relation to the diminished national income that debts became unsupportable. Hence, our entire financial structure collapsed and general economic paralysis resulted.

Had the government been like an individual, nothing could have been done to help the situation. We ultimately found that only the government, under such conditions as existed, was able by its lending and spending to stop the tide of deflation and bring about the upturn that we have since had, though it is still far short of the goal of full recovery. However, acting on the advice of the business and financial leaders of the country, the government did attempt to act like an individual from 1930 until the end of 1933 on the theory that the government could not afford to do otherwise, and that in order to maintain confidence and keep money sound, it must balance the budget. Most of you haven't forgotten the results.

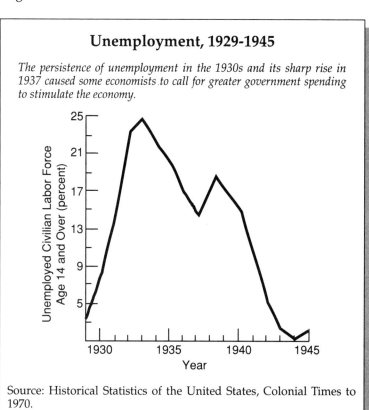

Unemployment, 1929-1945

The persistence of unemployment in the 1930s and its sharp rise in 1937 caused some economists to call for greater government spending to stimulate the economy.

Source: Historical Statistics of the United States, Colonial Times to 1970.

Of course, the government could not balance its budget because the incomes and profits of the taxpayers continued to fall or to disappear. Therefore, the government's revenues fell faster than it was possible to reduce expenses. Consequently, it had a total deficit of more than $7 billions for the calendar years of 1931, 1932 and 1933, while it was pursuing the policy advocated by those who believe as Senator Byrd does. And, mind you, all this happened during the period when everything was being done that business leaders thought would encourage business, even to the extent of setting up the RFC [Reconstruction Finance Corporation] to provide money to support the private financial structure. At the same time, the same business and financial leaders, some of whom were the beneficiaries of government lending, contended that the government's credit was such that it could not afford to come to the financial assistance of millions of unemployed through creation of beneficial public work in the absence of private work.

Past Deficits

The deficits incurred in 1931, 1932 and 1933 cannot be considered as being of what Senator Byrd chooses to call the "pump-priming" variety, because they resulted largely from decreased Federal revenues rather than from increased government expenditures. During this period we had no increase in the national income. In fact, during this period the sum of the annual losses in the national income, compared with the 1929 level, amounted to $120 billions. This staggering loss, to which Senator Byrd makes no reference, resulted from our failure to utilize our idle human and material resources. This is the kind of waste that the nation can ill afford. We had no increase in the national income until a comprehensive lending and spending program was launched, beginning in 1934, giving aid to farmers and home owners and creating jobs through relief and public works.

Let us now consider the years 1934-1937, inclusive. In this period, the government made cash loans and expenditures, including the soldiers' bonus, of $11 billions more than it collected, including payroll taxes. This largely resulted from a deliberate policy of stimulating recovery in private activity. During this period, the national income rose from approximately $40 billions in 1933 to about $70 billions in 1937. The combined increases in the national income for these four years, as compared with 1933, aggregated $70 billions, or more than six times the government's cash deficit of $11 billions for the same period.

And then what happened? During the year 1937, the government contributed about $3 billions less to the buying power of the public than it did in the year 1936, so that its cash receipts were only about $400 millions less than it spent. This too rapid withdrawal of the government's stimulus was accompanied by other important factors, including sharply increased construction costs, large scale speculative inventory buying, a too rapid expansion of short-term installment credit, serious conflicts between capital and labor, and a widening spread between agricultural and industrial prices. The result was another period of rapid deflation in the fall of 1937, which continued until the present spending program of the government was begun last summer. The national income has been rising steadily ever since that time.

In the light of this record of the last nine years—a record which Senator Byrd denounces as one of "fiscal insanity"—does it seem reasonable to believe that, as the Senator said in his letter to me— and I quote—"For every dollar the government borrows and spends in pump-priming, private enterprise is deterred from spending two"? If Senator Byrd really believes this, he should be exerting all of his influence in fighting for an immediate, instead of a gradual, balancing of the budget, in order to reduce government expenditures by at least $3 billions. Such a reduction, according to his unequivocal statement, would bring about an expansion in spending by private enterprise of $6 billions a year. I am convinced that the exact opposite is true. Accordingly, I believe that the country can well afford to have the government continue its stimulus to consumption and thus to business at this juncture.

We might have had about the same results with less government spending had some of it been directed into other channels or had it been better timed, or if private activity had not felt that there were deterrents due to government policy, but of one thing I am certain—whatever the deterrents have been, government spending has not been one of them.

Chapter 5

The Great Depression and the New Deal: Historical Assessments

Chapter Preface

Most historians mark the end of the Great Depression as occurring at the beginning of U.S. involvement in World War II. Economic activity and employment rose greatly as the U.S. government spent massive amounts retooling its industry and mobilizing its military forces. Whether or not the war, rather than the New Deal, deserves most of the credit for ending the depression is still a matter of some historical debate. Alan Brinkley writes in *The Reader's Companion to American History* that the New Deal "did not end the Great Depression and the massive unemployment that accompanied it; only the enormous public and private spending for World War II finally did that." However Robert Kelley, writing in *The Shaping of the American Past*, asserts:

> The American economy, contrary to the usual historical stereotypes, did not lie prostrate and shattered throughout the 1930s while the New Deal labored frantically to bring it alive. In 1937 real income was marginally higher (3 percent) than it had been in 1929; per capita income reached the 1929 level in 1939. . . . It did not require the mobilization of World War II to end the Great Depression.

The question of how the Great Depression ended is just one of many confronting historians of the period. Differing historical interpretations can be found concerning the cause of the 1929 stock market crash, how much that crash was a cause of the Great Depression, the role of U.S. monetary policy in the U.S. economy, and how the Great Depression and the New Deal affected specific groups of Americans, such as women, blacks, and organized labor.

One of the central questions about this period is whether the New Deal should be considered a true revolution, for good or bad, or whether it represented a missed opportunity of revolution. The consensus of historians over the New Deal has changed over time. For the first two decades following Roosevelt's death historians such as Carl Degler generally argued that the New Deal was a success that helped Americans during the Great Depression and prevented the United States from falling under fascist dictatorships similar to Germany or Italy.

During the 1960s, however, a new school of "New Left" historians came of age. Barton J. Bernstein, Paul Conkin, and others examined the New Deal and found it wanting in terms of helping most Americans. Oklahoma State history professor Roger Biles writes in his 1991 study *A New Deal for the American People*:

The disastrous economic conditions of the Great Depression created an opportunity for change unprecedented in America's history, but to the radical critics of the nation's political economy the piecemeal alterations that ensued proved disappointing. . . . The rigor of the New Left Critique made it impossible to gainsay the New Deal's shortcomings, particularly its failure to challenge entrenched elites and to address economic inequality. Having largely accepted the accuracy of Barton Bernstein's indictment, many historians have sought to explain the paucity of change by referring to the constraints limiting New Deal reform efforts.

Biles and other historians, including William E. Leuchtenburg, have responded to such criticism of the New Deal by noting that while it did not achieve many of its stated goals, the New Deal did achieve much in American society. Programs begun in the New Deal such as Social Security remain popular today, and the people's general perception of the proper role of the federal government was fundamentally changed. Biles writes:

Whether the New Deal went too far or not far enough, reforms implemented in the Roosevelt years indelibly shaped American life through the 1980s. And, its critics notwithstanding, New Deal reforms suited most of the American people well enough to secure an enduring place in the society.

The Great Depression and the New Deal had a lasting impact on American life and society. As personal memories of the era fade, the questions historians ask about that time raise significant issues for Americans today.

Viewpoint 1

"The New Deal failed to solve the problem of depression, it failed to raise the impoverished."

The New Deal Achieved Little

Barton J. Bernstein (1936-)

Barton J. Bernstein is a history professor at Stanford University in California. Among the books he has written and/or edited are *Understanding the American Experience* and *Hiroshima Reconsidered*. Since the 1960s he has been one of the main figures of the New Left historical school, which has reexamined American history from a radical perspective.

The following viewpoint is taken from an influential and frequently cited essay first published in 1968. In it, Bernstein challenges the overwhelmingly positive view of Franklin D. Roosevelt and critiques the New Deal from a New Left perspective. He argues that Roosevelt should have responded to the Great Depression by redistributing wealth and reshaping American society. He maintains that the New Deal was a fundamentally conservative phenomenon that did little to help the poor or the typical American.

Writing from a liberal democratic consensus, many American historians in the past two decades have praised the Roosevelt administration for its nonideological flexibility and for its far-ranging reforms. To many historians, particularly those who reached intellectual maturity during the depression, the government's accomplishments, as well as the drama and passion, marked the decade as a watershed, as a dividing line in the American past.

Enamored of Franklin D. Roosevelt and recalling the bitter opposition to welfare measures and restraints upon business, many liberal historians have emphasized the New Deal's discontinuity with the immediate past. For them there was a "Roosevelt Revolution," or at the very least a dramatic achievement of a beneficent liberalism which had developed in fits and spurts during the preceding three decades. . . . For most liberal historians the New Deal meant the replenishment of democracy, the rescuing of the federal government from the clutches of big business, the significant redistribution of political power. Breaking with laissez faire, the new administration, according to these interpretations, marked the end of the passive or impartial state and the beginning of positive government, of the interventionist state acting to offset concentrations of private power, and affirming the rights and responding to the needs of the unprivileged.

These themes no longer seem adequate to characterize the New Deal. The liberal reforms of the New Deal did not transform the American system; they conserved and protected American corporate capitalism, occasionally by absorbing parts of threatening programs. There was no significant redistribution of power in American society, only limited recognition of other organized groups, seldom of unorganized peoples. Neither the bolder programs advanced by New Dealers nor the final legislation greatly extended the beneficence of government beyond the middle classes or drew upon the wealth of the few for the needs of the many. Designed to maintain the American system, liberal activity was directed toward essentially conservative goals. Experimentalism was most frequently limited to means; seldom did it extend to ends. Never questioning private enterprise, it operated within safe channels, far short of Marxism or even of native American radicalisms that offered structural critiques and structural solutions.

All of this is not to deny the changes wrought by the New Deal—the extension of welfare programs, the growth of federal power, the strengthening of the executive, even the narrowing of property rights. But it is to assert that the elements of continuity are stronger, that the magnitude of change has been exaggerated. The New Deal failed to solve the problem of depression, it failed to raise the impoverished, it failed to redistribute income, it failed to extend equality and generally countenanced racial discrimination and segregation. It failed generally to make business more responsible to the social welfare or to threaten business's preeminent political power. In this sense, the New Deal, despite the shifts in tone and spirit from the earlier decade, was profoundly conservative and continuous with the 1920s.

The 1920s

Rather than understanding the 1920s as a "return to normalcy," the period is more properly interpreted by focusing on the continuation of progressive impulses, demands often frustrated by the rivalry of interest groups, sometimes blocked by the resistance of Harding and Coolidge, and occasionally by Hoover. Through these years while agriculture and labor struggled to secure advantages from the federal government, big business flourished. Praised for creating American prosperity, business leaders easily convinced the nation that they were socially responsible, that they were fulfilling the needs of the public. Benefitting from earlier legislation that had promoted economic rationalization and stability, they were opponents of federal benefits to other groups but seldom proponents of laissez faire.

In no way did the election of Herbert Hoover in 1928 seem to challenge the New Era. An heir of Wilson, Hoover promised an even closer relationship with big business and moved beyond Harding and Coolidge by affirming federal responsibility for prosperity. As Secretary of Commerce, Hoover had opposed unbridled competition and had transformed his department into a vigorous friend of business. Sponsoring trade associations, he promoted industrial self-regulation and the increased rationalization of business. He had also expanded foreign trade, endorsed the regulation of new forms of communications, encouraged relief in disasters, and recommended public works to offset economic declines.

By training and experience, few men in American political life seemed better prepared than Hoover to cope with the depression. Responding promptly to the crisis, he acted to stabilize the economy and secured the agreement of businessmen to maintain production and wage rates. Unwilling to let the economy "go through the wringer," the President requested easier money, self-liquidating public works, lower personal and corporate income taxes, and stronger commodity stabilization corporations. In reviewing these unprecedented actions, Walter Lippmann wrote, "The national government undertook to make the whole economic order operate prosperously."

Hoover's Efforts

But these efforts proved inadequate. The tax cut benefitted the wealthy and failed to raise effective demand. The public works were insufficient. The commodity stabilization corporations soon ran out of funds, and agricultural prices kept plummeting. Businessmen cut back production, dismissed employees, and finally cut wages. As unemployment grew, Hoover struggled to inspire confidence, but his words seemed hollow and his understanding of the depression limited. Blaming the collapse on European failures, he could not admit that American capitalism had failed. When prodded by Congress to increase public works, to provide direct relief, and to further unbalance the budget, he doggedly resisted. Additional deficits would destroy business confidence, he feared, and relief would erode the principles of individual and local responsibility. Clinging to faith in voluntarism, Hoover also briefly rebuffed the efforts by financiers to secure the Reconstruction Finance Corporation (RFC). Finally endorsing the RFC, he also supported expanded lending by Federal Land Banks, recommended home-loan banks, and even approved small federal loans (usually inadequate) to states needing funds for relief. In this burst of activity, the President had moved to the very limits of his ideology. . . .

Even though constitutional scruples restricted his efforts, Hoover did more than any previous American president to combat depression. He "abandoned the principles of laissez faire in relation to the business cycle, established the conviction that prosperity and depression can be publicly controlled by political action, and drove out of the public consciousness the old idea that depressions must be overcome by private adjustment," wrote Walter Lippmann. Rather than the last of the old presidents, Herbert Hoover was the first of the new.

Franklin D. Roosevelt

A charismatic leader and a brilliant politician, his successor expanded federal activities on the basis of Hoover's efforts. Using the federal government to stabilize the economy and advance the interests of the groups, Franklin D. Roosevelt directed the campaign to save large-scale corporate capitalism. Though recognizing new political interests and extending benefits to them, his New Deal never effectively challenged big business or the organization of the economy. In providing assistance to the needy and by rescuing them from starvation, Roosevelt's humane efforts also protected the established system: he sapped organized radicalism of its waning strength and of its potential constituency among the unorganized and discontented. Sensitive to public opinion and fearful of radicalism, Roosevelt acted from a mixture of motives that rendered his liberalism cautious and limited, his experimentalism narrow. Despite the flurry of activity, his government was more vigorous and flexible about means than goals, and the goals were more conservative than historians usually acknowledge.

Roosevelt's response to the banking crisis emphasizes the conservatism of his administration and its self-conscious avoidance of more radical means that might have transformed American capitalism. Entering the White House when banks were failing and Americans had lost faith in the financial system, the President could have nationalized it—"without a word of protest," judged Senator Bronson Cutting. "If ever there was a moment when things hung in the balance," later wrote Raymond Moley, a member of the original "brain trust," "it was on March 5, 1933—when unorthodoxy would have drained the last remaining strength of the capitalistic system." To save the system, Roosevelt relied upon collaboration between bankers and Hoover's Treasury officials to prepare legislation extending federal assistance to banking. So great was the demand for action that House members, voting even without copies, passed it unanimously, and the Senate, despite objections by a few Progressives, approved it the same evening. "The President," remarked a cynical congressman, "drove the money-changers out of the Capitol on March 4th—and they were all back on the 9th."

Undoubtedly the most dramatic example of Roosevelt's early conservative approach to recovery was the National Recovery Administration (NRA). . . .

Designed largely for industrial recovery, the NRA legislation provided for minimum wages and maximum hours. It also made concessions to pro-labor congressmen and labor leaders who demanded some specific benefits for unions—recognition of the worker's right to organization and to collective bargaining. In practice, though, the much-heralded Section 7a was a disappointment to most friends of labor. . . . To many frustrated workers and their disgusted leaders, NRA became "National Run Around." The clause, unionists found (in the words of Brookings economists), "had the practical effect of placing NRA on the side of anti-union employers in their struggle against trade unions. . . . [It] thus threw its weight against labor in the balance of bargaining power.". . .

Not only did the NRA provide fewer advantages than unionists had anticipated, but it also failed as a recovery measure. It probably even retarded recovery by supporting restrictionism and price increases, concluded a Brookings study. Placing effective power for code-writing in big business, NRA injured small businesses and contributed to the concentration of American industry. . . .

The Broker State

Viewing the economy as a "concert of organized interests," the New Deal also provided benefits for farmers—the Agricultural Adjustment Act. Reflecting the political power of larger commercial farmers and accepting restrictionist economics, the measure assumed that the agricultural problem was overproduction, not underconsumption. Financed by a processing tax designed to raise prices to parity, payments encouraged restricted production and cutbacks in farm labor. With benefits accruing chiefly to the larger owners, they frequently removed from production the lands of sharecroppers and tenant farmers, and "tractored" them and hired hands off the land. In assisting agriculture, the AAA, like the NRA, sacrificed the interests of the marginal and the unrecognized to the welfare of those with greater political and economic power.

In large measure, the early New Deal of the NRA and AAA was a "broker state." Though the government served as a mediator of interests and sometimes imposed its will in divisive situations, it was generally the servant of powerful groups. "Like the mercantilists, the New Dealers protected vested interests with the authority of the state," acknowledges William Leuchtenburg. But it was some improvement over the 1920s when business was the only interest capable of imposing its will on the government. While extending to other groups the benefits of the state, the New Deal, however, continued to recognize the pre-eminence of business interests. . . .

It was not the disaffection of a portion of the business community, nor the creation of the Liberty League, that menaced the broker state. Rather it was the threat of the Left—expressed, for example, in such overwrought statements as Minnesota Governor Floyd Olson's: "I am not a liberal . . . I am a radical. . . . I am not satisfied with hanging a laurel wreath on burglars and thieves . . . and calling them code authorities or something else." While Olson, along with some others who succumbed to the rhetoric of militancy, would back down and soften their meaning, their words dramatized real grievances: the failure of the early New Deal to end misery, to re-create prosperity. The New Deal excluded too many. Its programs were inadequate. While Roosevelt reluctantly endorsed relief and went beyond Hoover in support of public works, he too preferred self-liquidating projects, desired a balanced budget, and resisted spending the huge sums required to lift the nation out of depression.

Challenge from the Left

For millions suffering in a nation wracked by poverty, the promises of the Left seemed attractive. Capitalizing on the misery, Huey Long offered Americans a "Share Our Wealth" program—a welfare state with prosperity, not subsistence, for the disadvantaged, those neglected by most politicians. "Every Man a King": pensions for the elderly, college for the deserving, homes and cars for families—that was the promise of American life. Also proposing minimum wages, increased public works, shorter work weeks, and a generous farm program, he demanded a "soak-the-rich" tax program. Despite the economic defects of his plan, Long was no hayseed, and his forays into the East revealed support far beyond the bayous and hamlets of his native South. . . .

A Taste of Reconstruction

Howard Zinn is a professor emeritus at Boston University. His books include A People's History of the United States. *In 1966 Zinn edited* New Deal Thought, *a collection of writings from that time. In the book's introduction he expressed his own views on the limits of the New Deal.*

When the reform energies of the New Deal began to wane around 1939 and the depression was over, the nation was back to its normal state: a permanent army of unemployed; twenty or thirty million poverty-ridden people effectively blocked from public view by a huge, prosperous, and fervently consuming middle class; a tremendously efficient yet wasteful productive apparatus that was efficient because it could produce limitless supplies of what it decided to produce, and wasteful because what it decided to produce was not based on what was most needed by society but on what was most profitable to business.

What the New Deal did was to refurbish middle-class America, which had taken a dizzying fall in the depression, to restore jobs to half the jobless, and to give just enough to the lowest classes (a layer of public housing, a minimum of social security) to create an aura of good will. Through it all, the New Dealers moved in an atmosphere thick with suggestions, but they accepted only enough of these to get the traditional social mechanism moving again, plus just enough more to give a taste of what a truly far-reaching reconstruction might be.

Challenged by the Left, and with the new Congress more liberal and more willing to spend, Roosevelt turned to disarm the discontent. "Boys—this is our hour," confided Harry Hopkins. "We've got to get everything we want—a works program, social security, wages and hours, everything—now or never. Get your minds to work on developing a complete ticket to provide security for all the folks of this country up and down and across the board." Hopkins and the associates he addressed were not radicals: they did not seek to transform the system, only to make it more humane. They, too, wished to preserve large-scale corporate capitalism, but unlike Roosevelt . . . , they were prepared for more vigorous action. Their commitment to reform was greater, their tolerance for injustice far less. Joining them in pushing the New Deal left were the leaders of industrial unions, who, while also not wishing to transform the system, sought for workingmen higher wages, better conditions, stronger and larger unions, and for themselves a place closer to the fulcrum of power. . . .

Limited Reforms

Responding to the threat from the left, Roosevelt also moved during the Second Hundred Days to secure laws regulating banking, raising taxes, dissolving utility-holding companies, and creating social security. Building on the efforts of states during the Progressive Era, the Social Security Act marked the movement toward the welfare state, but the core of the measure, the old-age provision, was more important as a landmark than for its substance. While establishing a federal-state system of unemployment compensation, the government, by making workers contribute to their old-age insurance, denied its financial responsibility for the elderly. The act excluded more than a fifth of the labor force leaving, among others, more than five million farm laborers and domestics without coverage.

Though Roosevelt criticized the tax laws for not preventing "an unjust concentration of wealth and economic power," his own tax measure would not have significantly redistributed wealth. Yet his message provoked an "amen" from Huey Long and protests from businessmen. Retreating from his promises, Roosevelt failed to support the bill, and it succumbed to conservative forces. They removed the inheritance tax and greatly reduced the proposed corporate and individual levies. The final law did not "soak the rich." But it did engender deep resentment among the wealthy for increasing taxes on gifts and estates, imposing an excess-profits tax (which Roosevelt had not requested), and raising surtaxes. When combined with such regressive levies as social security and local taxes, however, the Wealth Tax of 1935 did not drain wealth from higher-income groups, and the top 1 percent even increased their shares during the New Deal years.

Those historians who have characterized the events of 1935 as the beginning of a second New Deal have imposed a pattern on those years which most participants did not then discern. In moving to social security, guarantees of collective bargaining, utility regulation, and progressive taxation, the government did advance the nation toward greater liberalism, but the shift was exaggerated and most of the measures accomplished far less than either friends or foes suggested. Certainly, despite a mild bill authorizing destruction of utilities-holding companies, there was no effort to atomize business, no real threat to concentration. . . .

Though vigorous in rhetoric and experimental in tone, the New

Deal was narrow in its goals and wary of bold economic reform. Roosevelt's sense of what was politically desirable was frequently more restricted than others' views of what was possible and necessary. Roosevelt's limits were those of ideology; they were not inherent in experimentalism. For while the President explored the narrow center, and some New Dealers considered bolder possibilities, John Dewey, the philosopher of experimentalism, moved far beyond the New Deal and sought to reshape the system. Liberalism, he warned, "must now become radical. . . . For the gulf between what the actual situation makes possible and the actual state itself is so great that it cannot be bridged by piecemeal policies undertaken *ad hoc*." The boundaries of New Deal experimentalism, as Howard Zinn has emphasized, could extend far beyond Roosevelt's cautious ventures. Operating within very safe channels, Roosevelt not only avoided Marxism and the socialization of property, but he also stopped far short of other possibilities—communal direction of production or the organized distribution of surplus. The President and many of his associates were doctrinaires of the center, and their maneuvers in social reform were limited to cautious excursions.

Running Out of Ideas

Usually opportunistic and frequently shifting, the New Deal was restricted by its ideology. It ran out of fuel not because of the conservative opposition, but because it ran out of ideas. Acknowledging the end in 1939, Roosevelt proclaimed, "We have now passed the period of internal conflict in the launching of our program of social reform. Our full energies may now be released to invigorate the processes of recovery in order to preserve our reforms. . . ."

The sad truth was that the heralded reforms were severely limited, that inequality continued, that efforts at recovery had failed. Millions had come to accept the depression as a way of life. A decade after the Great Crash, when millions were still unemployed, Fiorello LaGuardia recommended that "we accept the inevitable, that we are now in a new normal." "It was reasonable to expect a probable minimum of 4,000,000 to 5,000,000 unemployed," Harry Hopkins had concluded. Even that level was never reached, for business would not spend and Roosevelt refused to countenance the necessary expenditures. "It was in economics that our troubles lay," Rexford Tugwell wrote. "For their solution his [Roosevelt's] progressivism, his new deal was pathetically insufficient. . . .

Clinging to faith in fiscal orthodoxy even when engaged in deficit spending, Roosevelt had been unwilling to greatly unbalance the budget. Having pledged in his first campaign to cut expenditures and to restore the balanced budget, the President had at first adopted recovery programs that would not drain government finances. Despite a burst of activity under the Civil Works Administration during the first winter, public works expenditures were frequently slow and cautious. Shifting from direct relief, which Roosevelt (like Hoover) considered "a narcotic, a subtle destroyer of the human spirit," the government moved to work relief. ("It saves his skill. It gives him a chance to do something socially useful," said Hopkins.) By 1937 the government had poured enough money into the economy to spur production to within 10 percent of 1929 levels, but unemployment still hovered over seven million. Yet so eager was the President to balance the budget that he cut expenditures for public works and relief, and plunged the economy into a greater depression. While renewing expenditures, Roosevelt remained cautious in his fiscal policy, and the nation still had almost nine million unemployed in 1939. After nearly six years of struggling with the depression, the Roosevelt administration could not lead the nation to recovery, but it had relieved suffering. In most of America, starvation was no longer possible. Perhaps that was the most humane achievement of the New Deal.

Its efforts on behalf of humane *reform* were generally faltering and shallow, of more value to the middle classes, of less value to organized workers, of even less to the marginal men. In conception and in practice, seemingly humane efforts revealed the shortcomings of American liberalism. For example, public housing, praised as evidence of the federal government's concern for the poor, was limited in scope (to 180,000 units) and unfortunate in results. It usually meant the consolidation of ghettos, the robbing of men of their dignity, the treatment of men as wards with few rights. And slum clearance came to mean "Negro clearance" and removal of the other poor. Of much of this liberal reformers were unaware, and some of the problems can be traced to the structure of bureaucracy and to the selection of government personnel and social workers who disliked the poor. But the liberal conceptions, it can be argued, were also flawed for there was no willingness to consult the poor, nor to encourage their participation. Liberalism was elitist. Seeking to build America in their own image, liberals wanted to create an environment which they thought would restructure character and personality more appropriate to white, middle-class America. . . .

Liberalism's Failure

The New Deal was neither a "third American Revolution," as Carl Degler suggests, nor even a "half-way revolution," as William Leuchtenburg concludes. Not only was the extension of representation to new groups less than full-fledged partnership, but the New Deal neglected many Americans—sharecroppers, tenant farmers, migratory workers and farm laborers, slum dwellers, unskilled workers, and the unemployed Negroes. They were left outside the new order. As Roosevelt asserted in 1937 (in a classic understatement), one third of the nation was "ill-nourished, ill-clad, ill-housed."

Yet, by the power of rhetoric and through the appeals of political organization, the Roosevelt government managed to win or retain the allegiance of these peoples. Perhaps this is one of the crueller ironies of liberal politics, that the marginal men trapped in hopelessness were seduced by rhetoric, by the style and movement, by the symbolism of efforts seldom reaching beyond words. In acting to protect the institution of private property and in advancing the interests of corporate capitalism, the New Deal assisted the middle and upper sectors of society. It protected them, sometimes, even at the cost of injuring the lower sectors. Seldom did it bestow much of substance upon the lower classes. Never did the New Deal seek to organize these groups into independent political forces. Seldom did it risk antagonizing established interests. For some this would constitute a puzzling defect of liberalism; for some, the failure to achieve true liberalism. To others it would emphasize the inherent shortcomings of American liberal democracy. As the nation prepared for war, liberalism, by accepting private property and federal assistance to corporate capitalism, was not prepared effectively to reduce inequities, to redistribute political power, or to extend equality from promise to reality.

VIEWPOINT 2

"It is hard to think of another period in the whole history of the republic that was so fruitful or of a crisis that was met with as much imagination."

The New Deal Was a Great Achievement

William E. Leuchtenburg (1922-)

William E. Leuchtenburg, a history professor at the University of North Carolina at Chapel Hill, taught history for more than thirty years at Columbia University in New York. He has also been president of the Society of American Historians and a senior fellow of the National Endowment for the Humanities. Recognized as one of the leading historians of the New Deal era, his books include the award-winning *Franklin D. Roosevelt and the New Deal, 1932-1940*; *The New Deal: A Documentary History*; and *In the Shadow of FDR*.

In the following viewpoint, written around the time of the fiftieth anniversary of the start of the Roosevelt administration, Leuchtenburg defends the New Deal from what he believes are unfair attacks by historians such as Barton J. Bernstein, author of the previous viewpoint. The New Deal should not be regarded as a failure or as an essentially conservative movement that preserved the status quo, he argues. Rather, it should be recognized as a series of imaginative initiatives and programs that helped innumerable Americans during the Great Depression and transformed the way American government works.

Excerpted from William E. Leuchtenburg, "The Achievement of the New Deal." In *Fifty Years Later: The New Deal Reevaluated*, edited by Howard Sitkoff. Philadelphia: Temple University Press, 1985. Copyright © 1985 by Alfred A. Knopf, Inc. Reprinted by permission of McGraw-Hill, Inc.

The fiftieth anniversary of the New Deal, launched on March 4, 1933, comes at a time when it has been going altogether out of fashion. Writers on the left, convinced that the Roosevelt experiment was either worthless or pernicious, have assigned it to the dustbin of history. Commentators on the right, though far less conspicuous, see in the New Deal the origins of the centralized state they seek to dismantle. . . .

To be sure, the New Deal has always had its critics. In Roosevelt's own day Marxists said that the New Deal had not done anything for agriculture that an earthquake could not have done better at the same time that conservatives were saying that FDR was unprincipled. Hoover even called him "a chameleon on plaid." Most historians have long since accepted the fact that New Deal policies were sometimes inconsistent, that Roosevelt failed to grasp countercyclical fiscal theory, that recovery did not come until armaments orders fueled the economy, that the President was credited with certain reforms like insurance of bank deposits that he, in fact, opposed, that a number of New Deal programs, notably aid for the marginal farmer, were inadequately financed, and that some New Deal agencies discriminated against blacks.

During the 1960s historians not only dressed up these objections as though they were new revelations but carried their disappointment with contemporary liberalism to the point of arguing either that the New Deal was not just inadequate but actually malign or that the New Deal was so negligible as to constitute a meaningless episode. . . . The New Deal was now perceived to be elitist, since it had neglected to consult the poor about what legislation they wanted, or to encourage the participation of ghetto-dwellers in decision-making. Roosevelt's policies, historians maintained, redounded to the benefit of those who already had advantages—wealthier staple farmers, organized workers, business corporations, the "deserving poor"—while displacing share-croppers and neglecting the powerless. An "antirevolutionary response to a situation that had revolutionary potentialities," the New Deal, it was said, missed opportunities to nationalize the banks and restructure the social order. Even "providing assistance to the needy and . . . rescuing them from starvation" served conservative ends, historians complained, for these efforts "sapped organized radicalism of its waning strength and of its potential constituency among the unorganized and discontented." The Roosevelt Administration, it has been asserted, failed to achieve more than it did not as a result of the strength of conservative opposition but because of the intellectual deficiencies of the New Dealers and because Roosevelt deliberately sought to save "large-scale corporate capitalism." In *Towards a New Past*, the New Left historian Barton Bernstein summed up this point of view: "The New Deal failed to solve the problem of depression, it failed to raise the impoverished, it failed to redistribute income, it failed to extend equality and generally countenanced racial discrimination and segregation."

Although the characterization of Bernstein as "New Left" suggests that he represents a deviant persuasion, the New Left perspective has, in fact, all but become the new orthodoxy, even though there is not yet any New Left survey of the domestic history of the United States in the 1930s. This emphasis has so permeated writing on the New Deal in the past generation that an instructor who wishes to assign the latest thought on the age of Roosevelt has a wide choice of articles and anthologies that document the errors of the New Deal but no assessment of recent vintage that explores its accomplishments.

The fiftieth anniversary of the New Deal provides the occasion for a modest proposal—that we reintroduce some tension into the argument over the interpretation of the Roosevelt years. If historians are to develop a credible synthesis, it is important to regain a sense of the achievement of the New Deal. As it now stands, we have a dialectic that is all antithesis with no thesis. The so-called "debate" about the New Deal is not truly a debate, for even some of the historians who dispute the New Left assertions agree that one can only take a melancholy view of the period. The single question asked is whether the failure of the New Deal was the fault of the Roosevelt Administration or the result of the strength of conservative forces beyond the government's control; the fact of failure is taken as the basic postulate. As a first step toward a more considered evaluation, one has to remind one's self not only of what the New Deal did not do, but of what it achieved.

New Deal Changes

Above all, one needs to recognize how markedly the New Deal altered the character of the State in America. Indeed, though for decades past European theorists had been talking about *der Staat*, there can hardly be said to have been a State in America in the full meaning of the term before the New Deal. If you had walked into an American town in 1932, you would have had a hard time detecting any sign of a federal presence, save perhaps for the post office and even many of today's post offices date from the 1930s. Washington rarely affected people's lives directly. There was no national old-age pension system, no federal unemployment compensation, no aid to dependent children, no federal housing, no regulation of the stock market, no withholding tax, no federal school lunch, no farm subsidy, no national minimum wage law, no welfare state. As late as Herbert Hoover's presidency, it was regarded as axiomatic that government activity should be minimal. In the pre-Roosevelt era, even organized labor and the National Conference of Social Workers opposed federal action on behalf of the unemployed. The New Deal sharply challenged these shibboleths. From 1933 to 1938, the government intervened in a myriad of ways from energizing the economy to fostering unionization. . . .

Although the New Deal always operated within a capitalist matrix and the government sought to enhance profitmaking, Roosevelt and his lieutenants rejected the traditional view that government was the handmaiden of business or that government and business were coequal sovereigns. As a consequence, they adopted measures to discipline corporations, to require a sharing of authority with government and unions, and to hold businessmen accountable. In the early days of the National Recovery Administration, the novelist Sherwood Anderson wrote:

> I went to several code hearings. No one has quite got their significance. Here for the first time you see these men of business, little ones and big ones, . . . coming up on the platform to give an accounting. It does seem the death knell of the old idea that a man owning a factory, office or store has a right to run it in his own way.
>
> There is at least an effort to relate it now to the whole thing, man's relations with his fellow men etc. Of course it is crude and there will be no end to crookedness, objections, etc. but I do think an entire new principle in American life is being established.

Through a series of edicts and statutes, the administration invaded the realm of the banker by establishing control over the nation's money supply. The government clamped an embargo on gold, took the United States off the gold standard, and nullified the requirement for the payment of gold in private contracts. In 1935 a resentful Supreme Court sustained this authority, although a dissenting justice said that this was Nero at his worst. The Glass-Steagall Banking Act (1933) stripped commercial banks of the privilege of engaging in investment banking, and established federal insurance of bank deposits, an innovation which the leading monetary historians have called "the structural change most conducive to monetary stability since bank notes were taxed out of existence immediately after the Civil War." The Banking Act of 1935 gave the United States what other industrial nations had long had, but America lacked—central banking. This series of changes transformed the relationship between the government and the financial community from what it had been when Grover Cleveland had gone, hat in hand, to beseech J. P. Morgan for help. As Charles Beard observed: "Having lost their gold coins and bullion to the Federal Government and having filled their vaults with federal bonds and other paper, bankers have become in a large measure mere agents of the Government in Washington. No longer do these powerful interests stand, so to speak, 'outside the Government' and in a position to control or dictate to it."

A number of other enactments helped transfer authority from Wall Street to Washington. The Securities Act of 1933 established government supervision of the issue of securities, and made company directors civilly and criminally liable for misinformation on the statements they were required to file with each new issue. The Securities and Exchange Act of 1934 initiated federal supervision of the stock exchanges, which to this day operate under the lens of the Securities and Exchange Commission (SEC). The Holding Company Act of 1935 levelled some of the utility pyramids, dissolving all utility holding companies that were more than twice removed from their operating companies, and increased the regulatory powers of the SEC over public utilities. Robert Sobel has concluded that the 1934 law marked "a shift of economic power from the lower part of Manhattan, where it had been for over a century, to Washington." To be sure, financiers continued to make important policy choices, but they never again operated in the uninhibited universe of the Great Bull Market. By the spring of 1934, one writer was already reporting:

> Financial news no longer originates in Wall Street. . . . News of a financial nature in Wall Street now is merely an echo of events which take place in Washington. . . . The pace of the ticker is determined now in Washington not in company boardrooms or in brokerage offices. . . . In Wall Street it is no longer asked what some big trader is doing, what some important banker thinks, what opinion some eminent lawyer holds about some pressing question of the day. The query in Wall Street has become: "What's the news from Washington?"

The age of Roosevelt focused attention on Washington, too, by initiatives in fields that had been regarded as exclusively within the private orbit, notably in housing. The Home Owners' Loan Corporation, created in 1933, saved tens of thousands of homes from foreclosure by refinancing mortgages. In 1934 the Federal Housing Administration (FHA) began its program of insuring loans for the construction and renovation of private homes, and over the next generation more than 10 million FHA-financed units were built. Before the New Deal, the national government had never engaged in public housing, except for the World War I emergency, but agencies like the Public Works Administration now broke precedent. The Tennessee Valley Authority laid out the model town of Norris, the Federal Emergency Relief Administration (FERA) experimented with subsistence homesteads, and the Resettlement Administration created greenbelt communities, entirely new towns girdled by green countryside. When in 1937 the Wagner-Steagall Act created the U.S. Housing Authority, it assured public housing a permanent place in American life.

A New Deal for the Common Man

The New Deal profoundly altered industrial relations by throwing the weight of government behind efforts to unionize workers. At the outset of the Great Depression, the American labor movement was "an anachronism in the world," for only a tiny minority of factory workers were unionized. Employers hired and fired and imposed punishments at will, used thugs as strikebreakers and private police, stockpiled industrial munitions, and ran company towns as feudal fiefs. In an astonishingly short period in the Roosevelt years a very different pattern emerged. Under the umbrella of Section 7(a) of the National Industrial Recovery Act of 1933 and of the far-reaching Wagner Act of 1935, union organizers gained millions of recruits in such open-shop strongholds as steel, automobiles, and textiles. Employees won wage rises, reductions in hours, greater job security, freedom from the tyranny of company guards, and protection against arbitrary punishment. Thanks to the National Recovery Administration and the Guffey acts, coal miners achieved the outlawing of compulsory company houses and stores. Steel workers, who in 1920 labored twelve-hour shifts seven days a week at the blast furnaces, were to become so powerful that in the postwar era they would win not merely paid vacations but sabbatical leaves. A British analyst has concluded: "From one of the most restrictive among industrially advanced nations, the labour code of the United States (insofar as it could be said to exist before 1933) was rapidly transformed into one of the most liberal," and these reforms, he adds, "were not the harvest of long-sustained agitation by trade unions, but were forced upon a partly sceptical labor movement by a government which led or carried it into maturity."

Years later, when David E. Lilienthal, the director of the Tennessee Valley Authority, was being driven to the airport to fly to Roosevelt's funeral, the TVA driver said to him:

> I won't forget what he did for me. . . . I spent the best years of my life working at the Appalachian Mills . . . and they didn't even treat us like humans. If you didn't do like they said, they always told you there was someone else to take your job. I had my mother and my sister to take care of. Sixteen cents an hour was what we got; a fellow can't live on that, and you had to get production even to get that, this Bedaux system; some fellows only got twelve cents. If you asked to get off on a Sunday, the foreman would say, "All right you stay away Sunday, but when you come back Monday someone else will have your job." No, sir, I won't forget what he done for us.

Helen Lynd has observed that the history of the United States is that of England fifty years later, and a half century after the welfare state had come to Western Europe, the New Deal brought it to America. The NRA wiped out sweatshops, and removed some 150,000 child laborers from factories. The Walsh-Healey Act of 1936 and the Fair Labor Standards Act of 1938 established the principle of a federally imposed minimal level of working conditions, and added further sanctions against child labor. If the New Deal did not do enough for the "one-third of a nation" to whom Roosevelt called attention, it at least made a beginning, through agencies like the Farm Security Administration, toward helping sharecroppers, tenant farmers, and migrants like John Steinbeck's Joads. Most important, it originated a new system of social rights to replace the dependence on private charity. The Social Security Act of 1935 created America's first national system of old-age pensions and initiated a federal-state program of unemployment insurance. It also authorized grants for the blind, for the incapacitated, and for dependent children, a feature that would have unimaginable long-range consequences. . . .

Roosevelt himself affirmed the newly assumed attitudes in Washington in his annual message to Congress in 1938 when he declared: "Government has a final responsibility for the well-being of its citizenship. If private co-operative endeavor fails to provide work for willing hands and relief for the unfortunate, those suffering hardship from no fault of their own have a right to call upon the Government for aid; and a government worthy of its name must make fitting response."

A New Deal for the Unemployed

Nothing revealed this approach so well as the New Deal's attention to the plight of the millions of unemployed. During the ten years between 1929 and 1939, one scholar has written, "more progress was made in public welfare and relief than in the three hundred years after this country was first settled." A series of alphabet agencies— the FERA, the CWA, the WPA—provided government work for the jobless, while the National Youth Administration (NYA) employed college students in museums, libraries, and laboratories, enabled high school students to remain in school, and set up a program of apprentice training. In Texas, the twenty-seven-year-old NYA director Lyndon Johnson put penniless young men like John Connally to work building roadside parks, and in North Carolina, the NYA employed, at 35 cents an hour, a Duke University law student, Richard Nixon.

In an address in Los Angeles in 1936, the head of FDR's relief operations, Harry Hopkins, conveyed the attitude of the New Deal toward those who were down and out:

I am getting sick and tired of these people on the W.P.A. and local relief rolls being called chiselers and cheats. . . . These people . . . are just like the rest of us. They don't drink any more than us, they don't lie any more, they're no lazier than the rest of us—they're pretty much a cross section of the American people. . . . I have never believed that with our capitalistic system people have to be poor. I think it is an outrage that we should permit hundreds and hundreds of thousands of people to be ill clad, to live in miserable homes, not to have enough to eat; not to be able to send their children to school for the only reason that they are poor. I don't believe ever again in America we are going to permit the things to happen that have happened in the past to people. We are never going back . . . to the days of putting the old people in the alms houses, when a decent dignified pension at home will keep them there. We are

---

Significant Change

David H. Bennett is a professor of history at Syracuse University in New York, specializing in the study of American radical movements. In an essay published in the anthology The Roosevelt New Deal: A Program Assessment Fifty Years Later, *he argues that the New Deal achieved significant change in American society by increasing the national government's responsibility to the economic well-being of the American people.*

The New Deal was more than just a relief expedition for a desperate middle class in the depth of the Depression. Its significance is more enduring than implied even in those terms of admiration and support used by its scholarly champions: "guarantor state," "welfare state," "interventionist state." It did establish the federal government's responsibility to intervene in order to guarantee the "collaboration of all of us to provide security for all of us." But beyond these reformed institutional arrangements and the heritage of its relief and recovery programs lay its larger achievement, the recognition that social and economic problems in this great nation required national political solutions and national political responsibility, that the old order would not and could not work any more. More important than its inconsistencies or its faltering conception of economic planning was this signal accomplishment. Franklin Roosevelt's New Deal did not bring the egalitarian utopia of the cooperative commonwealth, and it did not dramatically redistribute wealth or attend to racial wrongs and shames of the past. It brought no radical change, but it did create significant change. Yet even this required not only the skillful leadership of the President but the unparalleled collapse of the economic order in the Great Depression. Its very success is a measure of not what might have been, but a testament to how hard it is to make any significant new departures in political and socioeconomic relationships in America.

coming to the day when we are going to have decent houses for the poor, when there is genuine and real security for everybody. I have gone all over the moral hurdles that people are poor because they are bad. I don't believe it. A system of government on that basis is fallacious.

Under the leadership of men like Hopkins, "Santa Claus incomparable and privy-builder without peer," projects of relief agencies and of the Public Works Administration (PWA) changed the face of the land. The PWA built thoroughfares like the Skyline Drive in Virginia and the Overseas Highway from Miami to Key West, constructed the Medical Center in Jersey City, burrowed Chicago's new subway, and gave Natchez, Mississippi a new bridge, and Denver a modern water-supply system. Few New Yorkers today realize the long reach of the New Deal. If they cross the Triborough Bridge, they are driving on a bridge the PWA built. If they fly into La Guardia Airport, they are landing at an airfield laid out by the WPA. If they get caught in a traffic jam on the FDR Drive, they are using yet another artery built by the WPA. Even the animal cages in the Central Park Zoo were reconstructed by WPA workers. In New York City, the WPA built or renovated hundreds of school buildings; gave Orchard Beach a bathhouse, a mall, and a lagoon; landscaped Bryant Park and the campus of Hunter College in the Bronx; conducted examinations for venereal disease, filled teeth, operated pollen count stations, and performed puppet shows for disturbed children; it built dioramas for the Brooklyn Museum; ran street dances in Harlem and an open-air night club in Central Park; and, by combing neglected archives, turned up forgotten documents like the court proceedings in the Aaron Burr libel case and the marriage license issued to Captain Kidd. In New York City alone the WPA employed more people than the entire War Department. . . .

The New Deal showed unusual sensitivity toward jobless white-collar workers, notably those in aesthetic fields. The Public Works of Art Project gave an opportunity to muralists eager for a chance to work in the style of Rivera, Orozco, and Siqueiros. The Federal Art Project fostered the careers of painters like Stuart Davis, Raphael Soyer, Yasuo Kuniyoshi, and Jackson Pollock. . . .

The Federal Writers' Project provided support for scores of talented novelists and poets, editors and literary critics, men like Ralph Ellison and Nelson Algren, John Cheever and Saul Bellow. . . . When the magazine *Story* conducted a contest for the best contribution by a Project employee, the prize was won by an unpublished 29-year-old black who had been working on the essay on the Negro for the Illinois guide. With the prize money for his stories, subsequently published as *Uncle Tom's Children*, Richard Wright gained the time to complete his remarkable first novel,

274

Native Son. . . .

Roosevelt, it has been said, had a "proprietary interest in the nation's estate," and this helps account for the fact that the 1930s accomplished for soil conservation and river valley development what the era of Theodore Roosevelt had done for the forests. The Tennessee Valley Authority, which drew admirers from all over the world, put the national government in the business of generating electric power, controlled floods, terraced hillsides, and gave new hope to the people of the valley. In the Pacific Northwest the PWA constructed mammoth dams, Grand Coulee and Bonneville. Roosevelt's "tree army," the Civilian Conservation Corps, planted millions of trees, cleared forest trails, laid out picnic sites and campgrounds, and aided the Forest Service in the vast undertaking of establishing a shelterbelt—a windbreak of trees and shrubs: green ash and Chinese elm, apricot and blackberry, buffalo berry and Osage orange from the Canadian border to the Texas panhandle. Government agencies came to the aid of drought-stricken farmers in the Dust Bowl, and the Soil Conservation Service, another New Deal creation, instructed growers in methods of cultivation to save the land. As Alistair Cooke later said, the favorite of the New Dealers was the farmer with the will to "take up contour plowing late in life."

Saving American Farmers

These services to farmers represented only a small part of the government's program, for in the New Deal years, the business of agriculture was revolutionized. Roosevelt came to power at a time of mounting desperation for American farmers. Each month in 1932 another 20,000 farmers had lost their land because of inability to meet their debts in a period of collapsing prices. On a single day in May 1932, one-fourth of the state of Mississippi went under the sheriff's hammer. The Farm Credit Administration of 1933 came to the aid of the beleaguered farmer, and within eighteen months, it had refinanced one-fifth of all farm mortgages in the United States. In the Roosevelt years, too, the Rural Electrification Administration literally brought rural America out of darkness. At the beginning of the Roosevelt era, only one farm in nine had electricity; at the end, only one in nine did not have it. But more important than any of these developments was the progression of enactments starting with the first AAA (the Agricultural Adjustment Act) of 1933, which began the process of granting large-scale subsidies to growers. As William Faulkner later said, "Our economy is not agricultural any longer. Our economy is the federal government. We no longer farm in Mississippi cotton fields. We farm now in Washington corridors and Congressional committee rooms.". . .

Although in some respects the New Deal's performance with regard to blacks added to the sorry record of racial discrimination in America, important gains were also registered in the 1930s. Blacks, who had often been excluded from relief in the past, now received a share of WPA jobs considerably greater than their proportion of the population. Blacks moved into federal housing projects; federal funds went to schools and hospitals in black neighborhoods; and New Deal agencies like the Farm Security Administration (FSA) enabled 50,000 Negro tenant farmers and sharecroppers to become proprietors. "Indeed," one historian has written, "there is a high correlation between the location of extensive FSA operations in the 1930s and the rapidity of political modernization in black communities in the South in the 1960s." Roosevelt appointed a number of blacks, including William Hastie, Mary McLeod Bethune, and Robert Weaver, to high posts in the government. Negroes in the South who were disfranchised in white primaries voted in AAA crop referenda and in National Labor Relations Board plant elections, and a step was taken toward restoring their constitutional rights when Attorney General Frank Murphy set up a Civil Liberties Unit in the Department of Justice. The reign of Jim Crow in Washington offices, which had begun under Roosevelt's Democratic predecessor, Woodrow Wilson, was terminated by Secretary of the Interior Harold Ickes who desegregated cafeterias in his department. Ickes also had a role in the most dramatic episode of the times, for when the Daughters of the American Revolution (DAR) denied the use of their concert hall to the black contralto Marian Anderson, he made it possible for her to sing before thousands from the steps of Lincoln Memorial; and Mrs. Roosevelt joined in the rebuke to the DAR. Anderson's concert on Easter Sunday 1939 was heard by thousands at the Memorial, and three networks carried her voice to millions more. Blacks delivered their own verdict on the New Deal at the polling places. Committed to the party of Lincoln as late as 1932, when they voted overwhelmingly for Hoover, they shifted in large numbers to the party of FDR during Roosevelt's first term. This was a change of allegiance that many whites were also making in those years.

The Great Depression and the New Deal brought about a significant political realignment of the sort that occurs only rarely in America. The Depression wrenched many lifelong Republican voters from their moorings. In 1928, one couple christened their newborn son "Herbert Hoover Jones." Four years later they petitioned the court, "desiring to relieve the young man from the chagrin and mortification which he is suffering and will suffer," and asked that his name be changed to Franklin D. Roosevelt Jones. In 1932 FDR became the first Democrat to enter the White House with as much as 50 percent of the popular vote in eighty years—since Franklin K. Pierce in 1852. Roosevelt took advantage of this opportunity to mold "the FDR coalition," an alliance centered in the low-income districts of the great cities and, as recently as the 1980 election, the contours of the New Deal coalition could still be discerned. Indeed, over the past half-century, the once overpowering Republicans have won control of Congress only twice, for a total of four years. No less important was the shift in the character of the Democratic party from the conservative organization of John W. Davis and John J. Raskob to the country's main political instrumentality for reform. "One political result of the Roosevelt years," Robert Burke has observed, "was a basic change in the nature of the typical Congressional liberal." He was no longer a maverick, who made a fetish of orneriness, no longer one of the men Senator Moses called "the sons of the wild jackass," but "a party Democrat, labor-oriented, urban, and internationalist-minded."

Furthermore, the New Deal drastically altered the agenda of American politics. When Arthur Krock of the *New York Times* listed the main programmatic questions before the 1932 Democratic convention, he wrote: "What would be said about the repeal of prohibition that had split the Republicans? What would be said about tariffs?" By 1936, these concerns seemed altogether old fashioned, as campaigners discussed the Tennessee Valley Authority and industrial relations, slum clearance and aid to the jobless. That year, a Little Rock newspaper commented: "Such matters as tax and tariff laws have given way to universally human things, the living problems and opportunities of the average man and the average family.". . .

Accomplishments

What then did the New Deal do? It gave far greater amplitude to the national state, expanded the authority of the presidency, recruited university-trained administrators, won control of the money supply, established central banking, imposed regulation on Wall Street, rescued the debt-ridden farmer and homeowner, built model communities, financed the Federal Housing Administration, made federal housing a permanent feature, fostered unionization of the factories, reduced child labor, ended the tyranny of company towns, wiped out many sweatshops, mandated minimal working standards, enabled tenants to buy their own farms, built camps for migrants, introduced the welfare state with old-age pensions, unemployment insurance, and aid for dependent children, provided jobs for millions of unemployed, created a special program for the jobless young and for students, covered the American landscape with new edifices, subsidized painters and novelists, composers and ballet dancers, founded

America's first state theater, created documentary films, gave birth to the impressive Tennessee Valley Authority, generated electrical power, sent the Civilian Conservation Corps boys into the forests, initiated the Soil Conservation Service, transformed the economy of agriculture, lighted up rural America, gave women greater recognition, made a start toward breaking the pattern of racial discrimination and segregation, put together a liberal party coalition, changed the agenda of American politics, and brought about a Constitutional Revolution. . . .

The New Deal accomplished all of this at a critical time, when many were insisting that fascism was the wave of the future and denying that democracy could be effective. For those throughout the world who heard such jeremiads with foreboding, the American experience was enormously inspiriting. . . .

By restoring to the debate over the significance of the New Deal acknowledgment of its achievements, we may hope to produce a more judicious estimate of where it succeeded and where it failed. For it unquestionably did fail in a number of respects. There were experiments of the 1930s which miscarried, opportunities that were fumbled, groups who were neglected, and power that was arrogantly used. Over the whole performance lies the dark cloud of the persistence of hard times. The shortcomings of the New Deal are formidable, and they must be recognized. But I am not persuaded that the New Deal experience was negligible. Indeed, it is hard to think of another period in the whole history of the republic that was so fruitful or of a crisis that was met with as much imagination.

For Discussion

Chapter One

1. Which of the authors support greater federal government help for the depression? Which oppose it? What common arguments do you find among these groupings?

2. What is the purpose behind the numerous anecdotes and depiction used by Joseph L. Heffernan? Who or what is being criticized?

3. Does the fact that Henry Ford was a wealthy industrialist worth millions of dollars strengthen or weaken his arguments?

4. Why does Charles R. Walker describe the unemployed autoworker he profiles as lucky? Do you agree or disagree? What does this say about the Great Depression?

5. Does Ray Vance believe depressions are inevitable? Why or why not?

6. What does Herbert Hoover mean by the "American system"? How does he believe it is threatened by Franklin D. Roosevelt? List three specific warnings Hoover gives about what would happen if Roosevelt was elected.

7. Why has Herbert Hoover failed, according to Franklin D. Roosevelt? List three specific promises Roosevelt makes to the American people in his acceptance speech.

Chapter Two

1. Which of the authors believe the New Deal constitutes a revolution? What criteria do they use in determining this?

2. What important and fundamental principle does the New Deal embrace, according to Allan Nevins? How does this principle affect government actions?

3. How does Suzanne La Follette classify Franklin D. Roosevelt on the political spectrum? Is her analysis similar to those of Norman Thomas and Allan Nevins? Explain.

4. Does Henry Wallace defend agriculture production reductions as a permanent a temporary measure? What are his goals for agriculture?

5. What are the fundamental limits of capitalism, according to

Norman Thomas? How does he believe the New Deal reveals these limitations?

6. What does Rexford G. Tugwell believe is the essence of the New Deal? Which early and later New Deal programs were consistent with his vision? Which were not?

7. How does H. L. Mencken contrast presidents Hoover and Roosevelt? Who does he think made the better president?

Chapter Three

1. What does Huey P. Long promise the American people? How does he propose to keep his promises? How might he respond to David Lawrence's arguments on the folly of redistributing wealth?

2. What objections does John C. Gall have about Social Security? Did his fears prove to be justified by subsequent events? Explain.

3. What relevance do the arguments of Frances Perkins and John C. Gall have for contemporary disputes over Social Security benefits?

4. Both John C. Gall and Malcolm Muir were presenting their views on behalf of the National Association of Manufacturers, a business lobbying group. How might this help explain their positions? How does their association affect your judgment of their arguments?

5. John Davis and Robert C. Weaver, respectively, give negative and positive evaluations of the New Deal's impact on blacks. Are there any issues on which they agree? Does Davis acknowledge benefits of the New Deal? Does Weaver acknowledge shortcomings? Does the fact that blacks voted overwhelmingly for Roosevelt in 1936 strengthen Weaver's arguments?

6. What arguments does Hugo L. Black make concerning the Constitution? Why might he consider such arguments necessary?

Chapter Four

1. Does Franklin D. Roosevelt argue the Great Depression is over? How does he defend his New Deal programs?

2. Does Robert A. Taft support a return to the policies of Herbert Hoover? What changes does he propose? What New Deal changes would he retain?

3. What beliefs does Harry Hopkins express concerning work and giving people direct relief? Does he believe in "deserving" and "undeserving" poor?

4. How do the conditions described by Samuel Lubell and Walter

Everett compare with those described by Joseph L. Heffernan in the first chapter? How has the New Deal changed things?

5. What differing beliefs of Marriner S. Eccles and Harry F. Byrd concerning the economy underlay their arguments concerning budget deficits?

6. From 1932 to 1938 the highest level of annual government spending was $8.42 billion—in 1936—and the highest budget deficit was $4.42 billion the same year. The budget deficits of the 1980s and 1990s run into the hundreds of billions. Are the arguments of Byrd and Eccles still relevant today?

Chapter Five

1. How does Barton J. Bernstein describe the differences between Herbert Hoover and Franklin D. Roosevelt? How does his evaluation of the two presidents differ from that of William E. Leuchtenburg?

2. List five specific achievements of the New Deal that William E. Leuchtenburg cites as evidence of its success. Do you believe them to have been positive, lasting changes? What do you think Barton J. Bernstein might say about them?

General Questions

1. Judging from the viewpoints presented, how did the Great Depression change thinking on the economy? On the role of the federal government?

2. What predictions concerning the Roosevelt administration are made in chapters 1 and 2? How accurate were the predictions?

3. Which of the criticisms of the New Deal seem valid today? Which do not? Why?

Chronology

October 1929	Stock market crashes on Wall Street.
November 1929	President Hoover recommends a doubling of federal spending for public buildings, dams, highways, and harbors.
June 1930	Congress passes the Hawley-Smoot Tariff in an effort to fight the depression by raising tariff rates substantially.
October 1930	The president of the National Association of Manufacturers delivers a speech in which he blames the jobless for their own plight.
	Hoover speaks to the American Bankers Association where he denounces "economic fatalists" and contends that the "genius of American business" will restore prosperity.
December 1930	Hoover administration announces that 4.5 million Americans are out of work.
	The large and once-powerful Bank of the United States fails.
	Governor Franklin D. Roosevelt of New York declares Hoover administration anti-depression measures to be too radical and too costly.
February 1931	President Hoover vetoes a bill to permit World War I veterans to borrow up to half of their bonus scheduled for payment in 1945.
September 1931	Gerald Swope, chairman of General Electric, calls for a relaxation of antitrust laws in the name of combatting the depression.
	The American Legion demands early payment of veterans' bonus.
	Farmers openly rebel in Iowa and Minnesota. They block farm foreclosure proceedings in both states.
1932-1936	A four-year drought creates the "Dust Bowl" from Texas to the Dakotas.

January 1932	President Hoover signs into law the creation of the Reconstruction Finance Corporation, allowing the expenditure of $1.5 billion to aid businesses and banks.
	Congressional representative Fiorello La-Guardia denounces the legislation as a "millionaires' dole."
	Congressional representative Wright Patman of Texas demands impeachment of Treasury secretary Andrew Mellon for using government experts to assist him in avoiding payment of personal income tax.
	President Hoover takes a 20% cut in salary.
	President Hoover calls for a tax increase from 24% to 55% on upper-income Americans.
	Financier J. P. Morgan tells a Senate committee that a higher income tax will destroy the "leisure class" and with it "civilization."
March 1932	Congress decisively rejects a national sales tax.
April 1932	Government officials estimate that more than 4,000 working men return to Europe.
April 1932	One-fourth of the land in the state of Mississippi goes on the auction block.
	President Hoover publicly encourages a congressional investigation of Wall Street "bears" who are "raiding" the stock market.
April-May 1932	The "Brains Trust" is organized to advise candidate Roosevelt on the key issues for the 1932 election.
May 1932	Congress passes the Revenue Act of 1932, which includes hefty increases in excise taxes to offset the defeated sales tax.
	Democratic liberals announce that they are firmly behind the presidential candidacy of Franklin Roosevelt.
July 1932	Milo Reno organizes the Farm Holiday Association.
	General Electric and U.S. Steel announce jointly that their stock is worth 8% of its pre-crash value.
	Governor Franklin D. Roosevelt of New York secures the presidential nomination of the

Democratic party.

The Bonus Army, a group of veterans demanding their cash bonuses promised for military service, is driven out of the Anacostia Flats on the edge of Washington, D.C., by General Douglas MacArthur on the order of President Hoover.

September 1932 — In a Pittsburgh campaign speech candidate Roosevelt calls for reducing government spending by 25%.

November 1932 — Roosevelt crushes Hoover in the general election.

December 1932 — Unemployment reaches nearly 13 million.

Father Charles Coughlin estimates that his weekly radio audience is between 30 and 45 million people.

January 1933 — The president of the United States, in a speech to the Chamber of Commerce, advocates a $1 billion slash in government spending.

February 1933 — President-elect Roosevelt breaks off transition negotiations with Hoover administration.

March 1933 — Unemployment reaches more than 15 million.

March 4, 1933 — Franklin D. Roosevelt is inaugurated the thirty-second president of the United States.

March 6, 1933 — President Roosevelt shuts down the American banking system by declaring a bank holiday.

March 8, 1933 — President Roosevelt holds his first press conference.

March 9, 1933 — The 73rd Congress convenes. That same evening it passes the Emergency Banking Act.

March 10, 1933 — Roosevelt delivers a special message to Congress calling for spending cuts to eliminate a $5 billion deficit.

March 12, 1933 — President Roosevelt gives his first "fireside chat" to assure the American people of the safety of bank deposits.

March 16, 1933 — Congress votes to legalize the sale of 3.2% beer.

Roosevelt calls for national planning for American agriculture.

March 31, 1933 — The Civilian Conservation Corps is established.

April 1, 1933	U.S. Steel announces that its payroll of full-time workers has fallen to zero.
April 19, 1933	The United States abandons the gold standard.
May 12, 1933	The Federal Emergency Relief Act is passed, setting up the first national system of relief programs.
	The Emergency Farm Mortgage Act provides for the refinancing of farm mortgages.
	The Agricultural Adjustment Act creates a national plan for agriculture through a system of paying farmers to take land out of cultivation.
May 18, 1933	The Tennessee Valley Authority Act provides for federal funding for the development of the Tennessee Valley.
May 27, 1933	The Truth-in-Securities Act requires full disclosure in the issuance of new securities.
June 13, 1933	The Home Owners' Loan Act provides for the refinancing of home mortgages.
June 16, 1933	The National Industrial Recovery Act provides for a system of industrial codes and for a $3.3 billion public works program.
	The Glass-Steagall Banking Act divorces commercial from investment banking and guarantees bank deposits.
September 1933	Socialist Upton Sinclair organizes his End Poverty in California (EPIC) movement, which culminates with his unsuccessful race for governor in 1934.
October 1933	The Commodity Credit Corporation is created to lend money to farmers who agree to take land out of production in 1934.
December 1933	The Eighteenth Amendment, prohibiting the sale of alcoholic beverages, is repealed.
January 1934	Roosevelt signs the Gold Reserve Act on his birthday, thereby giving the Treasury greater control of credit and currency.
	Senator Huey Long founds his national organization of "Share Our Wealth" clubs.
	Dr. Francis Townsend proposes an old-age pension program of $200 a month to those over sixty, with the provision that the money

be spent in its entirety each month.

The Civil Works Administration under the administration of Harry Hopkins reaches its peak as it employs 4,230,000 people.

March 1934 Roosevelt creates the National Recovery Review Board to study monopolistic tendencies in National Recovery Administration codes.

May-July 1934 Teamster strike in Minneapolis leads to great violence and a settlement which leaves the radical Teamsters Union the most powerful labor voice in the upper Midwest.

June 1934 Roosevelt signs the Silver Purchase Act, which directs the Treasury to buy silver until it reaches 25% of United States monetary reserve.

Roosevelt signs Securities Exchange Act, which places trading practices under federal regulations.

July 1934 The Southern Tenant Farmers' Union is organized to aid tenant farmers and sharecroppers, many of whom had been thrown off the land by the effects of crop restrictions under the Agricultural Adjustment Administration.

The Federal Communications Commission is created, placing radio, telegraph, and cable businesses under federal regulation.

A general strike organized by San Francisco longshoremen sweeps the Bay area.

The National Housing Act is passed, creating the Federal Housing Administration to federally insure home loans made by private lending institutions.

August 1934 Budget director Lewis Douglas resigns, thereby eliminating a conservative voice within the Roosevelt White House.

The American Liberty League is organized to spearhead conservative opposition to the New Deal.

November 1934 The Democratic party defies American political history by gaining seats in the House and Senate in an off-year election when the party in power also holds the presidency. The new

House contains 322 Democrats, 103 Republicans, and 10 Progressives or Farmer-Laborites. The new Senate has 69 Democrats.

Convinced that capitalism is finished, Father Charles Coughlin announces the formation of his National Union for Social Justice.

January 1935	President Roosevelt proposes a gigantic program of emergency public employment to give work to 3.5 million jobless.
April 1935	President Roosevelt sets up the Resettlement Administration under Rexford G. Tugwell to deal with the problems of rural poverty.
May 1935	The Supreme Court declares the National Recovery Act unconstitutional.
	The Rural Electrification Administration comes into being to begin to change the face of rural America, where nine out of ten farms do not have electricity.
June 1935	Roosevelt asks Congress to pass steep increases in individual, corporate, and inheritance taxes.
July 1935	Roosevelt signs the National Labor Relations Act, which guarantees the right of collective bargaining to American workers.
	Congress passes the Public Utilities Holding Company Act, which strikes at holding companies more than twice removed from the operating company.
August 1935	Congress passes the Wealth Tax Act, which increases taxes on the wealthy but not as severely as Roosevelt had requested.
	Roosevelt signs the Social Security Act providing workers with retirement annuities financed by taxes on their wages and on their employer's payroll.
August 27, 1935	The first session of the 74th Congress comes to a close and with it ends the second "hundred days" of the New Deal.
September 1935	Senator Huey P. Long, a leading political opponent of Roosevelt and the New Deal, is assassinated in Baton Rouge, Louisiana.
October 1935	The CIO (Congress of Industrial Organizations) is formed, having split away from the

American Federation of Labor.

January 1936   New York politician and former presidential candidate Al Smith tells a Liberty League gathering that the New Deal has headed in a "socialistic" direction.

February 1936   The Supreme Court declares the Agricultural Adjustment Act unconstitutional.

June 1936   The Union Party is created under the leadership of Al Smith and Father Coughlin. Representative William Lemke of North Dakota is nominated to run for president.

November 1936   President Roosevelt soundly defeats Republican candidate Governor Alf Landon of Kansas and is reelected to the presidency.

December 1936   The United Auto Workers stage a "sit down" strike at General Motors.

January 20, 1937   President Roosevelt's Second Inaugural Address heralds a more radical turn as he looks out over "one-third of a nation ill-housed, ill-clad, ill-nourished."

February 1937   Roosevelt sends Congress his plan for reorganizing the Supreme Court by adding a new justice (up to a maximum of fifteen) for each sitting justice who refuses to retire at age seventy.

February 11, 1937   General Motors surrenders to United Auto Workers demands.

April 1937   The Supreme Court invalidates a New York state minimum wage law.

Firestone capitulates to the United Rubber Workers after an eight-week strike.

The American economy finally returns to 1929 level of output.

May 1937   The Supreme Court upholds the constitutionality of the Social Security Act.

May 30, 1937   Police kill ten strikers in one violent day of the United Steel Workers strike against Republic Steel in Chicago.

July 1937   The Farm Security Administration is organized to provide, among other things, labor camps for migratory workers.

Congress kills the Roosevelt "court packing"

scheme.

August 1937	A new economic downturn, which comes to be labeled the "Roosevelt recession," begins and does not level out until mid-1938.
September 1937	Roosevelt signs the Wagner-Steagall Housing Act, which makes available $500 million in loans for low-cost housing.
December 1937	Blaming the new recession on "monopolists," the Roosevelt Justice Department announces an antitrust crusade.
February 1938	Congress passes a new agriculture act authorizing crop loans and crop insurance.
June 1938	Congress authorizes a $3.75 billion public works package to alleviate the "Roosevelt recession."
	Congress passes the Fair Labor Standards Act which sets the minimum wage at forty cents an hour and the maximum working hours at forty hours per week.
September 1938	Roosevelt joins the campaign against conservatives within his own party.
November 1938	Democrats suffer serious setbacks in both houses of Congress as Republicans gain eighty-one seats in the House and eight in the Senate, thereby giving conservatives from both parties a working majority in the Congress.
1939	Congress repeatedly rejects mild housing and spending measures to combat renewed economic depression.
	Congress begins to move in a piecemeal fashion to dismantle the New Deal.
September 1939	War erupts in Europe and President Roosevelt begins to change hats from "Dr. New Deal" to "Dr. Win the War."
1941-1945	American participation in World War II slowly pulls the American economy the rest of the way out of the Great Depression.

Annotated
Bibliography

Daniel Aaron, *Writers on the Left*. New York: Harcourt, Brace, 1961. A literary and cultural history of the United States between 1912 and the early 1940s, with a focus on those American writers who turned to politics and to the left during the 1930s.

Henry Adams, *Harry Hopkins*. New York: G.P. Putnam's Sons, 1977. A political biography of Roosevelt's "Man Friday" evenly balanced between his pre-World War II domestic policy and World War II foreign policy duties.

William Akin, *Technology and the American Dream*. Berkeley: University of California Press, 1977. A study of twentieth-century utopian plans for technology, culminating with the New Deal.

Joseph Alsop and Turner Catledge, *The 168 Days*. Garden City, NY: Doubleday, 1938. A journalistic account of the Roosevelt court-packing scheme and the political fight surrounding it.

Thurman Arnold, *The Folklore of Capitalism*. New Haven, CT: Yale University Press, 1937. A study of the evolution of capitalism, written by the Justice Department official who presided over the antitrust actions of the second Roosevelt term.

Sidney Baldwin, *Poverty and Politics: The Rise and Decline of the Farm Security Administration*. Chapel Hill: University of North Carolina Press, 1968. A history of the FSA that is sympathetic toward it but critical of inadequate Roosevelt administration efforts to support it.

John Barnard, *Walter Reuther and the Rise of the Auto Workers*. Boston: Little, Brown, 1983. A brief biography of one of the important labor leaders of the 1930s.

Bernard Bellush, *The Failure of the NRA*. New York: Norton, 1975. A history of the National Recovery Administration, but also an indictment of the Roosevelt administration and Congress for turning over too much power to private business and the trade associations.

Bernard Bellush, *Franklin D. Roosevelt as Governor of New York*. New York: Columbia University Press, 1955. A detailed history, topically arranged, of programs that contained the seeds of the New Deal.

David Bennett, *Demagogues in the Depression*. New Brunswick, NJ: Rutgers University Press, 1969. Primarily a history of the Union party and its role in the election of 1936.

Andrew Bergman, *We're in the Money*. New York: New York University Press, 1971. An analysis of more than one hundred depression-era films of the gangster, G-man, and screwball comedy varieties.

Adolph A. Berle, *Navigating the Rapids*. New York: Harcourt, Brace, 1973. A memoir by a liberal member of the Roosevelt Brains Trust.

Michael Bernstein, *The Great Depression*. New York: Cambridge University Press, 1987. A provocative study that examines the causes of the Great Depression and the reasons for its persistence and that seeks to place it in its international context.

Irving Bernstein, *The Lean Years*. Boston: Houghton Mifflin, 1960. A social and economic history of the American worker during the years of Republican rule that preceded the New Deal.

Irving Bernstein, *The Turbulent Years*. Boston: Houghton Mifflin, 1970. A sympathetic history of the American worker and the American labor movement from 1933 through 1941.

Neil Betten, *Catholic Activism and the Industrial Worker*. Gainesville, FL: University Presses of Florida, 1976. A study of Dorothy Day and the Catholic Worker movement and of the relations between the Catholic church and the CIO.

Alan Brinkley, *Voices of Protest*. New York: Vintage Books, 1983. A dual biography of Huey Long and Fr. Charles Coughlin, two of the most important anti-Roosevelt demagogues of the 1930s.

Karl Brunner, ed., *The Great Depression Revisited*. Boston: Martinus Mijhoff Publishing, 1981. Anthology of economists debating the causes of the Great Depression.

David Burner, *The Politics of Provincialism*. New York: Knopf, 1967. A history of the Democratic party during the 1920s and its years out of power just prior to the New Deal.

James M. Burns, *Roosevelt: The Lion and the Fox*. New York: Harcourt, Brace, 1956. A balanced political biography of Franklin Roosevelt, whom the author describes as a fox with an ability to recognize traps and a lion who was able to frighten the wolves among his enemies, but who was ultimately unable to create a political coalition to sustain his reform policies.

Sean Dennis Cashman, *America in the Twenties and Thirties*. New York: New York University Press, 1989. Third in a series of interdisciplinary studies of the United States since the Civil War.

Henry M. Christman, ed., *Kingfish to America: Share Our Wealth: Selected Senatorial Papers of Huey P. Long*. New York: Schocken Books, 1985. A collection of speeches by Long in which he attacks the New Deal and promotes his "Share Our Wealth" program.

Bert Cochran, *Labor and Communism: The Conflict That Shaped American Unions*. Princeton, NJ: Princeton University Press, 1978. Written by an activist in the 1930s, this history attempts to demonstrate the efforts by Moscow to control certain American labor unions.

Lizabeth Cohen, *Making a New Deal: Industrial Workers in Chicago, 1919-1939*. New York: Cambridge University Press, 1990. A history of the working class in Chicago and the divisions between men and women, whites and blacks, natives and ethnics.

Paul Conkin, *The New Deal*. New York: Thomas Crowell, 1967. A slender overview of the New Deal written from a slightly left-of-center perspective.

Paul Conkin, *Tomorrow a New World*. Ithaca, NY: Cornell University Press, 1958. A general history of the origins and implementation of New Deal community-based programs.

Blanche Wiesen Cook, *Eleanor Roosevelt, 1884-1933*. New York: Viking Press, 1992. The first volume of what promises to be the definitive biography of Roosevelt and which seeks to strike a balance between her private and public lives.

Roger Daniels, *The Bonus March*. Westport, CT: Greenwood Press, 1971. A fair-minded but occasionally didactic history of the national roots of the war of nerves over the effort to secure early payment bonus money owed to veterans of World War I.

Kenneth Davis, *FDR: The Beckoning of Destiny*. New York: Random House, 1972. A sympathetic, but not hero-worshipping, treatment of the early years of Franklin Roosevelt.

Kenneth Davis, *FDR: The New Deal Years*. New York: Random House, 1986. Takes Roosevelt's story through 1937.

Kenneth Davis, *FDR: The New York Years*. New York: Random House, 1985. A study of Roosevelt from his governorship through his election to the presidency and assembling of the Brains Trust.

Nelson Dawson, *Louis Brandeis, Felix Frankfurter, and the New Deal*. Hamden, CT: Archon Books, 1980. An examination of the legal opinions of two of the giants of the Supreme Court, who served during portions of the New Deal.

Carl N. Degler, ed., *The New Deal*. Chicago: Quadrangle Books, 1970. A collection of 1930s articles from the *New York Times Magazine*.

Milton Derber and Edwin Young, *Labor and the New Deal*. Madison: University of Wisconsin Press, 1957. A history that emphasizes the role of unions during the New Deal.

Melvyn Dubofsky and Warren Van Tine, *John L. Lewis*. Chicago: Quadrangle Books, 1977. A biography of John L. Lewis that emphasizes his role in the founding of the CIO.

Marriner S. Eccles, *Beckoning Frontiers*. New York: Knopf, 1951. The memoir of one of Roosevelt's key economic advisers in the early years of the New Deal.

James Farley, *Behind the Ballots*. New York: Harcourt, Brace, 1938. Autobiography and apologia of the politics that led to the 1932 nomination of Franklin Roosevelt and the politics of the New Deal through 1938.

292

Sidney Fine, *The Automobile Under the Blue Eagle*. Ann Arbor: University of Michigan Press, 1963. A case study of the workings of the National Recovery Administration with the automobile industry as the focus.

Sidney Fine, *Frank Murphy: The New Deal Years*. Chicago: University of Chicago Press, 1979. A partial biography of one of Roosevelt's attorneys general and a subsequent Roosevelt appointee to the Supreme Court.

Sidney Fine, *Sit-Down*. Ann Arbor: University of Michigan Press, 1969. A detailed history of the General Motors strike of 1936-37.

Frank Freidel, *FDR: The Apprenticeship*. Boston: Little, Brown, 1952. The first volume of a biography of Franklin Roosevelt that takes the story through World War I and sets the model for the balanced and meticulous scholarship in the succeeding volumes.

Frank Freidel, *FDR: The Ordeal*. Boston: Little, Brown, 1954. The second volume of a Roosevelt biography, which takes the story through his election as governor of New York.

Frank Freidel, *FDR: Rendezvous with Destiny*. Boston: Little, Brown, 1990. A single-volume summation of the work of the most prolific Roosevelt scholar.

Frank Freidel, *FDR: The Triumph*. Boston: Little, Brown, 1956. The third volume of the biography, taking the story through FDR's election to the presidency.

Frank Freidel, *The New Deal and the South*. Baton Rouge: Louisiana State University Press, 1965. A series of lectures on the political and cultural aspects of the New Deal and of the connections between the two.

David Fusfeld, *The Economic Thought of Franklin D. Roosevelt and the Origins of the New Deal*. New York: Columbia University Press, 1956. Explores the roots both of Roosevelt's personality and of New Deal economic policy.

John Kenneth Galbraith, *The Great Crash*. Boston: Houghton Mifflin, 1955. A popular history of the background to the stock market collapse and of the crash of 1929.

Walter Galenson, *The CIO Challenge to the AFL*. Cambridge, MA: Harvard University Press, 1960. A descriptive history of the labor movement, focusing on the rise of the industrial unions.

John A. Garraty, *The Great Depression*. New York: Harcourt Brace Jovanovich, 1986. A collection of essays by the distinguished Columbia University historian in which he examines how the Great Depression affected economies throughout the world.

James Gilbert, *Writers and Partisans*. New York: Wiley, 1968. A history of literary radicals as seen through the eyes and thoughts of the editors of the *Partisan Review*.

Eric Goldman, *Rendezvous with Destiny*. New York: Vintage Books, 1952. A general and very readable history of American reform from the populists through the New Deal.

Otis Graham, *Encore for Reform*. New York: Oxford University Press, 1967. A collective portrait of leading old progressives of the pre-World War II era and their response to the New Deal.

James Gregory, *American Exodus: The Dust Bowl Migration and Okie Culture in California*. New York: Oxford University Press, 1989. A study of the Okie experience, which relies heavily and effectively on oral histories and personal interviews.

Tamara Haraven, *Eleanor Roosevelt: An American Conscience*. Chicago: Quadrangle Books, 1968. A portrait of Roosevelt and her involvement in a variety of social causes during her time as first lady and after.

Ellis Hawley, *The New Deal and the Problem of Monopoly*. Princeton, NJ: Princeton University Press, 1965. A thorough study of business-government interactions during the 1930s with special emphasis on the history of the National Recovery Administration.

Joan Hoff-Wilson and Marjorie Lightman, eds., *Without Precedent*. Bloomington: Indiana University Press, 1984. A series of essays dealing with various aspects of Roosevelt's career as a political figure and social reformer.

Richard Hofstadter, *The Age of Reform*. New York: Knopf, 1954. A path-breaking history of the reform impulse, which contends that the New Deal represented a sharp break with the past.

Herbert Hoover, *The Great Depression, 1929-1941*. New York: Macmillan, 1951. The third volume of the memoirs of the president whose single-term presidency coincided with the first four years of the Great Depression.

Joseph Huthmacher, *Senator Robert Wagner and the Rise of Urban Liberalism*. New York: Atheneum, 1968. A portrait of the democratic senator from New York who was the primary author of the National Labor Relations Act of 1935.

Harold Ickes, *The Autobiography of a Curmudgeon*. Westport, CT: Greenwood Press, 1985. A memoir of the New Deal written by Roosevelt's secretary of the interior.

Glen Jeansonne, *Gerald L. K. Smith: Minister of Hate*. New Haven, CT: Yale University Press, 1988. A highly critical biography of a disciple of Huey Long who struck out on his own path of demagoguery.

Bernard Johnpoll, *Pacifist's Progress*. Chicago: Quadrangle Books, 1970. A biography of Norman Thomas and a history of the decline of the socialist movement during the 1930s.

Matther Josephson, *Sidney Hillman*. Garden City, NY: Doubleday, 1952. A sympathetic biography of one of the major labor leaders, and a leading Roosevelt supporter, during the 1930s.

Laurence Kelly, *The Assault on Assimilation: John Collier and the Origins of Indian Policy Reform*. Albuquerque: University of New Mexico Press, 1983. A favorable biography of a New Deal reformer who challenged the orthodoxies of federal policy toward the native American.

Thomas Kessner, *Fiorello H. LaGuardia and the Making of Modern New York*. New York: McGraw-Hill, 1989. A sprawling but effective biography of the mayor of New York during much of the Great Depression.

John Kirby, *Black Americans in the Roosevelt Era*. Knoxville: University of Tennessee Press, 1980. A study of white liberals and the limits of their efforts to build and support programs for black America.

Harvey Klehr, *The Heyday of American Communism*. New York: Basic Books, 1984. A history of the American Communist party during the 1930s, emphasizing its subservience to Moscow.

Fiorello LaGuardia, *The Making of an Insurgent*. Westport, CT: Greenwood Press, 1985. The colorful memoirs of the colorful New York mayor who held that office during much of the Great Depression.

Joseph Lash, *Dreamers and Dealers*. New York: Doubleday, 1988. A collection of New Deal-era portraits, with special emphasis on the careers of Tommy Corcoran and Ben Cohen, written by a friend of Eleanor Roosevelt and someone in general sympathy with the New Deal.

Joseph Lash, *Eleanor and Franklin*. New York: Norton, 1971. A dual biography of the president and the first lady written by a youthful supporter of the New Deal who befriended Eleanor Roosevelt when she was the president's wife.

R. Alan Lawson, *The Failure of Independent Liberalism*. New York: G. P. Putnam, 1971. An intellectual history of those inside and outside the New Deal who wanted to replace capitalism with some aspects of a non-Marxist communitarian society.

William E. Leuchtenburg, *Franklin Roosevelt and the New Deal*. New York: Harper and Row, 1963. A model of careful scholarship and a general survey of the first two terms of the Roosevelt presidency.

William E. Leuchtenburg, *The New Deal: A Documentary History*. New York: Harper and Row, 1968. A collection of primary source articles, speeches, and documents by supporters, opponents, and chroniclers of the New Deal.

David Lilienthal, *TVA: Dam on the March*. New York: Harper, 1953. A history of the TVA written by its most important New Deal administrator.

Walter Lippmann, *The Good Society*. Boston: Little Brown, 1937. A philosophical inquiry into the nature of the good society and a commentary on the differences between liberalism and collectivism.

Huey P. Long, *Every Man a King*. New Orleans: National Book Company, 1933. The political autobiography of the Kingfish and an outline of his prescriptions for reform.

Richard Lowitt, *George Norris: The Persistence of a Progressive*. Urbana: University of Illinois Press, 1971. The second volume of the biography of one of the leading western progressive Republican senators and his career through the Hoover presidency.

Richard Lowitt, *George Norris: The Triumph of a Progressive*. Urbana: University of Illinois Press, 1978. Final volume of the Norris trilogy, which stresses his role in the formation of the TVA and his progressive Republican response to the Democratic New Deal.

Roy Lubove, *The Struggle for Social Security*. Cambridge, MA: Harvard University Press, 1968. A history of the background to, debate over, and passage and implementation of the Social Security Act of 1935.

Everett Luoma, *The Farmer Takes a Holiday*. New York: Exposition Press, 1967. A general history of the Farm Holiday movement in the Midwest during the 1930s.

Robert Lynd and Helen Lynd, *Middletown in Transition*. New York: Harcourt, Brace, 1937. A sequel to *Middletown* and a return to Muncie, Indiana, a microcosm of American society during the depression.

Donald McCoy, *Angry Voices*. Lawrence: University of Kansas Press, 1958. A study of the left-of-center protest politics of the 1930s, with special emphasis on farm protest politics.

Thomas McCraw, *TVA and the Power Fight*. Philadelphia: Lippincott, 1970. A political and administrative history of the debate over public power in the 1930s.

Robert McElvaine, ed., *Down and Out in the Great Depression*. Chapel Hill: University of North Carolina Press, 1983. A careful compilation of letters to people in power by ordinary citizens who were feeling the impact of the depression.

Robert McElvaine, *The Great Depression: America, 1929-1941*. New York: Random House, 1985. A solid, single-volume survey of the impact of the depression on American life, which is in general sympathy with the New Deal but which criticizes it from the left.

George McJimsey, *Harry Hopkins: Ally of the Poor and Defender of Democracy*. Cambridge, MA: Harvard University Press, 1987. A sympathetic portrait of the former social worker Roosevelt often turned to for advice, especially when it was time to implement public works projects.

David Madden, ed., *Proletarian Writers of the Thirties*. Carbondale: University of Southern Illinois Press, 1967. A collection of essays by and about the leading proletarian writers of the "red decade."

Jerre Mangione, *The Dream and the Deal*. Philadelphia: University of Pennsylvania Press, 1983. A history of the Federal Writers' Project from 1935 to 1943.

George Mayer, *The Political Career of Floyd B. Olson*. Minneapolis: University of Minnesota Press, 1951. A political biography of Minnesota's Farmer-Labor governor from 1930 through 1936, who was a key Roosevelt ally in the Midwest.

Paul Mertz, *New Deal Policy and Southern Rural Poverty*. Baton Rouge: Louisiana State University Press, 1978. A history of the Agricultural Adjustment Administration and its impact on the growth of rural poverty during the early New Deal, and a history of the New Deal's efforts to solve those problems.

Broadus Mitchell, *Depression Decade*. New York: Rinehart, 1947. A general social history of the 1930s.

Raymond Moley, *After Seven Years*. Lincoln: University of Nebraska Press, 1971. A conservative critique of the New Deal, written by one of the original members of the Brains Trust, and a chronicle of his increasing disillusionment with the New Deal and of his frank refusal to tender to Roosevelt the loyalty the president demanded.

Chester Morgan, *Redneck Liberal: Theodore Bilbo and the New Deal*. Baton Rouge: Louisiana State University Press, 1985. A biography of one of the leading southern conservative critics of the New Deal.

Ted Morgan, *FDR: A Biography*. New York: Simon and Schuster, 1985. A highly readable, single-volume biography of the president.

William Starr Myers and Walter H. Newton, *The Hoover Administration: A Documented Narrative*. New York: Charles Scribner's Sons, 1936. A chronological narrative of the presidency of Herbert Hoover, with numerous extracts of the president's speeches and writings, compiled by the editor of Hoover's papers and his personal secretary.

David O'Brien, *American Catholics and Social Reform*. New York: Oxford University Press, 1968. A study of the rise of social activism within the American Catholic church as it sought to respond to the problems of the depression.

James Olson, *Herbert Hoover and the RFC, 1931-1933*. Ames: Iowa State University Press, 1977. A study of the Reconstruction Finance Corporation, which served as a transition to a more federally managed economy but which underestimated the severity of the depression.

James Patterson, *Congressional Conservatism and the New Deal*. Lexington: University of Kentucky Press, 1967. A collective biography of primarily southern conservatives and their activities, culminating with the congressional elections of 1938.

James Patterson, *The New Deal and the States*. Princeton, NJ: Princeton University Press, 1969. A study of the changing nature of federalism during the New Deal.

David Peeler, *Hope Among Us Yet: Social Criticism and Social Thought in the Depression Years*. Athens: University of Georgia Press, 1987. An intellectual history of depression-era painting, photography, and literature, charting the creative process during a time of social crisis.

Richard Pells, *Radical Visions and American Dreams: Cultural and Social Thought in the Depression Years*. New York: Harper and Row, 1973. A cultural and literary history that examines the attractions of Marxism and the impact of the depression on American intellectual history.

Frances Perkins, *The Roosevelt I Knew*. New York: Harper and Row, 1946. A personal memoir of the Roosevelt presidency written by his secretary of labor, the first woman cabinet member in American history.

Val Perkins, *Crisis in Agriculture*. Berkeley: University of California Press, 1969. A study of the background to, the passage and implementation of, and the demise of the Agricultural Adjustment Administration.

William R. Phillips and Bernard Sternsher, eds., *Hitting Home: The Great Depression in Town and Country*. Chicago: Ivan R. Dee, 1989. A collection of local history articles examining how the depression affected American communities.

Leo Ribuffo, *The Old Christian Right*. Philadelphia: Temple University Press, 1983. A critical study of fringe groups on the right during the 1930s.

Walter Rideout, *The Radical Novel in the United States, 1900-1954*. Cambridge, MA: Harvard University Press, 1956. A literary history and criticism of novels of the left.

Edgar Robinson, *The Roosevelt Leadership, 1933-1945*. Philadelphia: Lippincott, 1955. The most critical scholarly biography of Roosevelt, which argues that the president was both a demagogue and a very competent politician.

Alfred Rollins, *Roosevelt and Howe*. New York: Knopf, 1962. A political biography of a political friendship from 1912 until Howe's death in 1935.

Albert Romasco, *The Poverty of Abundance*. New York: Oxford University Press, 1965. A study of the response of the Hoover administration to the problems created by the depression.

Eleanor Roosevelt, *This I Remember*. New York: Harper and Row, 1949. The second volume of the autobiography of the first lady, which considers the years between 1928 and 1945.

Elliott Rosen, *Hoover, Roosevelt, and the Brains Trust*. New York: Columbia University Press, 1977. A study contrasting the Hoover and Roosevelt approaches to the depression; more critical of Hoover.

Samuel Rosenman, *Working with Roosevelt*. New York: Harper and Row, 1952. A memoir of the Roosevelt years written by one of his chief speechwriters.

John Salmond, *The Civilian Conservation Corps*. Durham, NC: Duke University Press, 1967. A history of one of the most popular New Deal agencies.

John Salmond, *A Southern Rebel: The Life and Times of Aubrey Williams, 1890-1965*. Chapel Hill: University of North Carolina Press, 1983. A sympathetic portrait of the head of the National Youth Administration.

Lois Scharf, *Eleanor Roosevelt: First Lady of American Liberalism*. Boston: Twayne, 1987. A brief but solid biography of Roosevelt.

Lois Scharf, *To Work and to Wed: Female Employment, Feminism, and the Great Depression*. Westport, CT: Greenwood Press, 1980. A social history of the choices women were making during this time of great economic difficulty and social dislocation.

Arthur M. Schlesinger, *The Age of Roosevelt*. Boston: Houghton Mifflin, 1957-60. A three-volume history of the New Deal and its antecedents, that is both openly partisan in its praise of Roosevelt and the New Deal and full of solid scholarship on domestic politics and policies between 1919 and 1936.

David Shannon, *The Great Depression*. Englewood Cliffs, NJ: Prentice-Hall, 1960. A general socioeconomic survey of the depression.

John Shover, *Cornbelt Rebellion*. Urbana: University of Illinois Press, 1965. A thorough study of the Farm Holiday Association and the accompanying Farm Holiday movement.

Howard Sitkoff, *Fifty Years: The New Deal*. New York: McGraw-Hill, 1985. A series of retrospective essays on New Deal policies and personalities.

Howard Sitkoff, *A New Deal for Blacks*. New York: Oxford University Press, 1978. Examines the roots of the civil rights movement, the rise of black expectations, and the role of Eleanor Roosevelt as a spokesperson for black America.

Richard Norton Smith, *An Uncommon Man*. New York: Simon and Schuster, 1984. A highly readable, sympathetic single-volume biography of President Hoover.

Bernard Sternsher, *Rexford G. Tugwell and the New Deal*. New Brunswick, NJ: Rutgers University Press, 1964. An intellectual biography of one of the important members of the Roosevelt Brains Trust.

Lela Stiles, *The Man Behind Roosevelt*. Cleveland: World Publications, 1954. A biography of Louis Howe, who was one of Roosevelt's key political operatives, emphasizing the 1932 election and written by a Howe associate.

W. A. Swanberg, *Norman Thomas: The Last Idealist*. New York: Scribner's, 1976. A biographical portrait of the leading American socialist of the twentieth century and a rival to Roosevelt for the presidency.

Peter Temin, *Did Monetary Forces Cause the Great Depression?* New York: Norton, 1976. A provocative economic history that argues that the decline in spending levels was a more crucial factor in causing the Great Depression than was monetary policy.

Studs Terkel, *Hard Times*. New York: Pantheon Books, 1970. Captivating oral histories of the impact of the Great Depression on the lives of then-famous, later-famous, and never-famous Americans.

Francis Townsend, *New Horizons*. Chicago: J. L. Stewart, 1943. The autobiography of the doctor who drafted an old-age pension plan that helped to push Congress to pass the Social Security Act.

Charles Trout, *The Great Depression and the New Deal*. New York: Oxford University Press, 1977. A case history of a city, stressing the inadequacy of the New Deal and the efforts of local politicians to block New Deal programs.

Rexford G. Tugwell, *The Brains Trust*. New York: Viking Press, 1968. A history of the leading academic advisers around Roosevelt, written by a leading member of the group.

Rexford G. Tugwell, *The Democratic Roosevelt*. Garden City, NY: Doubleday, 1957. A biography of FDR written by a member of his Brains Trust who is critical of the president's failure to move toward collectivization and who combines moral fervor with a fascination for the technical details of policy-making.

Charles Tull, *Father Charles Coughlin and the New Deal*. Syracuse, NY: Syracuse University Press, 1965. A biography of the "radio priest" and his proposals for reform and criticisms of the New Deal.

Jerome Tweton, *The New Deal at the Grass Roots*. St. Paul: Minnesota Historical Society Press, 1988. A case study of how the New Deal operated at the county level.

Jude Wanniski, *The Way the World Works*. New York: Simon and Schuster, 1978. Supply-side economist argues that the cause of the 1929 crash was the specter of rising protectionism, not maldistribution of wealth.

Susan Ware, *Beyond Suffrage*. Cambridge, MA: Harvard University Press, 1982. An administrative history of twenty-eight women in various New Deal agencies, most of whom had been social workers before their work for the Roosevelt administration.

Susan Ware, *Holding Their Own: American Women in the 1930s*. Boston: Twayne, 1982. A brief social history of women and feminism during the 1930s.

Harris Warren, *Herbert Hoover and the Great Depression*. New York: Oxford University Press, 1959. A political and economic history of the Hoover years that sees the president as too progressive for the conservatives and too conservative for the radicals.

T. H. Watkins, *Righteous Pilgrim: The Life and Times of Harold L. Ickes, 1874-1952*. New York: Henry Holt, 1990. A massive single-volume history of the tormented private life and highly visible public life of Roosevelt's secretary of the interior.

Dixon Wecter, *The Age of the Great Depression, 1929-1941*. New York: Macmillan, 1948. A cautious but very descriptive combined sociopolitical history of the 1930s.

Nancy Weiss, *Farewell to the Party of Lincoln*. Princeton, NJ: Princeton University Press, 1983. A study of American blacks' shift away from the Republican party to the Democratic party because of New Deal programs.

Jeane Westin, *Making Do: How Women Survived the '30s*. Chicago: Follet, 1976. A study of everyday life based on extensive personal interviews and oral histories.

T. Harry Williams, *Huey Long*. New York: Knopf, 1969. The massive, definitive biography of the Louisiana politician and challenger to the New Deal.

Joan Hoff Wilson, *Herbert Hoover: Forgotten Progressive*. Boston: Little, Brown, 1975. A brief but excellent biography of Hoover that stresses his connections to the old progressives and his distance from the two Republican presidents who came before him.

George Wolfskill, *Revolt of the Conservatives*. Boston: Houghton Mifflin, 1962. A history of the Liberty League, the organization that took the lead in opposing the New Deal in the mid-1930s.

Howard Zinn, ed., *New Deal Thought*. Indianapolis: Bobbs-Merrill, 1966. Key selections from the writings and speeches of key New Dealers.

Index